The Modern Age

Hulton Drama Series

Neil King

Hulton Educational

Acknowledgements

To Frank King

The publishers are very grateful to the following
for allowing them to reproduce copyright
photographs:

Alec Russell 15T, 22R
Angus McBean 12B
BBC Hulton Picture Library 7B, 9B, 12T, 13, 15B,
    19, 21, 22R
The British Broadcasting Corporation 110, 124, 127
Derek Balmer 28, 33, 36, 39, 47, 55
The Mary Evans Picture Library 6L, 6C, 20, 22L
The Raymond Mander & Joe Mitchenson Theatre
    Collection 6R, 7T, 11T
Robert Cheesmond 10
Zoe Dominic 17

The author wishes to acknowledge the help of John
Tranmer and to thank Kris Kingsland and Nick
Atkinson for permission to reproduce *You Can't
Take It With You*; Methuen, London Ltd for
permission to reproduce *Mother Figure* and
Gosforth's Fête from Alan Ayckbourn's
Confusions; and Margaret Ramsay Ltd for
permission to reproduce *Our Day Out*.
We would also like to acknowledge the help of Mrs
Anne Kaufman Schneider.

First published in Great Britain 1985
by Hulton Educational Publications Ltd
Old Station Drive, Leckhampton,
Cheltenham GL53 0DN
Revised and reprinted 1989

Text and adaptations © Neil King 1985
Illustrations © Hulton Educational Publications
    Ltd 1985
Edited and designed by James Shepherd
Artwork by Barney Aldridge

ISBN 0 7175 1236 3

Phototypeset by Input Typesetting Ltd, London
Printed and bound in Great Britain at The Bath
Press, Avon

Contents

INTRODUCTION

Modern Drama

Preface

The difficulty in talking about the drama of the Modern Age is that we are still a part of it. We cannot stand back and view it in true proportion, and the unimportant cannot always be distinguished from the important. Any selection of representative plays has to appear eccentric. The plays in this book may appear lightweight or unbalanced. Where is Osborne, Wesker, Pinter, Stoppard, Bond, Brenton, Griffiths? These 'New Wave' dramatists have been omitted for two reasons: first, because their best established work is already widely available in print (*Look Back in Anger, Chips with Everything, The Caretaker, Rosencrantz and Guildenstern Are Dead*); and second, because much of their work—particularly their 'topical' or 'political' pieces—will soon appear to be as transient as the theatre of the symbolists or expressionists. This is not to condemn; it is as important to be of the moment as to be enduring. However, it is obvious that I do not want this book quickly to assume a dated look.

The five plays chosen were all popular when first produced, and remain popular. All are perceptive in their handling of character and in their social awareness.

Background

At the turn of the twentieth century the best British dramatic writing was in the form of comedies by Oscar Wilde (1856–1900) and Arthur Pinero (1855–1934) in the English comic tradition of Vanbrugh and Sheridan. A spirit of wit, when combined with social realism, led to the penetrating social studies of George Bernard Shaw (1856–1950) and John Galsworthy (1867–1933). Their plays were thought-provoking, but lacked both the gloomy solemnity and the power of the great Continental drama of the period.

British drama was unwilling to follow the path of such psychological realists as the Norwegian Henrik Ibsen (1828–1906), the Swede August Strindberg (1849–1912) and the Russian Anton Chekhov (1860–1904), who are often regarded as the founding-fathers of modern drama.

August Strindberg (*left*), Anton Chekhov (*centre*) and Henrik Ibsen (*right*)

In the Modern Age actors, managers, directors, playwrights and many other skilled artists and craftsmen make up what we call 'the theatre'. It is curious how, at different times, different personnel working in the theatre have taken the limelight. Towards the end of the nineteenth century the great managers were revered, and audiences went to see a company such as that at the Lyceum, London, because it was managed by Henry Irving (1838–1905), who was the first actor to be knighted. In the early twentieth century the director became all-important (see the section entitled 'The Directors', page 11). Actors have always attracted acclaim, but this has been particularly so with actresses such as Sarah Bernhardt (1845–1923), Ellen Terry (1847–1928), Mrs Patrick Campbell (1865–1940), Sybil Thorndike (1882–1976), Edith Evans (1888–1976) and Peggy Ashcroft (born 1907), and actors of the stature of Johnston Forbes-Robertson (1853–1937), Gerald du Maurier (1873–1934), Ralph Richardson (1902–84), John Gielgud (born 1904) and Laurence Olivier (born 1907). We seem now to be in a period of playwrights' theatre, where audiences wish to see a Brenton or a Stoppard, although designers are coming to the fore with such spectacles as *Time* and *Starlight Express*. Of course, this kind of chronological breakdown is a very loose generalisation: in the 1890s audiences flocked to see Oscar Wilde's plays, and in 1970 they did the same for the Royal Shakespeare Company's production of Shakespeare's *A Midsummer Night's Dream* by the director Peter Brook (born 1925)—and the production became known as 'Brook's *Dream*'.

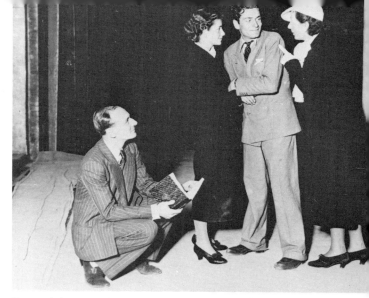

Four of the twentieth century's greatest players gathered together. John Gielgud rehearsing his memorable 1935 production of Shakespeare's *Romeo and Juliet* at the New Theatre, London, with Peggy Ashcroft as Juliet, Laurence Olivier as Romeo and Edith Evans as the Nurse

---

Movements

The different movements and 'isms' in modern theatre are bewildering. Here are a few definitions, in roughly chronological order, which may help you to see the wood for the trees.

Realism

Realism is a late nineteenth-century movement in which dramatists such as Ibsen wrote plays which aimed at a deep psychological realism in the portrayal of each character. The subject-matter of plays tended to deal as closely as possible with the perceived realities of life, and the playwright attempted to make members of the audience believe in the reality of the situation which they saw depicted in front of them, so that they forgot that they were only witnessing a play.

Naturalism

Naturalism is a development of and aid to realism, whereby the scenery, properties, language and every other aspect of theatrical presentation were as near as possible to real life. If the setting was a room, the audience were invited to believe that they were looking through a transparent fourth wall.

A scene from Ibsen's *Ghosts*, with Beatrix Lehmann as Mrs Alving and John Carol as Oswald

Symbolism

Symbolism is a reaction against naturalism, whereby attempts to represent faithfully the appearance of life were abandoned in favour of impressionistic sets and scenery which aimed at capturing the spirit of life. The main dramatist who advocated this style was the Belgian Maurice Maeterlinck (1862–1949).

Expressionism

Expressionism dominated the German theatre for a time in the 1920s. As symbolism was a reaction to naturalism, so expressionism was a reaction to realism. Expressionism tried to show that there are psychological forces which lie beneath the conscious surface of a person's mind. People such as the psychiatrist Sigmund Freud (1856–1939) and the surrealist artist Salvador Dali (born 1904) influenced playwrights such as Ernst Toller (1893–1939) in Germany, Karel Čapek (1890–1938) in Czechoslovakia and Elmer Rice (1892–1967) in the United States.

Constructivism

Constructivism is a product of theatre in Russia after the Revolution in 1917. The most important aspect of constructivism was the set, which was usually a mechanical collage of steps, platforms and scaffolds which were supposed to symbolise the dynamic qualities of the Russian way of life. Vsevolod Meyerhold (1874–?1940) developed this style of theatre. It was also experimented with outside Russia.

The Theatre of Cruelty

Growing out of expressionism and pioneered by Antonin Artaud (1896–1948), the idea was that the theatre of myth and magic and the spirit of Dionysus should be the driving forces of the theatre—not the theatre of narrative and psychological realism. The explosive forces beneath the civilised surface of a person's mind could be seen as crude and violent.

A design for one of Meyerhold's constructivist productions

Epic Theatre

Epic Theatre was developed in Germany in the 1920s, notably by Bertolt Brecht (1898–1956) and Erwin Piscator (1893–1966). The aim was to produce a play which depicted as simply as possible a procession of events, and to produce them in such a way that the audience were led towards detachment from the proceedings and to think about the implications of the play. In order to promote this end, 'alienation' devices were employed: stage-hands and lighting lanterns were kept in full view of the audience; each actor took several parts; a singer or narrator told the audience what was to happen before it occurred (this to eliminate the distracting element of suspense); the auditorium lights were sometimes left on during a performance; the audience was even encouraged to smoke (Brecht considered that nobody could be fooled whilst smoking!).

The essential point of Epic Theatre, according to Brecht, was that it appealed less to a spectator's feelings than to his reason. It may be seen that the objectives of Epic Theatre were exactly opposite to those of the naturalists.

Poetic Drama

Between the 1930s and the 1950s it was thought by some that the way forward for British drama might be through a return to the vigorous use of verse in the theatre. Notable verse plays were written by T. S. Eliot (1888–1965), Christopher Fry (born 1907) and W. H. Auden (1907–73). The movement petered out upon the arrival of the 'New Wave' of young British dramatists.

The Theatre of the Absurd

This was a kind of play which came to the fore in the 1950s, most notably with *Waiting for Godot* (1953) by Samuel Beckett (born 1906). 'Absurd' means literally 'out of harmony', and playwrights of the absurd wished to show how ridiculous Man's struggles are in a universe in which he lacks any purpose. The subject-matter of absurd plays were emphasised by their form, which seemed without logical construction and coherent dialogue. The main British playwrights of this genre are Harold Pinter (born 1930) and N. F. Simpson (born 1919).

Samuel Beckett's *Waiting for Godot* was first performed in Paris in 1953. It had its first London production at the Arts Theatre in 1955

The New Wave

This was the name given to the new breed of dramatists who changed the directions of the British theatre after the success of John Osborne's (born 1929) *Look Back in Anger* at London's Royal Court Theatre in 1956. Before that time, most plays staged in Britain, and especially in London, were revivals of classics, musicals and revues. Very little was seen of the work of new dramatists. Thanks largely to the policy of the English Stage Company at the Royal Court, the work of New Wave playwrights was staged during the late 1950s and the 1960s. Many of the new dramatists wanted to show some

John Osborne's *Look Back in Anger*, a harsh play with an embittered central character, is seen here being performed at the Royal Court Theatre, London. (*From left to right*) Mary Ure as Alison Porter, Alan Bates as Cliff Lewis, Helena Hughes as Helena Charles and Kenneth Haigh as Jimmy Porter

of the bitterness of real life or to attack the 'Establishment', and much of their output was rather contemptuously called 'kitchen-sink' drama by those who liked to go to the theatre only as an escape from 'real life'. Among the playwrights who began to make their names at this time are John Arden (born 1930), Donald Howarth (born 1931), Ann Jellicoe (born 1927), Harold Pinter and Arnold Wesker (born 1932).

The Second Wave

The 'Second Wave' is still rippling. Between the 1960s and 1980s a second generation of new playwrights emerged. They have extended the innovations of the first wave, and it is too early to assess the direction and value of their work. Much of their output is concerned with social and political problems, and they are often quick to seize upon a topical event and turn it into 'relevant' drama. Some of this is powerful and thought-provoking; some is tedious and ephemeral, and quickly forgotten. Among the best new writers are Alan Bleasdale (born 1946), Edward Bond (born 1935), Howard Brenton (born 1942), David Hare (born 1947), David Mercer (born 1928), Christopher Hampton (born 1946), Willy Russell, Tom Stoppard (born 1937) and David Storey (born 1933). These and others have written many excellent plays for television.

A scrum-down in Hull Truck Theatre Company's 1984 production of *Up 'n' Under*, by John Godber. (*From left to right*) Richard Ridings, Peter Geeves, Andrew Dunn and Jane Clifford

Alternative Theatre

This means just what it says: an alternative to mainstream theatre. Theatre of Cruelty, Absurd Drama and the German political theatre of the interwar years are all forerunners to the late twentieth-century alternative scene, which has grown up in a number of ways.

The first truly 'alternative' theatre appeared at the Edinburgh International Festival, which takes place in August and September each year. Over the past thirty-five years a 'fringe' has developed around the edges of the official festival, consisting of amateur, small professional touring, university and other groups. These companies perform in buildings ranging from Methodist church halls to abandoned warehouses, and often seek to present to the public shows which are more adventurous than those available within the official festival programme.

For a brief time before the New Wave became established, the Royal Court presented the alternative theatre of the 1950s. Since the abolition of stage censorship in 1968 fringe groups, both professional and amateur, have sprung up all over the country, presenting their shows in pubs or clubs, on the streets or on tour to any venue where they can perform. Often alternative theatre is dedicated to staging radical plays which protest against the way things are—and it is a bold expression of democracy that the Establishment, in the form of the Arts Council of Great Britain, often gives grants so that this work can carry on. Sometimes groups aspire to become a community theatre, attempting to draw in the local 'working classes' and those who do not regularly come to the theatre; but this ideal is rarely—if ever—achieved. If the products are good, reviews only appear in middle-class newspapers, and so it is that class who become interested and go along to see a group's work. Among the most interesting activities are those of a young American director and a Geordie fishmonger-turned-playwright who research and dramatise aspects of life in the North-east of England.

Much experimental theatre in Britain has been stimulated by young Americans who arrived in the 1960s—sometimes to avoid being drafted into the Vietnam War. One of these, Ed Berman, opened his Almost Free Theatre in London: theatre-goers could see a play by paying what they felt they could afford—but they had to pay *something*! Alternative theatre is vital to the growth of new ideas in subject-matter and style of presentation. Many companies such as Paines Plough, Shared Experience, Belt and Braces, 7—84 and Hull Truck are very talented and stage superb productions; others are enthusiastic and dedicated, but lack talent. Some experiments are dead-ends—but if they were assured of success then they could hardly be experiments. It is ironic that successful alternative theatre immediately ceases to be 'alternative', because it is then invariably taken up by the mainstream theatre.

The directors

Until the late nineteenth century, productions often simply 'happened'. A manager assembled a company, took a leading part himself, and sorted out the details of a production as he went along. He was usually more concerned with finance and scenery than in the style of the production. Leading actors of the day were engaged without so much as a single rehearsal before the performance. They knew their part, and the other members of the company fitted their performances as best they could around the lead actor, who 'did his own thing'.

Gradually, during the early years of the twentieth century, the director emerged: one man who did not act himself, but who stood in the auditorium outside the main action and controlled the actors and all other artistic aspects of a production, ensuring that a spectator received precisely the impression for which he, the director, was striving. The director's job may be described as follows:

(1) He decides upon the interpretation to be given to the play:
(2) He casts the actors;
(3) He works with the playwright, designers and technicians in planning the production;
(4) He rehearses the actors;
(5) He co-ordinates all the aspects into the finished stage-performance.

Many famous directors have come along during the twentieth century, creating productions which have so disturbed theatrical tradition that the theatre has not been the same after them. In Russia, Konstantin Stanislavsky (1865–1939) steered acting methods away from the histrionic and rhetorical and production techniques towards an emphasis of the

Konstantin Stanislavsky

realistic. His greatest successes in the theatre were in collaboration with Chekhov, whose plays perfectly suited Stanislavsky's style. He wrote several books expounding his theories.

The ideas of Gordon Craig (1872–1966), who

A design for Ibsen's *The Pretenders* by Gordon Craig

Peter Hall, a director of the RSC. Behind him can be seen the National Theatre, on London's South Bank

desired to see productions with complete artistic unity in the hands of one man, with actors little more than cogs in a machine, were taken up by the Austrian Max Reinhardt (1873–1943), who worked

One of the twentieth century's greatest actors, Laurence Olivier, in the title role in Shakespeare's *Othello*, with Frank Finlay as Iago (the Old Vic Theatre, London, 1964)

in Germany on all kinds of plays, from large-scale spectacle to performances in a room before a tiny audience. His influence spread abroad because he toured with his own productions (scoring a notable success in the United States in 1927–8), and directed productions in England and America. After Hitler's rise to power in the 1930s he settled in the United States.

Craig's ideas were developed in Russia by Meyerhold, who worked with Stanislavsky before the Russian Revolution. A keen Bolshevik, he worked hard to develop Soviet theatre, but eventually he came to be considered ideologically unsound by Stalin, and disappeared. It is presumed that he died in prison.

Political theatre was developed in Germany and elsewhere by Piscator and Brecht (see the section on 'Epic Theatre', page 9).

In Britain there have been many influential twentieth-century directors: John Gielgud; Michel St Denis (1897–1971)); Tyrone Guthrie (1900–71) at the Old Vic in the 1930s; Joan Littlewood (born 1914) and her workshop at the Theatre Royal, Stratford East (London); Peter Brook, who has done much of his experimental work abroad, particularly in France; Peter Hall (born 1930) with the Royal Shakespeare Company and at the National Theatre; Trevor Nunn (born 1940) and Terry Hands (born 1941) with the Royal Shakespeare and many other companies.

The actors

Actors during the later part of the nineteenth century experienced a steady rise in their social status, culminating in the knighthood of Henry Irving in 1895. Since then honours have been frequently bestowed upon actors, who lost their Bohemian image and were accepted as respectable—more or less. The profession became more organised, acting schools were founded, and a trade union was formed (Equity). Acting styles have generally tended to move towards a more naturalistic, less rhetorical, approach during the twentieth century, to the extent that underplaying is sometimes seen as an automatic virtue.

The playwrights

Until recently the playwrights of the twentieth century have not achieved the prominence of directors and actors. This may well be because, with a few exceptions, they have not been first-rate: plenty of talent but not much genius. It may also be because the exciting changes have not been so much in the subject-matter of the plays as in the style of their presentation; and hence the directors and actors have made the running.

At the end of the nineteenth century there was nobody writing for the English stage who matched Ibsen. Wilde's success was brilliant but short-lived. The light operas of W. S. Gilbert (1836–1911) and Arthur Sullivan (1842–1900) were popular and frivolous. Only Pinero and H. A. Jones (1851–1929) were writing socially realistic dramas, but they were not very profound works. Seeing all this, the music and theatre critic George Bernard Shaw decided to do better.

At first, Shaw wrote plays with prefaces for printing in book form: he hoped thereby to reach a wider reading public and the more widely to influence the direction of future theatrical developments. His characters are not very good; but his comic gifts, dramatic flair and abundance of ideas created a new type of play, and in many ways he brought the British theatre into the twentieth century.

Among those British dramatists of the first half of the twentieth century who are more than merely lightweight may be rated John Galsworthy, J. M. Barrie (1860–1937), W. B. Yeats (1865–1939) and Sean O'Casey (1880–1964) in Ireland, Somerset Maugham (1974–1965), James Bridie (1888–1951) in Scotland, Noel Coward (1899–1973), J. B. Priestley (1894–1984), Emlyn Williams (born 1905), T. S. Eliot, Christopher Fry (born 1907), Terence Rattigan (1911–1977) and John Whiting (1915–63). Among the best American playwrights are Eugene O'Neill (1888–1953), George S. Kaufman (1889–1961), Thornton Wilder (1897–1975), Moss Hart (1904–61), Tennessee Williams (1914–83) and Arthur Miller (born 1915).

In the mid-1950s the 'New Wave' of British dramatists arrived. It is impossible to refer to every good or potentially good playwright, but to those mentioned elsewhere in this introduction should be added two: Samuel Beckett, who, although an Irishman writing mainly in French, has had an incalculable impact upon the modern British theatre; and Joe Orton (1933–67), a brilliant playwright in the

The playwright and poet T. S. Eliot with members of the cast in his play *Murder in the Cathedral*, in 1951

tradition of the English Comedy of Manners whose violent early death was a great loss.

The Audience

Since the Second World War theatre managements have tried hard to draw into theatres people who do not normally go there (except perhaps to take the children to a Christmas pantomine). The aim has been to try to restore the kind of truly popular theatre which may have existed in Shakespeare's day, with businessmen and manual workers all within the same enthralled auditorium. It is a fine ideal, and breakthroughs do occur, as for a while at Nottingham Playhouse in the early 1960s. Yet, as we move towards the twenty-first century, it is still only a middle-class 5 per cent of the population, and mainly university graduates at that, who regularly attend the theatre. Even 'alternative theatre', which frequently attacks the complacency of this very audience, can usually attract only middle-class intellectuals. At Billingham Forum, Cleveland, an interesting experiment took place in the late 1960s whereby a theatre was built into a large complex which also housed under the same roof sports facilities and a cinema. All who went to the complex had to enter through the same doors and the hope was that, with basketball-players rubbing shoulders with theatre-goers, each might be tempted to sample the other's activity. Success was limited.

It is to be hoped that more and more people will, in the future, experience the magic of 'live' theatre, which happens 'before your very eyes'. It is not pre-packaged like video or film: it is flowing, even dangerous—no two performances are quite the same, and things can go wrong.

The theatres

Many expensive theatres were built in London and the provinces around the turn of the century. They were often criticised for their monumental architecture which, while impressive, did little to advance the art of the theatre. Often they were acoustically poor, and more regard was paid to packing in as many seats as possible in order to make big profits for their owners (who were businessmen rather than men of the theatre) than to creating good theatrical conditions. Moreover, they were all built with a proscenium arch—that is, the framework around the stage behind which the scenery was situated and the actors played; and theatrical taste was changing. If directors such as Brecht were going to succeed in breaking down the barrier between actor and audience and to destroy the illusion that one was watching 'real life' in the theatre, then the shape of the theatre-building itself would have to change. The proscenium arch was the physical barrier between the spectator and the player. Theatres had been constructed this way since the mid-seventeenth century. 'Abolish the proscenium!' was the cry in the early decades of the twentieth century; and accordingly theatres slowly began to be constructed which brought the actors into closer contact with the audience.

The first important development came in 1926 when Terence Gray converted an 1808 Georgian theatre on the outskirts of Cambridge. He called it the Festival Theatre, and in it he did abolish the proscenium arch, introducing a series of wide steps which led down from the stage to the audience. This area was intended to be used for the action as much as were the middle and back of the stage. The players were thus close to the audience for a larger proportion of the time.

Gray's initiative influenced later theatre-designers, and the importance of the proscenium has generally diminished. Except when a play, usually a traditional classic, demands proscenium treatment, directors have tended increasingly to organise their productions so as to take advantage of any 'thrust' or 'open' stage which projects into the auditorium and makes for greater intimacy between actors and audience. It may be that sometimes the illusion of real life is indeed lost, as Brecht desired; but this will not necessarily happen. If a director wishes the members of his audience to be absorbed in the action, then he can stimulate their imagination so that, however artificial, symbolic or expressionistic the setting, they will suspend their disbelief and imagine those things to be so which they are told *are* so.

The layout of the Festival Theatre, Cambridge. Steps led down into the audience and there was a revolving centre-stage and a raised and sliding back-stage

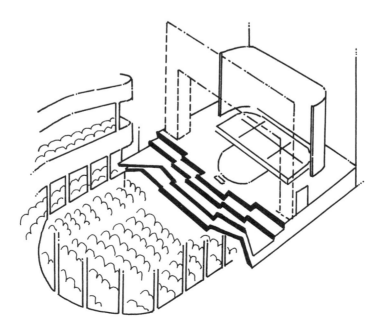

The Stephen Joseph Theatre-in-the-Round at Scarborough

Theatre-in-the-round has also developed in popularity—or rather, re-emerged: for medieval drama was often performed in an amphitheatre. The Stephen Joseph Theatre-in-the-Round at Scarborough is an excellent example of what can be done with a small space. Alan Ayckbourn is artistic director of this theatre, and it is here that all his plays are first presented. However, the major pioneering steps of modern theatre-in-the-round were taken in the United States which, lacking European theatrical tradition, has often been more adventurous in the creative arts.

After the Second World War there was little or no construction in Britain of new theatres for ten years. New houses and factories were more pressing needs. (Yet Germany, recognising that people need culture alongside their basic material needs, began to build and refurbish theatres immediately.) In the late 1950s a programme was begun of theatre-building which gathered momentum in the 1960s. New theatres were erected at Coventry (Belgrade), Leicester (Phoenix), Nottingham (Playhouse), Sheffield (Crucible), Bolton (Octagon), Leeds

(Playhouse—actually, a converted sports hall), Guildford (Yvonne Arnaud) and several other places. Nearly all new theatres were of arena-style construction, where either a thrust-stage came out into the auditorium or, like the ancient Greek theatres, seats were raked around or facing a flat open acting-space. The Mermaid theatre in the City of London, converted from a bombed-out warehouse and opened in 1959, was one of the first of the latter type.

A performance in progress at the Mermaid Theatre, London

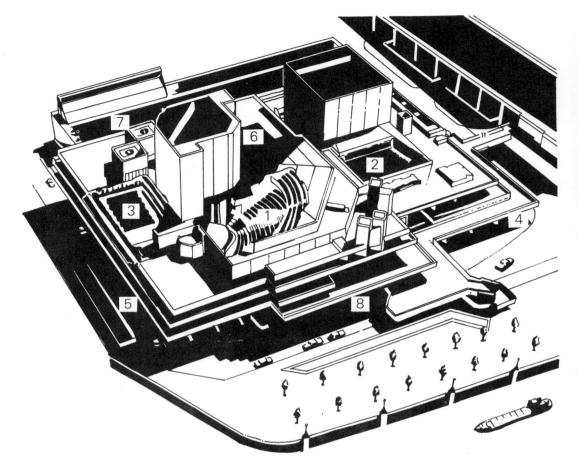

The National Theatre complex. 1 The Olivier Theatre; 2 the Lyttleton Theatre; 3 the Cottesloe Theatre; 4 Box Office; 5 stage door; 6 dressing-rooms; 7 workshops; 8 restaurant

Flexibility was often incorporated so that, if desired, a traditional proscenium theatre or orchestra pit could be created. Small studio theatres were sometimes built, either within the complex of a larger theatre or in their own right. The Gulbenkian Centre at Hull University's Department of Drama is an excellent example of all that a small, well-equipped flexible theatre can do; the auditorium and stage area can be altered to match almost any style of production from the ancient Greeks to the modern age.

When it came to the designing of a National Theatre for Britain, the architect decided that to try to design a truly flexible theatre within one auditorium was impossible. Accordingly, he planned three auditoria within one huge complex. The Lyttleton Theatre has a traditional proscenium arch; the Olivier Theatre is arena-style; and the Cottesloe is a small flexible theatre which can provide anything from an Elizabethan-type auditorium to a flat open space where the company may present 'promenade performances' (in which the audience and actors mingle, spectators sitting wherever they can in order to be a part of the actors' show).

The new National Theatre building was opened in London in 1976. In the same year the old Victorian Manchester Stock Exchange building was re-opened; within it squats an extraordinary circular structure with supporting legs and looking like a Victorian idea of a spacecraft. This is the Royal Exchange Theatre. It has proved to be a highly successful venture and offers productions of the highest standards with the best of actors.

The Arts Council of Great Britain, founded in the 1940s, gives much financial assistance for theatre-building and refurbishment. Many theatres which are so subsidised are also serving as social centres, offering such facilities as café, restaurant, bar, art gallery, bookshop, ticket-agency, conference-room and live music in the foyer—and all under the same roof as the theatre auditorium. Sadly, these amenities are rarely offered by commercial theatres, particularly in London; they are dead at those times when performances or rehearsals are not in progress.

During the past fifteen years or so another type of tiny theatre has developed:'pub' theatre. Small companies clear a space and perform among tables and chairs, or in a room above the bar. Mostly they present plays which can be described as alternative theatre (see page 10). The best-known pub theatre is probably The King's Head in Islington, London.

At the outbreak of the Second World War there were 130 provincial theatres; now there are 30. What seems like a disastrous decline has been in part a result of the coming of those two theatres in every home—radio and television. Bearing this is mind, it can be argued that there is more drama being listened to and watched than ever before, even though the dramatic standard of some of the 'soap opera' is rather low. Those 30 regional theatres which have survived always have financial problems, but they do survive and occasionally flourish. The amount of vigour to be found in small-scale theatre is also a sign of hope for the future.

One factor, however, must be weighed: the majority of the theatres, particularly in London, are still of the old proscenium-arch type. This must restrict the novelty of plays for the foreseeable future.

Scenery, costume and lighting

Two factors have led to simpler sets in the British theatre. The first is a shortage of money. The second was a visit to Britain in 1956 of Brecht's Berliner Ensemble. British audiences were astonished and excited to see how powerful an effect could be created by clear, direct uncluttered sets. A few carefully chosen props conveyed a sense of reality that a vast amount of naturalistic scenery could hardly have achieved.

Occasionally an audience may still see meticulously detailed or lavish sets, especially when attending an expensive commercial presentation in

An uncluttered set! The RSC's production of Harold Pinter's *Silence* in 1969, using only three chairs against a reflective backdrop and floor

London's West End or a play with a single room as the permanent set. However, naturalism has been largely abandoned. After the brief Constructivist period, set-designers have tended to create symbolic or impressionistic settings. A curtain is rarely raised or lowered to indicate beginnings or ends of scenes—this is normally now done by the raising or dimming of the stage lights, and is a part of the anti-illusion tendency which has been discussed elsewhere in this introduction. John Bury (born 1925) and Christopher Morley, successive heads of design at the RSC (as the Royal Shakspeare Company is known), have done much to develop this movement. Bury learnt his craft at Joan Littlewood's Theatre Royal at Stratford East. As so often, shortage of money directly influenced theatrical progress: Bury could not afford the high-quality wood which was used by such traditional designers as Cecil Beaton (1904–80). So he used old wood, corrugated iron, anything that came to hand, and created his sets as he went along rather than by sitting down at a drawing-board. He realised that skilful lighting could enhance scenic effects, producing contrasts of light and shade which the old-fashioned painted scenery never achieved. The lighting emphasised the texture of the material used.

Sean Kenney (1932–73), a designer at the Royal Court, Mermaid and other theatres, constantly attacked the British theatre's slowness to appreciate what could be achieved to enhance design by using the latest lighting equipment. Gradually, theatres are installing better lanterns, computerised lighting boards and so on, and the appointment of a lighting designer is now considered to be an important post in any company.

Scenery, lighting and costume were all developed as an integral house style at the RSC in the 1960s and 1970s. For Peter Hall's 1963 Shakespearean cycle *The Wars of the Roses*, into Bury's set of expanded metal textured with corrosive acids and copper solution were placed figures wearing costumes treated with plastics, rubber and latex to suggest the richness formerly created by embroidery and strong colours. Of the RSC style of the 1970s, the theatre commentator Peter Roberts has written:

> An important feature of the company's work . . . has been the use of costumes that are neither arbitrarily pegged to a certain period nor arbitrarily modern. They were designed to give simultaneously a hint of the play's period and a hint of relevant contemporary styles. The result has been that a young audience has not been made to feel they ought to be experts on period trimmings in order to get a revival's full flavour whilst, at the same time, they were given a visual opportunity to sample references to the world about them and so to receive the play both in terms of its period and in terms of the time of its revival.

Many designers today go into television work, but most television studio sets are naturalistic and less challenging to work on than those in the live theatre.

The companies

Many of the kinds of acting company to be found in Britain are mentioned elsewhere in this introduction. Tens of thousands of amateur companies flourish in towns, villages and institutions, drawing on faithful audiences who are unlikely to be regular attenders of the professional theatre. Professional companies may be categorised as follows:
(1) Large state-subsidised groups such as the National Theatre and the Royal Shakespeare Company. They each receive millions of pounds every year, and mount dozens of first-class productions in Britain and all over the world. By and large, they are well worth the financial help they receive.

The open stage of the theatre at Southampton University allows great flexibility, from the most simple set to the mechanical elaboration of Brecht

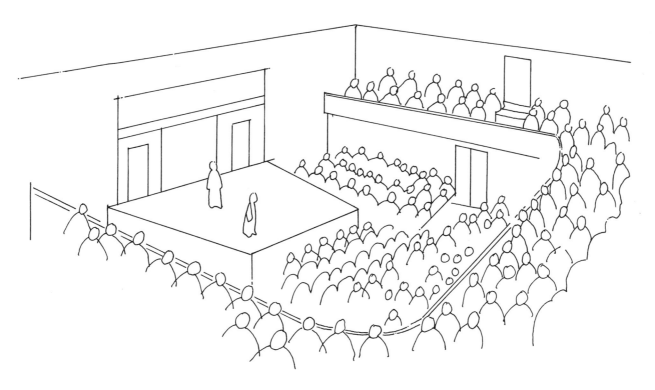

Two of the twentieth century's greatest actors, trained in repertory, in their dressing-rooms. (*Left*) Alec Guinness making up for a performance of *Cyrano* in 1947; (*right*) Ralph Richardson

The National Theatre is still not a truly national theatre. It is too much attached to London, and makes little attempt to tour the provinces or to invite good productions from elsewhere to appear within its walls. Some people object strongly to the idea of an institutional theatre which pretends to represent the best of what the nation has to offer. The headquarters of the RSC is divided between its Stratford home and the Barbican Theatre in London.

(2) Regional theatres. About 30 receive grants from the Arts Council, and most run the old repertory system. This system was created mainly by two people who spent on their theatres much of their personal wealth (in both cases derived from the wholesale grocery business). Annie Horniman (1860–1937) started the Abbey Theatre, Dublin, which virtually became the national theatre of Ireland, and then crossed the sea to Manchester and founded at the Gaiety Theatre a company dedicated to encouraging the work of northern playwrights and actors. Sir Barry Jackson (1879–1961) founded the Birmingham Repertory Company and did much to establish the idea of rep (as repertory is known), by which a company performs a new production every one, two or three weeks. Such a timetable is hard work for the actors who, even in a three-weekly rep, are studying one play, rehearsing a second and performing a third, all at the same time. One shudders to think what it is like for those in weekly reps (there are few of these left). Many actors such as

Sir Ralph Richardson have claimed that they were grateful to learn their craft in rep; others who have not eventually reached the top of their profession are more cynical.

Some regional theatres do not have residential companies, but are merely 'touring date' venues. This means that they are used by:

(3) Touring companies, who are based elsewhere and bring their productions on tour for several weeks or even months, usually playing in each theatre for a week before moving on.

(4) Companies are sometimes assembled for a single production, then disbanded afterwards. Commercial, non-subsidised plays are staged in London in this way. If a production is successful, then the actors involved may be in work for years (assuming they want to stay in one part for that long); if the production is a flop, then the actors are quickly back in the dole queue.

(5) Seasonal companies, such as those at Chichester, Sussex, or Pitlochry, Perthshire. Personnel are gathered together for a repertory season, and are usually headed by 'star' names. The company is disbanded at the end of the season.

(6) Small studio companies. A tiny staff sometimes perform in their own theatre and sometimes allow their premises to be used as a 'touring date' theatre for other small companies—perhaps while they themselves are on tour. These small companies often travel with all their scenery and props in a large van, and are true inheritors of the medieval tradition of wandering players.

(7) Theatre-in-Education companies are sometimes based at regional theatres or art centres. Their purpose is to travel around schools in their area, putting on performances and introducing school pupils to live theatre.

(8) Tiny companies exist who have no home theatre or perhaps, at most, a pub or club. They perform plays wherever they can—sometimes on the streets. In one eccentric 'performance' a group called The People Show approached passers-by in London's Sloane Square and asked them if they were interested in a 30-second show which would contain violence, drugs and sex. If keen, the 'audience' was taken to a phone box where he heard a brief sadistic story recited by a member of the group; he then watched a sugar cube being injected with a red fluid; and finally he/she was given a quick cuddle by a female/male member of the group. Not all small theatre groups are as 'alternative' as this!

(9) One-man companies: actors, jugglers, fire-eaters, mime-artists, buskers, or whatever, who perform wherever they can summon an audience. Here, as in many areas, theatre overlaps with circus, minstrelsy and other forms of live entertainment. Recently I saw a street performer in Bath who was drawing a large audience until he was moved on by the police. As he was escorted away I had time to

tell him how much pleasure he had given to my children and to many other people.

Between the 1950s and 1970s there was a fashion for actors to recreate famous men in one-man shows: Michael MacLiammoir (1899–1978) as Oscar Wilde, Max Adrian (1903–73) as George Bernard Shaw, Roy Dotrice (born 1923) as James Aubrey, Alec Guinness (born 1914) as Jonathan Swift, David Gooderson as William Cowper.

Most of the companies mentioned above receive some sort of subsidy from the Arts Council, with the exception of (4) and those under (3) which are merely insulting the regions by 'trying out' their production on tour before arrival in London for what they hope will be a long and commercially successful run.

Cinema, radio and television

These three new methods of presenting drama arrived in the order stated.

Cinema

When in the 1880s Edison invented a method of recording moving photogaphic images on celluloid, he created a great threat to live theatre. The audiences who had flocked to the theatre to see melodramas and musical hall deserted in favour of a form of entertainment which could offer more realistic illusions. The theatre responded by staging lavish comedy musicals and thrillers which only required one naturalistic set. The threat also prompted the theatre to question whether illusion was the essence of theatre, and triggered the developments discussed elsewhere in this introduction. Cinema, in turn, was to be robbed of its audiences by television.

Radio

Radio drama was first heard in the 1920s and, until the arrival of television, it was popular. Many people still like to listen to a radio play while they do hobbies or household chores; for their whole attention is not demanded, as with television, and yet they can use their imaginations to create their own illusion in their heads. This means that the most

A Lumière theatre in Paris in the early 1900s. The brothers Auguste and Louis Lumière were pioneers of photography, and their combined camera and projector using a 35-mm film is still the basis of modern ciné equipment

extravagant or fantastic settings can be used—and all for the cost of a few sound-effects. Radio gives life to a very enjoyable and satisfying form of drama. Radio 3 provides particular opportunities for new writers and experimental work, and has been responsible for bringing on modern playwrights such as Samuel Beckett, John Arden and Tom Stoppard.

Television

Television started up in the 1930s, and began to develop widely after the Second World War. It has been generally held that television is responsible for the decline of live theatre. This is true and false. Television has had some affect upon theatre-attendance; but cinema had already done most of the damage, and television in turn badly affected cinema audiences. People forsook the habit of a weekly visit to the cinema, as previously with the theatre. They stayed at home and watched the television.

Smaller audiences tended to mean more discriminating audiences, and the quality of drama rose in such theatres as were left. The arrival of Independent Television in 1956 (again and again a significant date), with its regional network, led to programmes which paid attention to local speech and subject-matter, and this had a spin-off effect in the theatre.

Many new playwrights developed through the increased opportunity which the small screen offered of their plays receiving a production. It has been lamented that many good dramatists have been encouraged by the high rewards to write only for television, or have become so used to writing for television that when they do write for the stage their plays appear fragmentary and thin (Alan Plater (born 1935) is a case in point). Few playwrights have mastered the different skills required in each medium (Harold Pinter and Willy Russell are exceptions). On the other hand, some theatrical works have reached a wider public thanks to television, and this has led people back to the theatre. After its theatrical failure in 1958, millions discovered Pinter's *The Birthday Party* when it appeared on television in 1960; and a televised extract of Osborne's *Look Back in Anger* drew audiences to the Royal Court, made the play a success, and set

A television studio transmitting a costume drama in 1938. Note the technician asking for silence — in dumb show

the English Stage Company on the road to great achievements in the theatre. The billing of television personalities and stars in stage plays also helps to draw non-regular attenders into the theatre. As the critic J. W. Lambert has said, the relationship between television and the theatre is a complex one.

The coming of video merely represents film and television in another form, and will do little to affect the present equation.

The playwrights represented in this book

John Galsworthy (1867–1933)

John Galsworthy was the son of a wealthy London solicitor and property-owner. He was educated at Harrow and Oxford, and in his early years was very much a gentleman-about-town. He trained as a lawyer, and this helped to give a precision to his choice of words when he began to write first novels and political pamphlets and then plays. He is now best remembered for a few plays and for his saga of stories concerning the Forsyte family. Although a wealthy man, he was very aware of social injustice, and gave generously of his time and money to many causes. In 1932 he won the Nobel Prize for Literature. Typically, he gave away the prize-money to a worthwhile cause.

John Galsworthy

Alan Ayckbourn

George S. Kaufman & Moss Hart

George S. Kaufman (1899–1961) and Moss Hart (1904–1961)

George S. Kaufman and Moss Hart met in 1930 when they collaborated on a comedy about Hollywood, *Once in a Lifetime*. Kaufman was forty and already a very successful playwright with such hits as *Merton and the Movies*, *June Moon*, *Theatre Royal* and *Dinner at Eight*, which he had written with various collaborators. Moss Hart was twenty-five, and *Once in a Lifetime* was his first play. Together they wrote eight plays; among the most successful were *The Man who Came to Dinner* and *You Can't take it with You*, which won the Pulitzer Prize in 1937. George Kaufman was also famous as the director of such successes as *The Front Page*, *Of Mice and Men*, *Guys and Dolls* and all of his own plays after 1928. Moss Hart went on to write *Lady in the Dark* and to direct *My Fair Lady* and *Camelot*. He also wrote a much-acclaimed autobiography *Act One*. Both men died in 1961, within six months of each other.

Alan Ayckbourn (Born 1939)

Alan Ayckbourn was born into a family with musical, literary and theatrical talents. After leaving Haileybury School, where he was encouraged by a master interested in the theatre, he joined as stage manager the touring company of Sir Donald Wolfit, the last of the great actor-managers. After various stage-management and acting jobs, he turned to directing and playwriting. From 1964 to 1970 he was Drama Producer for BBC Leeds. Since then he has been artistic director of two theatres-in-the-round in Scarborough, and currently directs his own and other plays in a converted school, re-named The Stephen Joseph Theatre-in-the-Round in honour of a man who did much for theatre-in-the-round, for theatre in Scarborough, and for Ayckbourn himself. A loyal company help him to create the first production of his plays, nearly every one of which is subsequently produced in the West End of London, in New York and around the world.

Willy Russell (Born 1947)

Willy Russell was born near Liverpool and did a variety of jobs, including song-writing, before writing his first play, a student production at St Katharine's College, Liverpool, in 1971. While teaching in Liverpool, throughout the 1970s he wrote many plays for all kinds of performance—primary schools, student productions, pubs, clubs, community centres, radio and television—with some of them being presented by the Everyman Theatre, Liverpool, the Liverpool Playhouse and the Whitehall Theatre, London. His most successful work to date is *Educating Rita* (1980), about a young woman with little education who decides to take an Open University course and finds herself assigned to a drunken tutor. The play won many awards when first presented by the Royal Shakespeare Company. The film version took most of the British Academy awards of 1984 and in the same year was nominated for several Oscars. Willy Russell is a founder and director of Quintet Films and an Honorary Director of the Liverpool Playhouse.

Things to do

1 Design a set for one of the plays in this book.
2 Find out more about (a) Alternative Theatre; (b) Arts Council of Great Britain funding—what is the present situation? (it changes every year); (c) the greatest twentieth-century actors; (d) the great twentieth-century directors; (c) the management policy and history of the nearest theatre to your school.
3 If you live in the north of England, try to visit The Stephen Joseph Theatre-in-the-Round, Valley Bridge Road, Scarborough, where Alan Ayckbourn works. He and his staff are very keen to welcome interested visitors, and he may even be available to talk to you himself.
4 If you live in the south of England, visit the National Theatre in London. Tours of the building can be booked in advance, and very interesting they are.
5 Arrange a production of one of the plays in this book. Try to involve artists, wood-workers, musicians and as many other departments of your school as possible. *Our Day Out* will need some adaptions for the stage, but skilful use of lighting and perhaps mime will enable a convincing production to be mounted fairly simply.

Willy Russell

23

THE PLAYS

John Galsworthy: *Strife*

Strife (1909) is a good example of the kind of well-made play with which the twentieth century is, in some ways, out of sympathy. Yet it has survived and is revived regularly by amateurs and professionals. Primarily a novelist and essayist, Galsworthy nonetheless displays a decisive grasp of stagecraft in this play. The dramatic structure is not in any way innovatory, Galsworthy being content to adapt the style of plays which he and his gentlemanly society had enjoyed for the previous twenty years. Where he was revolutionary is in his desire to write plays of ideas, to make his audience think.

The story in *Strife* is powerfully told, and that power is the result of the simplicity and impartiality with which Galsworthy unfolds the industrial dispute. Like the best of dramatists, he 'holds the mirror up to nature' and does not take sides. If we in the audience were to feel that he *was* taking sides, or if he had tried to caricature the workers as grasping socialists or the employers as fat capitalists, then the play would have been less good. By allowing both sides a share of credit and wrong-headedness he shows them to be human, and thus they are alive as dramatic characters. Some of today's political playwrights would do well to take another look at Galsworthy's balanced intelligence.

It is ironic that *Strife* has sometimes been viewed as propaganda. After a performance in Nottingham a prosperous businessman approached Galsworthy and praised him for Anthony's speech attacking the workers (see page 55); in Oxford a Labour 'fan' congratulated him on Roberts' speech (see page 47). Galsworthy was amused and disturbed by both reactions. He claimed that he used the theme of industrial strife, not because it was highly topical (as it ever has been during the twentieth century), but because it provided material which would well illustrate an idea close to his heart: namely, that there will always be a tragic waste when fanatics clash. The strikers' leader, Roberts, is an irresistible force; Anthony, the company chairman, is an immovable object. Both are stubborn idealists. Neither can win, but they have respect for each other's qualities.

Characters in the play

John Anthony, *Chairman of the Trenartha Tin Plate Works*
Edgar Anthony, *his son*
Frederic H. Wilder
William Scantlebury } *Directors of the same*
Oliver Wanklin
Henry Tench, *Secretary of the same*
Francis Underwood, C. E., *Manager of the same*
Simon Harness, *a trade union official*
David Roberts
James Green
John Bulgin } *the workmen's committee*
Henry Thomas
George Rous
Henry Rous
Lewis
Jago
Evans
A Blacksmith } *workmen at the Trenartha Tin Plate Works*
Davies
A Red-haired Youth
Brown
Frost, *valet to* **John Anthony**
Enid Underwood, *wife of* **Francis Underwood,** *daughter of* **John Anthony**
Annie Roberts, *wife of* **David Roberts**
Madge Thomas, *mother of* **George** *and* **Henry Rous**
Mrs Bulgin, *wife of* **John Bulgin**
Mrs Yeo, *wife of a workman*
A Parlourmaid *to the* **Underwoods**
Jan, **Madge's** *brother, a boy of ten*
A Crowd of Men on Strike

The action takes place on 7 February between the hours of noon and six in the afternoon, close to the Trenartha Tin Plate Works, on the borders of England and Wales, where a strike has been in progress throughout the winter.

Act I

It is noon. In the Underwoods' dining-room a bright fire is burning. On one side of the fireplace are double doors leading to the drawing-room, on the other side a door leading to the hall. In the centre of the room a long dining-table without a cloth is set out as a board table. At the head of it, in the Chairman's seat, sits **John Anthony**, *an old man, big, clean-shaven, and high-coloured, with thick white hair, and thick dark eyebrows. His movements are rather slow and feeble, but his eyes are very much alive. There is a glass of water by his side. On his right sits his son* **Edgar**, *an earnest-looking man of thirty, reading a newspaper. Next him* **Wanklin**, *a man with jutting eyebrows, and silver-streaked light hair, is bending over transfer papers.* **Tench**, *the secretary, a short and rather humble, nervous man, with side-whiskers, stands helping him. On* **Wanklin's** *right sits* **Underwood**, *the Manager, a quiet man, with a long, stiff jaw, and steady eyes. Back to the fire is* **Scantlebury**, *a very large, pale, sleepy man, with grey hair, rather bald. Between him and the Chairman are two empty chairs.*

Wilder (*Who is lean, cadaverous, and complaining, with drooping grey moustaches, stands before the fire*) I say, this fire's the devil! Can I have a screen, Tench?

Scantlebury A screen, ah!

Trench Certainly, Mr. Wilder. (*He looks at* **Underwood**) That is—perhaps the Manager—perhaps Mr Underwood—

Scantlebury These fireplaces of yours, Underwood—

Underwood (*Roused from studying some papers*) A screen? Rather! I'm sorry. (*He goes to the door with a little smile*) We're not accustomed to complaints of too much fire down here just now. (*He speaks as though he holds a pipe between his teeth, slowly, ironically*)

Wilder (*In an injured voice*) You mean the men. H'm!

(**Underwood** *goes out*)

Scantlebury Poor devils!

Wilder It's their own fault, Scantlebury.

Edgar (*Holding out his paper*) There's great distress amongst them, according to the *Trenartha News*.

Wilder Oh, that rag! Give it to Wanklin. Suit his Radical views. They call us monsters, I suppose. The editor of that rubbish ought to be shot.

Edgar (*Reading*) 'If the Board of worthy gentlemen who control the Trenartha Tin Plate Works from their armchairs in London, would condescend to come and see for themselves the conditions prevailing amongst their workpeople during this strike—'

Wilder Well, we *have* come.

Edgar (*Continuing*) 'We cannot believe that even their leg-of-mutton hearts would remain untouched.'

(**Wanklin** *takes the paper from him*)

Wilder Ruffian! I remember that fellow when he hadn't a penny to his name; little snivel of a chap that's made his way by blackguarding everybody who takes a different view to himself.

(**Anthony** *says something that is not heard*)

Wilder What does your father say?

Edgar He says 'The kettle and the pot'.

Wilder H'm!

(*He sits down next to* **Scantlebury**)

Scantlebury (*Blowing out his cheeks*) I shall boil if I don't get that screen.

(**Underwood** *and* **Enid** *enter with a screen, which they place before the fire.* **Enid** *is tall; she has a small, decided face, and is twenty-eight years old*)

Enid Put it closer, Frank. Will that do, Mr Wilder? It's the highest we've got.

Wilder Thanks, capitally.

Scantlebury (*Turning, with a sigh of pleasure*) Ah! Merci, Madame!

Enid Is there anything else you want, father? (**Anthony** *shakes his head*) Edgar—anything?

Edgar You might give me a 'J' nib, old girl.

Enid There are some down there by Mr Scantlebury.

Scantlebury (*Handing a little box of nibs*) Ah! your brothers uses 'J's. What does the manager use? (*With expansive politeness*) What does your husband use, Mrs Underwood?

Underwood A quill!

Scantlebury The homely product of the goose.

(*He holds out quills*)

Underwood (*Dryly*) Thanks, if you can spare me one.

(*He takes a quill*) What about lunch, Enid?

Enid (*Stopping at the double doors and looking back*) We're going to have lunch here, in the drawing-room, so you needn't hurry with your meeting.

(**Wanklin** *and* **Wilder** *bow, and she goes out*)

Scantlebury (*Rousing himself, suddenly*) Ah! Lunch! That hotel—Dreadful! Did you try the whitebait last night? Fried fat!

Wilder Past twelve! Aren't you going to read the

Anthony (Derek Smith) signs the minutes, while the Board looks on. (From a production at the Theatre Royal, Bristol, 1967)

minutes, Tench?

Tench (*Looking for the Chairman's assent, reads in a rapid and monotonous voice*) 'At a Board Meeting held the 31st of January at the Company's Offices, 512, Cannon Street, E. C. Present—Mr Anthony in the chair, Messrs F. H. Wilder, William Scantlebury, Oliver Wanklin, and Edgar Anthony. Read letters from the Manager dated January 20th, 23rd, 25th, 28th, relative to the strike at the Company's Works. Read letters to the Manager of January 21st, 24th, 26th, 29th. Read letter from Mr Simon Harness, of the Central Union, asking for an interview with the Board. Read letter from the Men's Committee signed David Roberts, James Green, John Bulgin, Henry Thomas, George Rous, desiring conference with the Board; and it was resolved that a special Board Meeting be called for February 7th at the house of the Manager, for the purpose of discussing the situation with Mr Simon Harness and the Men's Committee on the spot. Passed twelve transfers, signed and sealed nine certificates and one balance certificate.'

(*He pushes the book over to the Chairman*)

Anthony (*With a heavy sigh*) If it's your pleasure, sign the same.

(*He signs, moving the pen with difficulty*)

Wanklin What's the Union's game, Tench? They haven't made up their split with the men. What does Harness want this interview for?

Tench Hoping we shall come to a compromise, I

think, sir; he's having a meeting with the men this afternoon.

Wilder Harness! Ah! He's one of those cold-blooded, cool-headed chaps. I distrust them. I don't know that we didn't make a mistake to come down. What time'll the men be here?

Underwood Any time now.

Wilder Well, if we're not ready, they'll have to wait—won't do 'em any harm to cool their heels a bit.

Scantlebury (*Slowly*) Poor devils! It's snowing. *What* weather!

Underwood (*With meaning slowness*) This house'll be the warmest place they've been in this winter.

Wilder Well, I hope we're going to settle this business in time for me to catch the 6.30. I've got to take my wife to Spain tomorrow. (*Chattily*) My old father had a strike at his works in '69; just such a February as this. They wanted to shoot him.

Wanklin What! In the close season?

Wilder By George, there was no close season for employers then! He used to go down to his office with a pistol in his pocket.

Scantlebury (*Faintly alarmed*) Not seriously?

Wilder (*With finality*) Ended in his shootin' one of 'em in the legs.

Scantlebury (*Unavoidably feeling his thigh*) No? God bless me!

Anthony (*Lifting the agenda paper*) To consider the policy of the Board in relation to the strike.

(*There is a silence*)

Wilder It's this infernal three-cornered duel—the Union, the men, and ourselves.

Wanklin We needn't consider the Union.

Wilder It's my experience that you've always got to consider the Union, confound them! If the Union were going to withdraw their support from the men, as they've done, why did they ever allow them to strike at all?

Edgar We've had that over a dozen times.

Wilder Well, I've never understood it! It's beyond me. They talk of the engineers' and furnacemen's demands being excessive—so they are—but that's not enough to make the Union withdraw their support. What's behind it?

Underwood Fear of strikes at Harper's and Tinewell's.

Wilder (*With triumph*) Afraid of other strikes—now, that's a reason! Why couldn't we have been told that before?

Underwood You were.

Tench You were absent from the Board that day, sir.

Scantlebury The men must have seen they had no chance when the Union gave them up. It's madness.

Underwood It's Roberts!

Wilder Just our luck, the men finding a fanatical firebrand like Roberts for leader.

(*A pause*)

Wanklin (*Looking at* **Anthony**) Well?

Wilder (*Breaking in fussily*) It's a regular mess. I don't like the position we're in; I don't like it; I've said so for a long time. (*Looking at* **Wanklin**) When Wanklin and I came down here before Christmas it looked as if the men must collapse. You thought so too, Underwood.

Underwood Yes.

Wilder Well, they haven't! Here we are, going from bad to worse—losing our customers—shares going down!

Scantlebury (*Shaking his head*) M'm! M'm!

Wanklin What loss have we made by this strike, Tench?

Tench Over fifty thousand, sir!

Scantlebury (*Pained*) You don't say!

Wilder We shall never get it back.

Tench No, sir.

Wilder Who'd have supposed the men were going to stick out like this—nobody suggested that. (*Looking angrily at* **Tench**)

Scantlebury (*Shaking his head*) I've never liked a fight—never shall.

Anthony No surrender!

(*All look at him*)

Wilder Who wants to surrender? (**Anthony** *looks at him*) I—I want to act reasonably. When the men sent Roberts up to the Board in December—then was the time. We ought to have humoured him; instead of that, the Chairman—(*Dropping his eyes before* **Anthony**'s)—er—we snapped his head off. We could have got them in then by a little tact.

Anthony No compromise!

Wilder There we are! This strike's been going on now since October, and as far as I can see it may last another six months. Pretty mess we shall be in by then. The only comfort is, the men'll be in a worse!

Edgar (*To* **Underwood**) What sort of state are they really in, Frank?

Underwood (*Without expression*) Damnable!

Wilder Well, who on earth would have thought they'd have held on like this without support!

Underwood Those who know them.

Wilder I defy anyone to know them! And what about tin? Price going up daily. When we do get started we shall have to work off our contracts at the top of the market.

Wanklin What do you say to that, Chairman?

Anthony Can't be helped!

Wilder Shan't pay a dividend till goodness knows when!

Scantlebury (*With emphasis*) We ought to think of the shareholders. (*Turning heavily*) Chairman, I say we ought to think of the shareholders.

(**Anthony** *mutters*).

Scantlebury What's that?

Tench The Chairman says he *is* thinking of you, sir.

Scantlebury (*Sinking back into torpor*) Cynic!

Wilder It's past a joke. *I* don't want to go without a dividend for years if the Chairman does. We can't go on playing ducks and drakes with the Company's prosperity.

Edgar (*Rather ashamedly*) I think we ought to consider the men.

(*All but* **Anthony** *fidget in their seats*).

Scantlebury (*With a sigh*) We mustn't think of our private feelings, young man. That'll never do.

Edgar (*Ironically*) I'm not thinking of our feelings. I'm thinking of the men's.

Wilder As to that—we're men of business.

Wanklin That *is* the little trouble.

Edgar There's no necessity for pushing things so far in the face of all this suffering—it's—it's cruel.

(*No-one speaks, as though* **Edgar** *had uncovered something whose existence no man prizing his self-respect could afford to recognise*)

Wanklin (*With an ironical smile*) I'm afraid we mustn't base our policy on luxuries like sentiment.

Edgar I detest this state of things.

Anthony We didn't seek the quarrel.

Edgar I know that, sir, but surely we've gone far enough.

Anthony No.

(*All look at one another*)

Wanklin Luxuries apart, Chairman, we must look out what we're doing.

Anthony Give way to the men once and there'll be no end to it.

Wanklin I quite agree, but—(**Anthony** *shakes his head*) You make it a question of bedrock principle? (**Anthony** *nods*) Luxuries again, Chairman!

The shares are below par.

Wilder Yes, and they'll drop to a half when we pass the next dividend.

Scantlebury (*With alarm*) Come, come! Not so bad as that.

Wilder (*Grimly*) You'll see! (*Craning forward to catch* **Anthony's** *speech*) I didn't catch—

Tench (*Hesitating*) The Chairman says, sir, 'Fais que—que—devra—'

Edgar (*Sharply*) My father says: 'Do what we ought—and let things rip.'

Wilder Tcha!

Scantlebury (*Throwing up his hands*) The Chairman's a Stoic—I always said the Chairman was a Stoic.

Wilder Much good that'll do us.

Wanklin (*Suavely*) Seriously, Chairman, are you going to let the ship sink under you, for the sake of—a principle?

Anthony She won't sink.

Scantlebury (*With alarm*) Not while I'm on the Board I hope.

Anthony (*With a twinkle*) Better rat, Scantlebury.

Scantlebury What a man!

Anthony I've always fought them; I've never been beaten yet.

Wanklin We're with you in theory, Chairman. But we're not all made of cast-iron.

Anthony We've only to hold on.

Wilder (*Rising and going to the fire*) And go to the devil as fast as we can!

Anthony Better go to the devil than give in!

Wilder (*Fretfully*) That may suit you, sir, but it doesn't suit me, or anyone else I should think.

(**Anthony** *looks him in the face—a silence*)

Edgar I don't see how we can get over it that to go on like this means starvation to the men's wives and families.

(**Wilder** *turns abruptly to the fire, and* **Scantlebury** *puts out a hand to push the idea away*)

Wanklin I'm afraid again that sounds a little sentimental.

Edgar Men of business are excused from decency, you think?

Wilder Nobody's more sorry for the men than I am, but if they (*lashing himself*) choose to be such a pig-headed lot, it's nothing to do with us; we've quite enough on *our* hands to think of ourselves and the shareholders.

Edgar (*Irritably*) It won't kill the shareholders to miss a dividend or two; I don't see that *that's*

reason enough for knuckling under.

Scantlebury (*With grave discomfort*) You talk very lightly of your dividends, young man; I don't know where we are.

Wilder There's only one sound way of looking at it. We can't go on ruining *ourselves* with this strike.

Anthony No caving in!

Scantlebury (*With a gesture of despair*) Look at him! (**Anthony** *is leaning back in his chair. They do look at him*)

Wilder (*Returning to his seat*) Well, all I can say is, if that's the Chairman's view, I don't know what we've come down here for.

Anthony To tell the men that we've got nothing for them—(*Grimly*) They won't believe it till they hear it spoken in plain English.

Wilder H'm! Shouldn't be a bit surprised if that brute Roberts hadn't got us down here with the very same idea. I hate a man with a grievance.

Edgar (*Resentfully*) We didn't pay him enough for his discovery. I always said that at the time.

Wilder We paid him five hundred and a bonus of two hundred three years later. If that's not enough! What does he want for goodness' sake?

Tench (*Complainingly*) Company made a hundred thousand out of his brains, and paid him seven hundred— that's the way he goes on, sir.

Wilder The man's a rank agitator! Look here, I hate the Unions. But now we've got Harness here let's get him to settle the whole thing.

Anthony No!

(*Again they look at him*)

Underwood Roberts won't let the men assent to that.

Scantlebury Fantastic! Fanatic!

Wilder (*Looking at* **Anthony**) And not the only one! (**Frost** *enters from the hall*)

Frost (To **Anthony**) Mr Harness from the Union, waiting, sir. The men are here too, sir.

(**Anthony** *nods.* **Underwood** *goes to the door, returning with* **Harness**, *a pale, clean-shaven man with hollow cheeks, quick eyes and lantern jaw.* **Frost** *has retired*)

Underwood (*Pointing to* **Tench's** *chair*) Sit there next to the Chairman, Harness, won't you?

(*At* **Harness's** *appearance, the Board have drawn together, as it were, and turned a little to him, like cattle at a dog*)

Harness (*With a sharp look round, and a bow*) Thanks! (*He sits—his accent is slightly nasal*) Well, gentlemen, we're going to do business at last, I hope.

Wilder Depends on what you *call* business, Harness. Why don't you make the men come in?

Harness (*Sardonically*) The men are far more in the right than you are. The question with us is whether we shan't begin to support them again.

(*He ignores them all, except* **Anthony**, *to whom he turns in speaking*)

Anthony Support them if you like; we'll put in free labour and have done with it.

Harness That won't do, Mr Anthony. You can't get free labour, and you know it.

Anthony We shall see that.

Harness I'm quite frank with you. We were forced to withhold our support from your men because some of their demands are in excess of current rates. I expect to make them withdraw those demands today: if they do, take it straight from me, gentlemen, we shall back them again at once. Now, I want to see something fixed up before I go back tonight. Can't we have done with this old-fashioned tug-of-war business? What good's it doing you? Why don't you recognise once for all that these people are men like yourselves, and want what's good for them just as you want what's good for you—(*Bitterly*) Your motor-cars, and champagne, and eight-course dinners.

Anthony If the men will come in, we'll do something for them.

Harness (*Ironically*) Is that your opinion too, sir—and yours—and yours? (*The Directors do not answer*) Well, all I can say is: It's a kind of high and mighty aristocratic tone I thought we'd grown out of—seems I was mistaken.

Anthony It's the tone the men use. Remains to be seen which can hold out longest—they without us, or we without them.

Harness As businessmen, I wonder you're not ashamed of this waste of force, gentlemen. You know what it'll all end in.

Anthony What?

Harness Compromise—it always does.

Scantlebury Can't you persuade the men that their interests are the same as ours?

Harness (*Turning ironically*) I could persuade them of that, sir, if they were.

Wilder Come, Harness, you're a clever man, you don't believe all the Socialistic claptrap that's talked nowadays. There's no real difference between their interests and ours.

Harness There's just one very simple little question I'd like to put to you. Will you pay your men one penny more than they force you to pay them?

(**Wilder** *is silent*)

Wanklin (*Chiming in*) I humbly thought that not to pay more than was necessary was the ABC of commerce.

Harness (*With irony*) Yes, that seems to be the ABC of commerce, sir; and the ABC of commerce is between your interests and the men's.

Scantlebury (*Whispering*) We ought to arrange something.

Harness (*Dryly*) Am I to understand then, gentlemen, that your Board is going to make no concessions?

(**Wanklin** *and* **Wilder** *bend forward as if to speak, but stop*)

Anthony (*Nodding*) None.

(**Wanklin** *and* **Wilder** *again bend forward, and* **Scantlebury** *gives an unexpected grunt*)

Harness You were about to say something, I believe?

(*But* **Scantlebury** *says nothing*)

Edgar (*Looking up suddenly*) We're sorry for the state of the men.

Harness (*Icily*) The men have no use for your pity, sir. What they want is justice.

Anthony Then let *them* be just.

Harness For that word 'just' read 'humble' Mr Anthony. Why should they be humble? Barring the accident of money, aren't they as good men as you?

Anthony Cant!

Harness Well, I've been five years in America. It colours a man's notions.

Scantlebury (*Suddenly, as though avenging his uncompleted grunt*) Let's have the men in and hear what they've got to say!

(**Anthony** *nods, and* **Underwood** *goes out by the single door*)

Harness (*Dryly*) As I'm to have an interview with them this afternoon, gentlemen, I'll ask you to postpone your final decision till that's over.

(*Again,* **Anthony** *nods, and taking up his glass, drinks.* **Underwood** *comes in again, followed by* **Roberts, Green, Bulgin, Thomas, Rous**. *They file in, hat in hand, and stand silent in a row.* **Roberts** *is lean, of middle height, with a slight stoop. He has a little rat-gnawn, brown-grey beard, moustaches, high cheek-bones, hollow cheeks, small fiery eyes. He wears an old and grease-stained blue serge suit, and carries an old bowler hat. He stands nearest the Chairman.* **Green**, *next to him, has a clean, worn* *face, wih a small grey goatee beard and drooping moustaches, iron spectacles, and mild, straightforward eyes. He wears an overcoat, green with age, and a linen collar. Next to him is* **Bulgin,** *a tall, strong man, with a dark moustache, and fighting jaw, wearing a red muffler, who keeps changing his cap from one hand to the other. Next to him is* **Thomas,** *an old man with a grey moustache, full beard, and weatherbeaten, bony face, whose overcoat discloses a lean, plucked-looking neck. On his right,* **Rous,** *the youngest of the five, looks like a soldier; he has a glitter in his eyes)*

Underwood (*Pointing*) There are some chairs there against the wall, Roberts; won't you draw them up and sit down?

Roberts Thank you, Mr Underwood; we'll stand—in the presence of the Board. (*He speaks in a biting and staccato voice, rolling his r's, pronouncing his a's like an Italian a, and his consonants short and crisp*) How are you, Mr Harness? Didn't expect t' have the pleasure of seeing you till this afternoon.

Harness (*Steadily*) We shall meet again then, Roberts.

Roberts Glad to hear that; we shall have some news for you to take to your people.

Anthony What do the men want?

Roberts (*Acidly*) Beg pardon, I don't quite catch the Chairman's remark.

Tench (*From behind the Chairman's chair*) The Chairman wishes to know what the men have to say.

Roberts It's what the Board has to say we've come to hear. It's for the Board to speak first.

Anthony The Board has nothing to say.

Roberts (*Looking along the line of men*) In that case we're wasting the Directors' time. We'll be taking our feet off this pretty carpet.

(*He turns, the men move slowly, as though hypnotically influenced*)

Wanklin (*Suavely*) Come, Roberts, you didn't give us this long cold journey for the pleasure of saying that.

Thomas (*a pure Welshman*) No, sir, an' what I say iss—

Roberts (*Bitingly*) Go on, Henry Thomas, go on. You're better able to speak to the—Directors than me.

(**Thomas** *is silent*)

Tench The Chairman means, Roberts, that it was the men who asked for the Conference. The Board wish to hear what they have to say.

Roberts Gad! If I was to begin to tell ye all they have to say, I wouldn't be finished today. And there'd be some that'd wish they'd never left their London palaces.

Harness What's your proposition, man? Be reasonable.

Roberts You want reason, Mr Harness? Take a look round this afternoon before the meeting. (*He looks at the men; no sound escapes them*) You'll see some very pretty scenery.

Harness All right, my friend; you won't put me off.

Roberts (*To the men*) We shan't put Mr Harness off. Have some champagne with your lunch, Mr Harness; you'll want it, sir.

Harness Come, get to business, man!

Thomas What we're asking, look you, is just simple justice.

Roberts (*Venomously*) Justice from London? What are you talking about, Henry Thomas? Have you gone silly? (**Thomas** *is silent*) We know very well what we are—discontented dogs—never satisfied. What did the Chairman tell me up in London? That I didn't know what I was talking about. I was a foolish, uneducated man, that knew nothing of the wants of the men I spoke for.

Edgar Do please keep to the point.

Anthony (*Holding up his hand*) There can only be one master, Roberts.

Roberts Then, be Gad, it'll be us.

(*There is a silence;* **Anthony** *and* **Roberts** *stare at one another*)

Underwood If you've nothing to say to the Directors, Roberts, perhaps you'll let Green or Thomas speak for the men.

(**Green** *and* **Thomas** *look anxiously at* **Roberts,** *at each other, and the other men*)

Green (*An Englishman*) If I'd been listened to, gentlemen—

Thomas What I'fe got to say iss what we'fe all got to say—

Roberts Speak for yourself, Henry Thomas.

Scantlebury (*With a gesture of deep spiritual discomfort*) Let the poor men call their souls their own!

Roberts Aye, they shall keep their souls, for it's not much body that you've left them, Mr (*with biting emphasis, as though the word were an offence*) Scantlebury! (*To the men*) Well, will you speak, or shall I speak for you?

Rous (*Suddenly*) Speak out, Roberts, or leave it to others.

Roberts (*Ironically*) Thank you, George Rous.

'There can only be one master, Roberts.' Anthony (Derek Smith) confronts Roberts (Anthony Webb) in the 1967 production at the Theatre Royal, Bristol

(*Addressing himself to* **Anthony**) The Chairman and Board of Directors have honoured us by leaving London and coming all this way to hear what we've got to say; it would not be polite to keep them any longer waiting.

Wilder Well, thank God for that!

Roberts Ye will not dare to thank Him when I have done, Mr Wilder, for all your piety. May be your God up in London has no time to listen to the working man. I'm told He is a wealthy God; but if He listens to what I tell Him, He will know more than ever He learned in Kensington.

Harness Come, Roberts, you have your own God. Respect the God of other men.

Roberts That's right, sir. We have another God down here; I doubt He is rather different to Mr Wilder's. Ask Henry Thomas; he will tell you whether his God and Mr Wilder's are the same.

(**Thomas** *lifts his hand, and cranes his head as though to prophesy*)

Wanklin For goodness' sake, let's keep to the point, Roberts.

Roberts I rather think it is the point, Mr Wanklin. If you can get the God of Capital to walk through the streets of Labour, and pay attention to what he sees, you're a brighter man than I take you for, for all that you're a Radical.

Anthony Attend to me, Roberts! (**Roberts** *is silent*) You are hear to speak for the men, as I am here to speak for the Board.

(*He looks slowly round.* **Wilder, Wanklin,** *and* **Scantlebury** *make movements of uneasiness, and* **Edgar** *gazes at the floor. A faint smile comes on* **Harness**'s *face*)

Now then, what is it?

Roberts Right, sir? (*Throughout all that follows, he*

and **Anthony** *look fixedly upon each other. Men and Directors show in their various ways suppressed uneasiness, as though listening to words that they themselves would not have spoken*) The men can't afford to travel up to London; and they don't trust you to believe what they say in black and white. They know what the post is (*he darts a look at* **Underwood** *and* **Tench**), and what Directors' meetings are: 'Refer it to the manager—let the manager advise us on the men's condition. Can we squeeze them a little more?'

Underwood (*In a low voice*) Don't hit below the belt, Roberts!

Roberts Is it below the belt, Mr Underwood? The men know. When I came up to London, I told you the position straight. An' what came of it? I was told I didn't know what I was talkin' about. I can't afford to travel up to London to be told that again.

Anthony What have you to say for the men?

Roberts I have this to say—and first as to their condition. Ye shall 'ave no need to go and ask your manager. Ye can't squeeze them any more. Every man of us is well-nigh starving. (*A surprised murmur rises from the men.* **Roberts** *look round*) Ye wonder why I tell ye that? Every man of us is going short. We can't be no worse off than we've been these weeks past. Ye needn't think that by waiting ye'll drive us to come in. We'll die first, the whole lot of us. The men have sent for ye to know, once and for all, whether ye are going to grant them their demands. I see the sheet of paper in the Secretary's hand. (**Tench** *moves nervously*) That's it, I think, Mr Tench. It's not very large.

Tench (*Nodding*) Yes.

Roberts There's not one sentence of writing on that paper that we can do without. (*A movement amongst the men.* **Roberts** *turns on them sharply*) Isn't that so? (*The men assent reluctantly.* **Anthony** *takes from* **Tench** *the paper and peruses it*) Not one single sentence. All those demands are fair. We have not asked anything that we are not entitled to ask. What I said up in London, I say again now: there is not anything on that piece of paper that a just man should not ask, and a just man give.

(*A pause*)

Anthony There is not one single demand on this paper that we will grant.

(*In the stir that follows on these words* **Roberts** *watches the Directors and* **Anthony** *the men.* **Wilder** *gets up abruptly and goes over to the fire*)

Roberts D'ye mean that?

Anthony I do.

(**Wilder** *at the fire makes an emphatic movement of disgust*)

Roberts (*Noting it, with dry intensity*) Ye best know whether the condition of the Company is any better than the condition of the men. (*Scanning the Directors' faces*) Ye best know whether ye can afford your tyranny—but this I tell ye. If ye think the men will give way the least part of an inch, ye're making the worst mistake ye ever made. (*He fixes his eyes on* **Scantlebury**) Ye think because the Union is not supporting us—more shame to it!—that we'll be coming on our knees to you one fine morning. Ye think because the men have got their wives an' families to think of—that it's just a question of a week or two—

Anthony It would be better if you did not speculate so much on what we think.

Roberts Aye! It's not much profit to us! I will say this for you, Mr Anthony—ye know your own mind! (*Staring at* **Anthony**) I can reckon on ye!

Anthony (*Ironically*) I am obliged to you!

Roberts And I know mine. I tell ye this. The men will send their wives and families where the country will have to keep them; an' they will starve sooner than give way. I advise ye, Mr Anthony, to prepare yourself for the worst that can happen to your Company. We are not so ignorant as you might suppose. We know the way the cat is jumping. Your position is not all that it might be—not exactly!

Anthony Be good enough to allow us to judge of our position for ourselves. Go back, and reconsider your own.

Roberts (*Stepping forward*) Mr Anthony, you are not a young man now; from the time that I remember anything ye have been an enemy to every man that has come into your works. I don't say that ye're a mean man, or a cruel man, but ye've grudged them the say of any word in their own fact. Ye've fought them down four times. I've heard ye say ye love a fight—mark my words—ye're fighting the last fight ye'll ever fight—

(**Tench** *touches* **Roberts'** *sleeve*)

Underwood Roberts! Roberts!

Roberts Roberts! Roberts! I mustn't speak my mind to the Chairman, but the Chairman may speak his mind to me!

Wilder What are things coming to?

Anthony (*With a grim smile at* **Wilder**) Go on, Roberts; say what you like.

Roberts (*After a pause*) I have no more to say.

Anthony The meeting stands adjourned to five o'clock.

Wanklin (*In a low voice to* **Underwood**) We shall never settle anything like this.

Roberts (*Bitingly*) We thank the Chairman and Board of Directors for their gracious hearing.

(*He moves towards the door; the men cluster together stupefied; then* **Rous** *throwing up his head, passes* **Roberts** *and goes out. The others follow.* **Roberts** *stands with his hand on the door—maliciously*) Good-day gentlemen!

(*He goes out*)

Harness (*Ironically*) I congratulate you on the conciliatory spirit that's been displayed. With your permission, gentlemen, I'll be with you again at half-past five. Good morning!

(*He bows slightly, rests his eyes on* **Anthony** *who returns his stare unmoved, and, followed by* **Underwood**. *goes out. There is a moment of uneasy silence.* **Underwood** *reappears in the doorway*).

Wilder (*With emphatic disgust*) Well!

(*The double doors are opened*)

Enid (*Standing in the doorway*) Lunch is ready.

(**Edgar** *getting up abruptly, walks out past his sister*)

Wilder Coming to lunch, Scantlebury?

Scantlebury (*Rising heavily*) I suppose so, I suppose so. It's the only thing we can do.

(*They go out through the double doors*).

Wanklin (*In a low voice*) Do you really mean to fight to a finish, Chairman?

(**Anthony** *nods*)

Take care! The essence of things is to know when to stop.

(**Anthony** *does not answer*)

(*Very gravely*) This way disaster lies. The ancient Trojans were fools to your father, Mrs Underwood.

(*He goes out through the double doors*)

Enid I want to speak to father, Frank.

(**Underwood** *follows* **Wanklin** *out.* **Tench** *passing round the table, is restoring order to the scattered pens and papers*)

Aren't you coming, Dad?

(**Anthony** *shakes his head.* **Enid** *looks meaningly at* **Tench**)

Won't you go and have some lunch, Mr Tench?

Tench (*With papers in his hand*) Thank you, ma'am,

thank you!

(*He goes slowly, looking back*)

Enid (*Shutting the door*) I *do* hope it's settled, father!

Anthony No!

Enid (*Very disappointed*) Oh! Haven't you done anything?

(**Anthony** *shakes his head*)

Frank says they all want to come to a compromise, really, except that man Roberts.

Anthony *I* don't.

Enid It's such a horrid position for us. If you were the wife of the manager, and lived down here, and saw it all. You can't realise, Dad!

Anthony Indeed?

Enid We see *all* the distress. You remember my maid Annie, who married Roberts? (**Anthony** *nods*) It's so wretched, her heart's weak; since the strike began, she hasn't even been getting proper food. I know it for a fact, father.

Anthony Give her what she wants, poor woman!

Enid Roberts won't let her take anything from *us*.

Anthony (*Staring before him*) I can't be answerable for the men's obstinacy.

Enid They're all suffering. Father! Do stop it, for my sake!

Anthony (*With a keen look at her*) You don't understand, my dear.

Enid If I were on the Board, I'd do something.

Anthony What would you do?

Enid It's because you can't bear to give way. It's so—

Anthony Well?

Enid So unnecessary.

Anthony What do *you* know about necessity? Read your novels, play your music, talk your talk, but don't try and tell *me* what's at the bottom of a struggle like this.

Enid I live down here, and see it.

Anthony What d'you imagine stands between you and your class and these men that you're so sorry for?

Enid (*Coldly*) I don't know what you mean, father.

Anthony In a few years you and your children would be down in the condition they're in, but for those who have the eyes to see things as they are and the backbone to stand up for themselves.

Enid You don't know the state the men are in.

Anthony I know it well enough.

Enid You don't father; if you did, you wouldn't—

Anthony It's you who don't know the simple facts

Enid (Patricia Maynard) tries to console Anthony (Derek Smith) in the 1967 production at the Theatre Royal, Bristol

of the position. What sort of mercy do you suppose you'd get if no one stood between you and the continual demands of labour? This sort of mercy—(*he puts his hand up to his throat and squeezes it*). First would go your sentiments, my dear; then your culture, and your comforts would be going all the time!

Enid I don't believe in barriers between classes.

Anthony
You—don't—believe—in—barriers—between the classes?

Enid (*Coldly*) And I don't know what that has to do with this question.

Anthony It will take a generation or two for you to understand.

Enid It's only you and Roberts, father, and you know it!

(**Anthony** *thrusts out his lower lip*)
It'll ruin the Company.

Anthony Allow me to be the judge of that.

Enid (*Resentfully*) I won't stand by and let poor Annie Roberts suffer like this! And think of the children, father! I warn you.

Anthony (*With a grim smile*) What do you propose to do?

Enid That's my affair.

(**Anthony** *only looks at her*)

Enid (*In a changed voice, stroking his sleeve*) Father, you *know* you oughtn't to have this strain on you—you know what Dr Fisher said!

Anthony No old man can afford to listen to old women.

Enid But you *have* done enough, even if it really is such a matter of principle with you.

Anthony You think so?

Enid Don't, Dad! (*Her face works*) You—you might think of *us*!

Anthony I am.

Enid It'll break you down.

Anthony (*Slowly*) My dear, I am not going to funk; you may rely on that.

(*Re-enter* **Tench** *with papers; he glances at them, then plucking up courage*)

Tench Beg pardon, Madam, I think I'd rather see these papers were disposed of before I get my lunch.

(**Enid** *after an impatient glance at him, looks at her father, turns suddenly, and goes into the drawing-room.* **Tench** *holds the papers and a pen to* **Anthony** *very nervously*)

Would you sign these for me, please sir?

(**Anthony** *takes the pen and signs,* **Tench.** *standing with a sheet of blotting-paper behind* **Edgar**'s *chair, begins speaking nervously*)

I owe my position to you, sir.

Anthony Well?

Tench I'm obliged to see everything that's going on, sir; I—I depend upon the Company entirely. If anything were to happen to it, it'd be disastrous for me. (**Anthony** *nods*) And, of course, my wife's just had another; and so it makes me doubly anxious just now. And the rates are really terrible down our way.

Anthony (*With grim amusement*) Not more terrible than they are up mine.

Tench No, sir? (*Very nervously*) I know the Company means a great deal to you, sir.

Anthony It does; I founded it.

Tench Yes, sir. If the strike goes on it'll be very serious. I think the Directors are beginning to realise that, sir.

Anthony (*Ironically*) Indeed?

Tench I know you hold very strong views, sir, and it's always your habit to look things in the face; but I don't think the Directors—like it, sir, now they—they see it.

Anthony (*Grimly*) Nor you, it seems.

Tench (*With the ghost of a smile*) No, sir; of course I've got my children, and my wife's delicate; in my position I *have* to think of these things. (**Anthony** *nods*) It wasn't *that* I was going to say, sir, if you'll excuse me (*hesitates*)—

Anthony Out with it, then!

Tench I know—from my father, sir, that when you get on in life you do feel things dreadfully—

Anthony (*Almost paternally*) Come, out with it, Tench!

Tench I don't *like* to say it, sir.

Anthony (*Stonily*) You must.

Tench (*After a pause, desperately bolting it out*) I think the Directors are going to throw you over, sir.

Anthony (*Sits in silence*) Ring the bell!

(**Tench** *nervously rings the bell and stands by the fire*)

Tench Excuse me saying such a thing. I was *only* thinking of you, sir.

(**Frost** *enters from the hall. He comes to the foot of the table, and looks at* **Anthony**; **Tench** *covers his nervousness by arranging papers*)

Anthony Bring me a whisky and soda.

Frost Anything to eat, sir?

(**Anthony** *shakes his head.* **Frost** *goes to the sideboard, and prepares the drink*)

Tench (*In a low voice, almost supplicating*) If you could see your way, sir, it would be a great relief to my mind, it would indeed. (*He looks up at* **Anthony** *who has not moved*). It does make me so very anxious. I haven't slept properly for weeks, sir, and that's a fact.

(**Anthony** *looks in his face, then slowly shakes his head*)

Tench (*Disheartened*) No, sir?

(*He goes on arranging papers.* **Frost** *places the whisky and soda on a salver and puts it down by* **Anthony**'s *right hand. He stands away, looking gravely at* **Anthony**)

Frost *Nothing* I can get you, sir? (**Anthony** *shakes his head*) You're aware, sir, of what the doctor said, sir?

Anthony I am.

(*A pause.* **Frost** *suddenly moves closer to him, and speaks in a low voice*)

Frost This strike, sir; puttin' all this strain on you. Excuse me, sir, is it—is it worth it, sir? (**Anthony** *mutters some words that are inaudible*) Very good, sir!

(*He turns and goes out into the hall.* **Tench** *makes two attempts to speak; but meeting his Chairman's gaze he drops his eyes, and turning dismally, he too goes out.* **Anthony** *is left alone. He grips the glass, tilts it, and drinks deeply; then sets it down with a deep and rumbling sigh, and leans back in his chair*)

Act II, Scene 1

It is half past three. In the kitchen of **Roberts'** *cottage a meagre little fire is burning. The room is clean and tidy, very barely furnished, with a brick floor and white-washed walls, much stained with smoke. There is a kettle on the fire. A door opposite the fireplace opens inwards from a snowy street. On the wooden table are a cup and saucer, a teapot, knife, and plate of bread and cheese. Close to the fireplace in an old armchair, wrapped in a rug, sits* **Mrs Roberts**, *a thin and dark-haired woman about thirty-five, with patient eyes. Her hair is not done up, but tied back with a piece of ribbon. By the fire, too, is* **Mrs Yeo**; *a red-haired, broad-faced person. Sitting near the table is* **Mrs Rous**, *an old lady, ashen-white, with silver hair; by the door, standing, as if about to go, is* **Mrs Bulgin**, *a little pale, pinched-up woman. In a chair, with her elbows resting on the table and her face resting in her hands, sits* **Madge Thomas**, *a good-looking girl, of twenty-two, with high cheek-bones, deep-set eyes, and dark, untidy hair. She is listening to the talk but she neither speaks nor moves.*

Mrs Yeo So he gives me a sixpence, and that's the first bit o' money *I* seen this week. There an't much 'eat to this fire. Come and warm yerself, Mrs Rous, you're lookin' as white as the snow, you are.

Mrs Rous (*Shivering—placidly*) Ah! but the winter my old man was took was the proper winter. Seventy-nine that was, when none of you was hardly born—not Madge Thomas, nor Sue Bulgin. (*Looking at them in turn*) Annie Roberts, 'ow old were you, dear?

Mrs Roberts Seven, Mrs Rous.

Mrs Rous Seven—well ther'! A tiny little thing!

Mrs Yeo (*Aggressively*) Well, I was ten myself, I remembers it.

Mrs Rous (*Placidly*) The Company hadn't been started three years. Father was workin' on the acid, that's 'ow he got 'is pisoned leg. I kep' sayin' to 'im. 'Father, you've got a pisoned leg'. 'Well,' 'e said, 'Mother, pison or no pison, I can't afford to go a-laying up.' An' two days after he was on 'is back, and never got up again. It was Providence! There wasn't none o' these Compensation Acts then.

Mrs Yeo Ye hadn't no strike that winter! (*With grim humour*) This winter's 'ard enough for me. Mrs Roberts, you don't want no 'arder winter, do you?

Wouldn't seem natural to 'ave a dinner, would it, Mrs Bulgin?

Mrs Bulgin We've had bread and tea last four days.

Mrs Yeo You got that Friday's laundry job?

Mrs Bulgin (*Dispiritedly*) They said they'd give it me, but when I went last Friday, they were full up. I got to go again next week.

Mrs Yeo Ah! There's too many after that. I send Yeo out on the ice to put on the gentry's skates an' pick up what 'e can. Stops 'im from broodin' about the 'ouse.

Mrs Bulgin (*In a desolate, matter-of-fact voice*) Leavin' out the men—it's bad enough with the children. I keep 'em in bed, they don't get so hungry when they're not running about; but they're that restless in bed they worry your life out.

Mrs Yeo You're lucky they're all so small. It's the goin' to school that makes 'em 'ungry. Don't Bulgin give you *anythin'*?

Mrs Bulgin (*Shakes her head, then, as though by afterthought*) Would if he could, I s'pose.

Mrs Yeo (*Sardonically*) What! 'Aven't 'e got no shares in the Company?

Mrs Rous (*Rising with tremendous cheerfulness*) Well, goodbye, Annie Roberts, I'm going along home.

Mrs Roberts Stay an' have a cup of tea, Mrs Rous?

Mrs Rous (*With the faintest smile*) Roberts'll want 'is tea when he comes in. I'll just go an' get to bed; it's warmer there than anywhere.

(*She moves very shakily towards the door*)

Mrs Yeo (*Rising and giving her an arm*) Come on, Mother, take my arm; we're all goin' the same way.

Mrs Rous (*Taking the arm*) Thank you, my dearies!

(*They go out, followed by* **Mrs Bulgin**)

Madge (*Moving for the first time*) There, Annie, you see that! I told George Rous, 'Don't think to have my company till you've made an end of all this trouble. You ought to be ashamed,' I said, 'with your own mother looking like a ghost, and not a stick to put on the fire. So long as you're able to fill your pipes, you'll let us starve. 'I'll take my oath, Madge,' he said, 'I've not had smoke or drink these three weeks!' 'Well, then, why do you go on with it? 'I can't go back on Roberts!' . . . That's it! Roberts, always Roberts! They'd all drop it but for him. When *he* talks it's the devil that comes into them. (*A silence.* **Mrs Roberts** *makes a movement of pain*) Ah! *You* don't want

him beaten! He's your man. With everybody like their own shadows! (*She makes a gesture towards* **Mrs Roberts**) If Rous wants me he must give up Roberts. If *he* gave him up—they all would. They're only waiting for a lead. Father's against him—they're all against him in their hearts.

Mrs Roberts You won't beat Roberts! (*They look silently at each other.*)

Madge Won't I? The cowards—when their own mothers and their own children don't know where to turn.

Mrs Roberts Madge!

Madge (*Looking searchingly at* **Mrs Roberts**) I wonder he can look *you* in the face. (*She squats before the fire, with her hands out to the flame*) Harness is here again. They'll have to make up their minds today.

Mrs Roberts (*In a soft, slow voice, with a slight West-country burr*) Roberts will never give up the furnacemen and engineers. 'Twouldn't be right.

Madge You can't deceive me. It's just his pride.

(*A tapping on the door is heard. The women turn as* **Enid** *enters. She wears a round fur cap, and a jacket of squirrel's fur. She closes the door behind her*)

Enid Can I come in, Annie?

Mrs Roberts (*Flinching*) Miss Enid! Give Mrs Underwood a chair, Madge.

(**Madge** *gives* **Enid** *the chair she has been sitting on*)

Enid Thank you! (*To* **Mrs Roberts**) Are you any better?

Mrs Roberts Yes, M'm; thank you, M'm

Enid (*Looking at the sullen* **Madge** *as though requesting her departure*) Why did you send back the jelly? I call that really wicked of you!

Mrs Roberts Thank you, M'm, I'd no need for it.

Enid Of course! It was Roberts' doing, wasn't it? How can he let all this suffering go on amongst you?

Madge (*Suddenly*) What suffering?

Enid (*Surprised*) I beg your pardon!

Madge Who said there was suffering?

Mrs Roberts Madge?

Madge (*Throwing her shawl over her head*) Please to let us keep ourselves to ourselves. We don't want you coming here and spying on us.

Enid (*Confronting her, but without rising*) I didn't speak to you.

Madge (*In a low, fierce voice*) Keep your kind feelings to yourself. You think you can come amongst us, but you're mistaken. Go back and tell the Manager that.

Scene 1

Enid (*Stonily*) This is not your house.

Madge (*Turning to the door*) No, it is not my house; keep clear of my house, Mrs Underwood.

(*She goes out.* **Enid** *taps her fingers on the table*)

Mrs Roberts Please to forgive Madge Thomas, M'm; she's a bit upset today.

(*A pause*)

Enid (*Looking at her*) Oh, I think they're so *stupid*, all of them.

Mrs Roberts (*With a faint smile*) Yes, M'm.

Enid Is Roberts out?

Mrs Roberts Yes, M'm.

Enid It is *his* doing, that they don't come to an agreement. Now isn't it, Annie?

Mrs Roberts (*Softly, with her eyes on* **Enid** *and moving the fingers of one hand continually on her breast*) They do say that your father, M'm—

Enid My father's getting an old man, and you know what old men are.

Mrs Roberts I am sorry, M'm.

Enid (*More softly*) I don't expect *you* to feel sorry, Annie. I know it's his fault as well as Roberts'.

Mrs Roberts I'm sorry for anyone that gets old, M'm; it's dreadful to get old, and Mr Anthony was such a fine old man I always used to think.

Enid (*Impulsively*) He always liked you, don't you remember? Look here, Annie, what can I do? I do so want to know. You don't get what you ought to have. (*Going to the fire, she takes the kettle off, and looks for coals*) And you're so naughty sending back the soup and things!

Mrs Roberts (*With a faint smile*) Yes, M'm?

Enid (*Resentfully*) Why, you haven't even got coals?

Mrs Roberts If you please, M'm, to put the kettle on again; Roberts won't have long for his tea when he comes in. He's got to meet the men at four.

Enid (*Putting the kettle on*) That means he'll lash them into a fury again. Can't you stop his going, Annie? (**Mrs Roberts** *smiles ironically*) Have you tried? (*A silence*) Does he know how ill you are?

Mrs Roberts It's only my weak 'eart, M'm.

Enid You used to be so well when you were with us.

Mrs Roberts (*Stiffening*) Roberts is always good to me.

Enid But you ought to have everything you want, and you have nothing!

Mrs Roberts (*Appealingly*) They tell me I don't look like a dyin' woman?

Enid Of course you don't; if you could only have

Enid (Patricia Maynard) with the women in Roberts' cottage. (From the production at the Theatre Royal, Bristol, 1967)

proper—Will you see my doctor if I send him to you? I'm sure he'd do you good.

Mrs Roberts (*With faint questioning*) Yes, M'm.

Enid Madge Thomas oughtn't to come here; she only excites you. As if I didn't know what suffering there is amongst the men! I do feel for them dreadfully, but you know they *have* gone too far.

Mrs Roberts (*Continually moving her fingers*) They say there's no other way to get better wages, M'm.

Enid (*Earnestly*) But, Annie, that's why the Union won't help them. My husband's very sympathetic with the men, but he says they're not underpaid.

Mrs Roberts No, M'm?

Enid They never think how the Company could go on if we paid the wages they want.

Mrs Roberts (*With an effort*) But the dividends having been so big, M'm.

Enid (*Taken aback*) You all seem to think the shareholders are rich men, but they're not—most of them are really no better off than working men. (**Mrs Roberts** *smiles*) They have to keep up appearances.

Mrs Roberts Yes, M'm?

Enid You don't have to pay rates and taxes, and a hundred other things that they do. If the men didn't spend such a lot in drink and betting they'd be quite well off!

Mrs Roberts They say, workin' so hard, they must have some pleasure.

Enid But surely not low pleasure like that.

Mrs Roberts (*A little resentfully*) Roberts never touches a drop; and he's never had a bet in his life.

Enid Oh! but he's not a com— I mean he's an engineer—a superior man.

Mrs Roberts Yes, M'm. Roberts says they've no chance of other pleasures.

Enid (*Musing*) Of course, I know it's hard.

Mrs Roberts (*With a spice of malice*) And they say gentlefolk's just as bad.

Enid (*With a smile*) I go as far as most people, Annie, but you know, yourself, that's nonsense.

Mrs Roberts (*With painful effort*) A lot o' the men never go near the Public; but even they don't save but very little, and that goes if there's illness.

Enid But they've got their clubs, haven't they?

Mrs Roberts The clubs only give up to eighteen shillin's a week, M'm, and it's not much amongst a family. Roberts says workin' folk have always lived from hand to mouth. Sixpence to-day is worth more than a shillin to'morrow, that's what they say.

Enid But that's the spirit of gambling.

Mrs Roberts (*With a sort of excitement*) Roberts says a working man's life is all a gamble, from the time 'e's born to the time 'e dies. (**Enid** *leans forward, interested.* **Mrs Roberts** *goes on with a growing excitement that culminates in the personal feeling of the last words*) He says, M'm, that when a working man's baby is born, it's a toss-up from breath to breath whether it ever draws another, and so on all 'is life; an' when he comes to be old, it's the workhouse or the grave. He says that without a man is very near, and pinches and stints himself and 'is children to save, there can't be neither surplus nor security. That's why he wouldn't have no children (*she sinks back*), not though I *wanted* them.

Enid Yes, yes, I know!

Mrs Roberts No, you don't, M'm. You've got your children, and you'll never need to trouble for them.

Enid (*Gently*) You oughtn't to be talking so much, Annie. (*Then, in spite of herself*) But Roberts was paid a lot of money, wasn't he, for discovering that process?

Mrs Roberts (*On the defensive*) All Roberts' savin's have gone. He's always looked forward to this strike. He says he's no right to a farthing when the others are suffering. 'Tisn't so with all o'them!

Some don't seem to care no more than that—so long as they get their own.

Enid I don't see how they can be expected to when they're suffering like this. (*In a changed voice*) But Roberts ought to think of *you!* It's all terrible! The kettle's boiling. Shall I make the tea? (*She takes the teapot, and seeing tea there, pours water into it*) Won't you have a cup?

Mrs Roberts No, thank you, M'm. (*She is listening, as though for footsteps*) I'd sooner you didn't see Roberts, M'm, he gets so wild.

Enid Oh! but I must, Annie; I'll be quite calm, I promise.

Mrs Roberts It's life an' death to him, M'm.

Enid (*Very gently*) I'll get him to talk to me outside, we won't excite you.

Mrs Roberts (*Faintly*) No, M'm.

(*She gives a violent start.* **Roberts** *has come in, unseen*)

Roberts (*Removing his hat—with subtle mockery*) Beg your pardon for coming in; you're engaged with a lady, I see.

Enid Can I speak to you, Mr Roberts?

Roberts Whom have I the pleasure of addressing, Ma'am?

Enid But surely you know me! I'm Mrs Underwood.

Roberts (*With a bow of malice*) The daughter of our chairman.

Enid (*Earnestly*) I've come on purpose to speak to you; will you come outside a minute? (*She looks at* **Mrs Roberts**)

Roberts (*Hanging up his hat*) I have nothing to say, Ma'am.

Enid But I *must* speak to you, please.

(*She moves towards the door*)

Roberts (*With sudden venom*) I have not the time to listen!

Mrs Roberts David!

Enid Mr Roberts, *please!*

Roberts (*Taking off his overcoat*) I am sorry to disoblige a lady: Mr Anthony's daughter.

Enid (*Wavering, then with sudden decision*) Mr Roberts, I know you've another meeting of the men. (**Roberts** *bows*) I came to appeal to you. Please, please try to come to some compromise; give way a little, if it's only for your own sakes!

Roberts (*Speaking to himself*) The daughter of Mr Anthony begs me to give way a little, if it's only for our own sakes.

Enid For everybody's sake; for your wife's sake.

Roberts For my wife's sake, for everybody's

sake—for the sake of Mr Anthony.

Enid Why are you so bitter against my father? He has never done anything to you.

Roberts Has he not?

Enid He can't help his views, any more than you can help yours.

Roberts I really didn't know that I had a right to views!

Enid He's an old man, and you—

(*Seeing his eyes fixed on her, she stops*)

Roberts (*Without raising his voice*) If I saw Mr Anthony going to die, and I could save him by lifting my hand, I would not lift the little finger of it.

Enid You—you—

(*She stops again, biting her lips*)

Roberts I would not, and that's flat!

Enid (*Coldly*) You don't mean what you say, and you know it!

Roberts I mean every word of it.

Enid But why?

Roberts (*With a flash*) Mr Anthony stands for tyranny! That's why!

Enid Nonsense!

(**Mrs Roberts** *makes a movement as if to rise, but sinks back in her chair*)

Enid (*With an impetuous movement*) Annie!

Roberts Please not to touch my wife!

Enid (*Recoiling with a sort of horror*) I believe—you are mad.

Roberts The house of a madman then is not the fit place for a lady.

Enid I'm not afraid of you.

Roberts (*Bowing*) I would not expect the daughter of Mr Anthony to be afraid. Mr Anthony is not a coward like the rest of them.

Enid (*Suddenly*) I suppose you think it brave, then, to go on with this struggle.

Roberts Does Mr Anthony think it brave to fight against women and children? Mr Anthony is a rich man, I believe; does he think it brave to fight against those who haven't a penny? Does he think it brave to see the children crying with hunger, an' women shivering with cold?

Enid (*Putting up her hand, as though warding off a blow*) My father is acting on his principles, and you know it!

Roberts And so am I!

Enid You hate us; and you can't bear to be beaten.

Roberts Neither can Mr Anthony, for all that he may say.

Enid At any rate you might have pity on your wife.

(**Mrs Roberts**, *who has her hand pressed to her heart, takes it away, and tries to calm her breathing*)

Roberts Madam, I have no more to say.

(*He takes up the loaf. There is a knock at the door, and* **Underwood** *comes in. He stands looking at them.* **Enid** *turns to him, then seems undecided*)

Underwood Enid!

Roberts (*Ironically*) Ye were not needing to come for your wife, Mr Underwood. We are not rowdies.

Underwood I know that, Roberts. I hope Mrs Roberts is better. (**Roberts** *turns away without answering*) Come, Enid!

Enid I make one more appeal to you, Mr Roberts, for the sake of your wife.

Roberts (*With polite malice*) If I might advise ye, Ma'am—make it for the sake of your husband and your father.

(**Enid**, *suppressing a retort, goes out.* **Underwood** *opens the door for her and follows.* **Roberts**, *going to the fire, holds out his hands to the dying glow*)

Roberts How goes it, my girl? Feeling better, are you?

(**Mrs Roberts** *smiles faintly. He brings his overcoat and wraps it round her. Looking at his watch*)

Ten minutes to four! (*As though inspired*) I've seen their faces, there's no fight in them, except for that one old robber.

Mrs Roberts Won't you stop and eat, David? You've 'ad nothing all day!

Roberts (*Putting his hand to his throat*) Can't swallow till those old sharks are out o' the town. (*He walks up and down*) I shall have a bother with the men—there's no heart in them, the cowards. Blind as bats, they are—can't see a day before their noses.

Mrs Roberts It's the women, David.

Roberts Ah! So they say! They can remember the women when their own bellies speak! The women never stop them from the drink; but from a little suffering to themselves in a sacred cause, the women stop them fast enough.

Mrs Roberts But think o' the children, David.

Roberts Ah! If they will go breeding themselves for slaves, without a thought o' the future o' them they breed—

Mrs Roberts (*Gasping*) That's enough, David; don't begin to talk of that—I won't—I can't—

Roberts (*Staring at her*) Now, now, my girl!

Mrs Roberts (*Breathlessly*) No, no, David—I won't!

Roberts There, there! Come, come! That's right. (*Bitterly*) Not one penny will they put by for a day like this. Not they! Hand to mouth—Gad!—I know them! They've broke my heart. There was no holdin' them at the start, but now the pinch 'as come.

Mrs Roberts How can you expect it, David? They're not made of iron.

Roberts Expect it? Wouldn't I expect what I would do meself? Wouldn't I starve an' rot rather than give in? What one man can do, another can.

Mrs Roberts And the women?

Roberts This is not women's work.

Mrs Roberts (*With a flash of malice*) No, the women may die for all you care. That's their work.

Roberts (*Averting his eyes*) Who talks of dying? No one will die till we have beaten these— (*He meets her eyes again, and again turns his away, Excitedly*) This is what I've been waiting for all these months. To get the old robbers down, and send them home again without a farthin's worth o' change. I've seen their faces, I tell you, in the valley of the shadow of defeat.

(*He goes to the peg and takes down his hat*)

Mrs Roberts (*Following with her eyes—softly*) Take your overcoat, David; it must be bitter cold.

Roberts (*Coming up to her—his eyes are furtive*) No, no! There, there, stay quiet and warm. I won't be long, my girl!

Mrs Roberts (*With soft bitterness*) You'd better take it.

(*She lifts the coat. But* **Roberts** *puts it back, and wraps it round her. He tries to meet her eyes, but cannot.* **Mrs Roberts** *stays huddled in the coat. Her eyes, that follow him about, are half malicious, half yearning. He looks at his watch again, and turns to go. In the doorway he meets* **Jan Thomas,** *a boy of ten in clothes too big for him, carrying a penny whistle*)

Roberts Hallo, boy!

(*He goes.* **Jan** *stops within a yard of* **Mrs Roberts,** *and stares at her without a word*)

Mrs Roberts Well, Jan!

Jan Father's coming; sister Madge is coming.

(*He sits at the table, and fidgets with his whistle; he blows three vague notes; then imitates a cuckoo. There is a tap on the door. Old* **Thomas** *comes in*)

Thomas A very coot tay to you, Ma'am. It is petter that you are.

Mrs Roberts Thank you, Mr Thomas.

Thomas (*Nervously*) Roberts in?

Mrs Roberts Just gone on to the meeting, Mr Thomas.

Thomas (*With relief, becoming talkative*) This is fery unfortunate, look you! I came to tell him that we must make terms with London. It is a fery great pity he is gone to the meeting. He will be kicking against the pricks, I am thinking.

Mrs Roberts (*Half rising*) He'll never give in, Mr Thomas.

Thomas You must not be fretting, that is very pat for you. Look you, there iss hartly any mans for supporting him now, but the engineers and George Rous. (*Solemnly*) This strike is no longer coing with Chapel, look you! I have listened carefully, an' I have talked with her. (**Jan** *blows*) Sst! I don't care what th' others say, I say that *Chapel means us* to be stopping the trouble, that is what I make of her; and it is my opinion that this is the fery best thing for all of us. If it wasn't my opinion, I ton't say—but it is my opinion, look you.

Mrs Roberts (*Trying to suppress her excitement*) I don't know what'll come to Roberts, if you give in.

Thomas It iss no disgrace whateffer! All that a mortal man coult do he hass tone. It iss against Human Nature he hass gone; fery natural—any man may to that; but Chapel has spoken and he must not go against *her.* (**Jan** *initiates the cuckoo*) Ton't make that squeaking! (*Going to the door*) Here iss my taughter come to sit with you. A fery goot day, Ma'am—no fretting—remember!

(**Madge** *comes in and stands at the open door, watching the street*)

Madge You'll be late, Father; they're beginning. (*She catches him by the sleeve*) For the love of God, stand up to him, Father—this time!

Thomas (*Detaching his sleeve with dignity*) Leave me to do what's proper, girl!

(*He goes out.* **Madge** *in the centre of the open doorway, slowly moves in, as though before the approach of someone*)

Rous (*Appearing in the doorway*) Madge!

(**Madge** *stands with her back to* **Mrs Roberts,** *staring at him with her head up and her hands behind her*)

Rous (*Who has a fierce distracted look*) Madge! I'm going to the meeting. (**Madge,** *without moving, smiles contemptuously*) D'ye hear me?

(*They speak in quick low voices*)

Madge I hear! Go, and kill your own Mother, if you must.

(**Rous** *seizes her by both her arms. She stands rigid,*

with her head bent back. *He releases her, and he too stands motionless*)

Rous I swore to stand by Roberts. I swore that! Ye want me to go back on what I've sworn.

Madge (*With slow soft mockery*) You are a pretty lover!

Rous Madge!

Madge (*Smiling*) I've heard that lovers do what their girls ask them—(**Jan** *sounds the cuckoo's notes*) but that's not true, it seems!

Rous You'd make a blackleg of me!

Madge (*With her eyes half-closed*) Do it for me!

Rous (*Dashing his hand across his brow*) Damn! I can't!

Madge (*Swiftly*) Do it for me!

Rous (*Through his teeth*) Don't play the wanton with me!

Madge (*With a movement of her hand towards* **Jan**—*quick and low*) I'd do *that* to get the children bread!

Rous (*In a fierce whisper*) Madge! Oh, Madge!

Madge (*With soft mockery*) But *you* can't break your word with me!

Rous (*With a choke*) Then, Begod, I can!

(*He turns and rushes off.* **Madge** *stands with a faint smile on her face, looking after him. She moves to the table*)

Madge I have done for Roberts!

(*She sees that* **Mrs Roberts** *has sunk back in her chair*)

Madge (*Running to her, and feeling her hands*) You're as cold as a stone! You want a drop of brandy. Jan, run to the 'Lion'; say I sent you for Mrs Roberts.

Mrs Roberts (*With a feeble movement*) I'll just sit quiet, Madge. Give Jan—his—tea.

Madge (*Giving* **Jan** *a slice of bread*) There, ye little rascal. Hold your piping. (*Going to the fire, she kneels*) It's going out.

Mrs Roberts (*With a faint smile*) 'Tis all the same! **Jan** *begins to blow his whistle.* **Jan** *stops*)

Madge Tsht! Tsht!—you—

Mrs Roberts (*Smiling*) Let 'im play, Madge.

Madge (*On her knees at the fire, listening*) Waiting an' waiting. I've no patience with it; waiting an' waiting—that's what a woman has to do! Can you hear them at it—I can!

(*She leans her elbows on the table, and her chin on her hands. Behind her,* **Mrs Roberts** *leans forward, with painful and growing excitement, as the sounds of the strikers' meeting come in*)

Scene 2

It is past four. In a grey, failing light, an open muddy space is crowded with workmen. Beyond, divided from it by a barbed-wire fence, is the raised towing-path of a canal, on which is moored a barge. In the distance are marshes and snow-covered hills. The 'Works' high wall runs from the canal across the open space, and in the angle of this wall is a rude platform of barrels and boards. On it, **Harness** *is standing.* **Roberts,** *a little apart from the crowd, leans his back against the wall. On the raised towing-path two bargemen lounge and smoke indifferently.*

Harness (*Holding out his hand*) Well, I've spoken to you straight. If I speak till tomorrow I can't say more.

Jago (*A dark, sallow, Spanish-looking man, with a short, thin beard*) Mister, want to ask you! Can they get blacklegs?

Bulgin (*Meaning*) Let 'em try.

(*There are savage murmurs from the crowd*)

Brown (*A round-faced man*) Where could they get 'em then?

Evans (*A small restless, harassed man, with a fighting face*) There's always blacklegs; it's the nature of 'em. There's always men that'll save their own skins.

(*Another savage murmur. There is a movement, and old* **Thomas,** *joining the crowd, takes his stand in front*)

Harness (*Holding up his hand*) They can't get them. But that won't help you. Now, men, be reasonable. Your demands would have brought on us the burden of a dozen strikes at a time when we were not prepared for them. The Unions live by Justice, not to one, but all. Any fair man will tell you—you were ill-advised! I don't say you go too far for that which you're entitled to, but you're going too far for the moment; you've dug a pit for yourselves. Are you to stay there, or are you to climb out? Come!

Lewis (*A clean-cut Welshman with a dark moustache*) You've hit it, Mister! Which is it to be?

(*Another movement in the crowd, and* **Rous,** *coming quickly, takes his stand next* **Thomas**)

Harness Cut your demands to the right pattern, and we'll see you through; refuse, and don't expect me to waste my time coming down here again. I'm not the sort that speaks at random, as you ought to know by this time. If you're the sound men I take you for—no matter who advises you against it—(*he fixes his eyes on* **Roberts**) you'll make up your minds to come in, and trust to us to get your terms. Which is to be? Hands together, and victory—or—the starvation you've got now?

(*A prolonged murmur from the crowd*)

Jago (*Sullenly*) Talk about what you know.

Harness (*Lifting his voice above the murmur*) Know? (*With cold passion*) All that you've been through, my friend, I've been through—I was through it when I was no bigger than (*pointing to a youth*) that shaver there; the Unions then weren't what they are now. What's made them strong? It's hands together that's made them strong. I've been through it all, I tell you, the brand's on my soul yet. I know what you've suffered—there's nothing you can tell me that I don't know; but the whole is greater than the part, and you are only the part. Stand by us, and we will stand by you.

(*Quartering them with his eyes, he waits. The murmuring swells; the men form little groups.* **Green, Bulgin,** *and* **Lewis** *talk together*)

Lewis Speaks very sensible, the Union chap.

Green (*Quietly*) Ah! if I'd a been *listened* to, you'd 'ave 'eard sense these two months past.

(*The bargemen are seen laughing*)

Lewis (*Pointing*) Look at those two blanks over the fence there!

Bulgin (*With gloomy violence*) They'd best stop their cackle, or I'll break their jaws.

Jago (*Suddenly*) You say the furnace men's paid enough?

Harness I did not say they were paid enough; I said they were paid as much as the furnace men in similar works elsewhere.

Evans That's a lie. (*Hubbub*) What about Harper's?

Harness (*With cold irony*) You may look at home for lies, my man. Harper's shifts are longer, the pay works out the same.

Henry Rous (*A dark edition of his brother* **George**) Will ye support us in double pay overtime Saturdays?

Harness Yes, we will.

Jago What have ye done with our subscriptions?

Harness (*Coldly*) I have told you that we *will* do with them.

Evans Ah! *will*, it's always will! Ye'd have our mates desert us.

(*Hubbub*)

Bulgin (*Shouting*) Hold your row!

(**Evans** *looks round angrily*)

Harness (*Lifting his voice*) Those who know their right hands from their lefts know that the Unions are neither thieves nor traitors. I've said my say. Figure it out, my lads; when you want me you know where I shall be.

(*He jumps down, the crowd gives way, he passes through them, and goes away. A bargeman looks after him, jerking his pipe with a derisive gesture. The men close up in groups, and many looks are cast at* **Roberts,** *who stands alone against the wall*)

Evans He wants ye to turn blacklegs, that's what he wants. He wants ye to go back on us. Sooner than turn blackleg—I'd starve, I would.

Bulgin Who's talkin' o' blacklegs—mind what you're saying, will you?

Blacksmith (*A youth with yellow hair and huge arms*) What about the women?

Evans They can stand what we can stand, I suppose, can't they?

Blacksmith Ye've no wife?

Evans An' don't want one.

Thomas (*Raising his voice*) Aye! Give us the power to come to terms with London lads.

Davies (*A dark, slow-fly, gloomy man*) Go up the platform, if you got anything to say, go up an' say it.

(*There are cries of 'Thomas!' He is pushed towards the platform; he ascends it with difficulty, and bares his head, waiting for silence. A hush!*)

Red-haired Youth (*Suddenly*) Coot old Thomas!

(*A hoarse laugh; the bargemen exchange remarks; a hush again, and* **Thomas** *begins speaking*)

Thomas We are all in the tepth together, and it iss Nature that has put us there.

Henry Rous It's London put us there!

Evans It's the Union.

Thomas It iss not London; nor it iss not the Union—it iss Nature. It iss no disgrace whateffer to a potty to give in to Nature. For this Nature iss a fery pig thing; it is pigger than what a man is. There iss more years to my hett than to the hett of any one here. It is fery pat, look you, this coing against Nature. It is pat to make other potties suffer, when there is nothing to pe cot py it. (*A laugh.* **Thomas** *angrily goes on*) What are ye laughing at? It is pat, I say! We are fighting for a principle; there is nopotty that shall say I am not a peliever in principle. Putt when Nature says 'No further', then it is no coot snapping your fingers in her face.

(*A laugh from* **Roberts,** *and murmurs of approval*))
This Nature must pe humort. It is a man's pisiness
to be pure, honest, just and merciful. That's what
Chapel tells you. (*To* **Roberts,** *angrily*) And, look
you, David Roberts, Chapel tells you ye can do
that without coing against Nature.

Jago What about the Union?

Thomas I ton't trust the Union; they haf treated us
like tirt. 'Do what we tell you,' said they. I haf
peen captain of the furnace men twenty years,
and I say to the Union—(*excitedly*) 'Can you tell
me then, as well as I can tell you, what iss the
right wages for the work that these men do? For
fife and twenty years I haf paid my moneys to the
Union and—(*with great excitement*) for nothings!
What iss that but roguery, for all that this Mr
Harness says!

(*Murmur*)

Evans Hear, hear.

Henry Rous Get on with you! Cut on with it then!

Thomas Look you, if a man toes not trust me, am
I coing to trust him?

Jago That's right.

Thomas Let them alone for rogues, and act for
ourselves.

(*Murmurs*)

Blacksmith That's what we been doin', haven't we?

Thomas (*With increased excitement*) I wass brought
up to do for meself. I wass brought up to go
without a thing, if I hat not moneys to puy it.
There iss too much, look you, of doing things with
other people's moneys. We haf fought fair, and if
we haf peen beaten, it iss no fault of ours. Gif us
the power to make terms with London for ourself;
if we ton't succeed, I say it iss petter to take our
peating like men, than to tie like togs, or hang on
to others' coat-tails to make them do our pusiness
for us!

Evans (*Muttering*) Who wants to?

Thomas (*Craning*) What's that? If I stand up to a
potty, and he knocks me town, I am not to go
hollering to other potties to help me; I am to stand
up again; and if he knocks me town properly, I
am to stay there, isn't that right?

(*Laughter*)

Jago No Union!

Henry Rous Union!

(*Others take up the shout*)

Evans Blacklegs!

(**Bulgin** *and the* **Blacksmith** *shake their fists at* **Evans**)

Thomas (*With a gesture*) I am an old man, look you.

(*A sudden silence, then murmurs again*)

Lewis Olt fool, with his 'No Union!'

Bulgin Them furnace chaps! For twopence I'd smash
the faces o' the lot of them.

Green If I'd 'a been listened to at the first—

Thomas (*Wiping his brow*) I'm coming' now to what
I was coing to say—

Davies (*Muttering*) An' time too!

Thomas (*Solemnly*) Chapel says: Ton't carry on this
strike! Put an end to it!

Jago That's a lie! Chapel says go on!

Thomas (*Scornfully*) Inteet! I haf ears to my head.

Red-haired Youth Ah! long ones!

(*A laugh*)

Jago Yours ears have misled you then.

Thomas (*Excitedly*) Ye cannot be right if I am, ye
cannot haf it both ways.

Red-haired Youth Chapel can though!

('*The Shaver' laughs; there are murmurs from the
crowd*)

Thomas (*Fixing his eyes on 'The Shaver'*) Ah! ye're
coing the roat to tamnation. An' so I say to all of
you. If ye co against Chapel I will not pe with
you, nor will any other Got-fearing man.

(*He steps down from the platform.* **Jago** *makes his
way towards it. There are cries of 'Don't let 'im go
up!'*)

Jago Don't let him go up? That's free speech, that
is. (*He goes up*) I ain't got much to say to you.
Look at the matter plain; ye've come the road
this far, and now you want to chuck the journey.
We've all been in one boat; and now you want to
pull in two. We engineers have stood by you;
ye're ready now, are ye, to give us the go-by? If
we'd a-known that before, we'd not a-started out
with you so early one bright morning! That's all
I've got to say. Old man Thomas a'n't got his
Bible lesson right. If you give up to London, or
to Harness, now, it's givin' us the chuck—to save
your skins—you won't get over that, my boys; it's
a dirty thing to do.

(*He gets down; during his little speech, which is ironically spoken, there is a restless discomfort in the
crowd.* **Rous,** *stepping forward, jumps on the platform. He has an air of fierce distraction. Sullen
murmurs of disapproval from the crowd*)

Rous (*Speaking with great excitement*) I'm no blanky
orator, mates, but wot I say is drove from me.
What I say is yuman nature. Can a man set an'
see 'is mother starve? Can 'e now?

Roberts (*Starting forward*) Rous!

Rous (*Staring at him fiercely*) Sim 'Arness said fair! I've changed my mind.

Evans Ah! Turned your coat you mean!

(*The crowd manifests a great surprise*)

Lewis (*Apostrophising* **Rous**) Hallo! What's turned him round?

Rous (*Speaking with intense excitement*) 'E said fair. 'Stand by us,' 'e said, 'and we'll stand by you.' That's where we've been making' our mistake this long time past; and who's to blame for't? (*He points at* **Roberts**) That man there! 'No,' 'e said, 'fight the robbers,' 'e said, 'squeeze the breath out o' them!' But it's not the breath out o' them that's being squeezed; it's the breath out of *us* and *ours*, and that's the book of truth. I'm no orator, mates, it's the flesh and blood in me that's speakin', it's the heart o' me. (*With a menacing, yet half-ashamed movement towards* **Roberts**). He'll speak to you again, mark my words, but don't ye listen. (*The crowd groans*) It's hell fire that's on that man's tongue. (**Roberts** *is seen laughing*) Sim 'Arness is right. What are we without the Union—handful o' parched leaves—a puff o'smoke. I'm no orator, but I say: Chuck it up! Chuck it up! Sooner than go on starving the women and the children.

(*The murmurs of acquiescence almost drown the murmurs of dissent*)

Evans What's turned *you* to blacklegging?

Rous (*With a furious look*) Sim 'Arness knows what he's talkin' about. Give us power to come to terms with London; I'm no orator, but I say—have done wi' this black misery!

(*He gives his muffler a twist, jerks his head back and jumps off the platform. The crowd applauds and surges forward. Amid cries of 'That's enough!' 'Up Union!' 'Up Harness!'* **Roberts** *quietly ascends the platform. There is a moment of silence*)

Blacksmith We don't want to hear you. Shut it!

Henry Rous Get down!

(*Amid such cries they surge towards the platform*)

Evans (*Fiercely*) Let 'im speak! Roberts! Roberts!

Bulgin (*Muttering*) He'd better look out that I don't crack 'is skull.

(**Roberts** *faces the crowd, probing them with his eyes till they gradually become silent. He begins speaking. One of the bargemen rises and stands*)

Roberts You don't want to hear me, then? You'll listen to Rous and to that old man, but not to me. You'll listen to Sim Harness of the Union that's treated you *so fair*; maybe you'll listen to those men from London? Ah! You groan! What for? You love their feet on your necks, don't you? (*Then as* **Bulgin** *elbows his way towards the platform, with calm pathos*) You'd like to break my jaw, John Bulgin. Let me speak, then do your smashing, if it gives you pleasure. (**Bulgin** *stands motionless and sullen*) Am I a liar, a coward, a traitor? If only I were, ye'd listen to me, I'm sure. (*The murmurings cease, and there is now dead silence*) Is there a man of you here that has less to gain by striking? Is there a man of you that had more to lose? Is there a man of you that has given up *eight hundred* pounds since this trouble here began? Come now, is there? How much has Thomas given up—ten pounds or five, or what? You listened to him, and what had he to say? 'None can pretend,' he said, 'that I'm not a believer in principle—(*with biting irony*) but when Nature says: 'No further,' 'tes going agenst Nature.' *I* tell you if a man cannot say to Nature: 'Budge me from this if ye can!'—(*with a sort of exaltation*) his principles are but his belly. 'Oh, but,' Thomas says, 'a man can be pure and honest, just and merciful, and take off his hat to Nature!' *I* tell you Nature's neither pure nor honest, just nor merciful. You chaps that live over the hill, an' go home dead beat in the dark on a snowy night—don't ye fight your way every inch of it? Do ye go lyin' down an' trustin' to the tender mercies of this merciful Nature? Try it and you'll soon know with what ye've got to deal. 'Tes only by that—(*he strikes a blow with his clenched fist*) in Nature's face that a man can be a man. 'Give in,' says Thomas, 'go down on your knees; throw up your foolish fight, an' perhaps,' he said, 'perhaps your enemy will chuck you down a crust.'

Jago Never!

Evans Curse them!

Thomas I nefer said that.

Roberts (*Bitingly*) If ye did not say it, man, ye meant it. An' what did ye say about Chapel? 'Chapel's against it, ye said. 'She's against it!' Well, if Chapel and Nature go hand in hand, it's the first I've ever heard of it. That young man there—(*pointing to Rous*) said I 'ad 'ell fire on my tongue. If I had I would use it all to scorch and wither this talking of surrender. Surrendering's the work of cowards and traitors.

Henry Rous (*As* **George Rous** *moves forward*) Go for him, George—don't stand his lip!

Roberts (*Flinging out his finger*) Stop there, George

Roberts (Anthony Webb) addresses the strikers. (From the production at the Theatre Royal, Bristol, 1967)

Rous, it's no time this to settle personal matters. (**Rous** *stops*) But there was one other spoke to you—Mr Simon Harness. We have not much to thank Mr Harness and the Union for. They said to us 'Desert your mates, or we'll desert you.' An' they did desert us.

Evans They did.

Roberts Mr Simon Harness is a clever man, but he has come too late. (*With intense conviction*) For all that Mr Simon Harness says, for all that Thomas, Rous, for all that any man present here can say—*We've won the fight!* (*The crowd sags nearer, looking eagerly up. With withering scorn*). You've felt the pinch o't in your bellies. You've forgotten what that fight 'as been; many times I have told you; I will tell you now this once again. The fight o' the country's body and blood against a bloodsucker. The fight of those that spend theirselves with every blow they strike and every breath they draw, against a thing that fattens on them, and grows and grows by the law of *merciful* Nature. That thing is Capital! A thing that buys the sweat o' men's brows, and the tortures o' their brains, at its own price. *Don't I* know that? Wasn't the work o' *my* brains bought for seven hundred pounds, and hasn't one hundred thousand pounds been gained them by that seven hundred without the stirring of a finger? It is a thing that will take as much and give you as little as it can. That's *Capital*! A thing that will say—'I'm very sorry for you, poor fellows—you have a cruel time of it, I know,' but will not give one sixpence of its dividends to help you have a better time. That's Capital! Tell me, for all their talk is there one of them that will consent to another penny on the Income Tax to help the poor? That's Capital! A white-faced, stony-hearted monster! Ye have got it on its knees; are ye to give up at the last minute to save your miserable bodies pain? When I went

47

this morning to those old men from London, I looked into their very 'earts. One of them was sitting there—Mr Scantlebury, a mass of flesh nourished on us: sittin' there for all the world like the shareholders in this Company, that sit not moving tongue nor finger, takin' dividends—a great dumb ox that can only be roused when its food is threatened. I looked into his eyes and I saw *he was afraid*—afraid for himself and his dividends, afraid for his fees, afraid of the very shareholders he stands for; and all but one of them's afraid—like children that get into a wood at night, and start at every rustle of the leaves. I ask you, men—(*he pauses, holding out his hand till there is utter silence*) Give me a free hand to tell them: 'Go you back to London. The men have nothing for you!' (*A murmuring*) Give me that, an' I swear to you, within a week you shall have from London all you want.

Evans, Jago, *and* **Others** A free hand! Give him a free hand! Bravo—bravo!

Roberts 'Tis not for this little moment of time we're fighting (*the murmuring dies*), not for ourselves, our own little bodies, and their wants, 'tis for all those that come after throughout all time. (*With intense sadness*) Oh! men—for the love o' them, don't roll up another stone upon their heads, don't help to blacken the sky, an' let the bitter sea in over them. They're welcome to the worst that can happen to me, to the worst that can happen to us all, aren't they—aren't they? If we can shake (*passionately*) that white-faced monster with the bloody lips, that has sucked the life out of ourselves, our wives and children, since the world began. (*Dropping the note of passion, but with the utmost weight and intensity*) If we have not the hearts of men to stand against it breast to breast, and eye to eye, and force it backward till it cry for mercy, it will go on sucking life; and we shall stay for ever what we are (*in almost a whisper*) less than the very dogs.

(*An utters stillness, and* **Roberts** *stands rocking his body slightly, with his eyes burning the faces of the crowd*)

Evans *and* **Jago** (*Suddenly*) Roberts!

(*The shout is taken up. There is a slight movement in the crowd, and* **Madge** *passing below the towing-path stops by the platform, looking up at* **Roberts**. *A sudden doubting silence*)

Roberts 'Nature', says that old man, 'give in to Nature.' I tell you, strike your blow in Nature's face—an' let it do its worst!

(*He catches sight of* **Madge**; *his brows contract, he looks away*)

Madge (*in a low voice—close to the platform*) Your wife's dying!

(**Roberts** *glares at her as if torn from some pinnacle of exaltation*)

Roberts (*Trying to stammer on*) I say to you—answer them—answer them—

(*He is drowned by the murmur in the crowd*)

Thomas (*Stepping forward*) Ton't you hear her, then?

Roberts What is it?

(*A dead silence*)

Thomas Your wife, man!

(**Roberts** *hesitates, then with a gesture, he leaps down, and goes away below the towing-path, the men making way for him. The standing bargeman opens and prepares to light a lantern. Daylight is fast failing*)

Madge He needn't have hurried! Annie Roberts is dead. (*Then in the silence, passionately.*) You pack of blinded hounds! How many more women are you going to let die?

(*The crowd shrinks back from her, and breaks up in groups, with a confused, uneasy movement.* **Madge** *goes quickly away below the towing-path. There is a hush as they look after her*)

Lewis There's a spitfire, for ye!

Bulgin (*Growling*) I'll smash 'er jaw.

Green If I'd a-been listened to, that poor woman—

Thomas It's a judgment on him for coing against Chapel. I tolt him how 'twould be!

Evans All the more reason for sticking by 'im. (*A cheer*) Are you goin' to desert him now 'e's down? Are you goin' to chuck him over, now 'e's lost 'is wife?

(*The crowd is murmuring and cheering all at once*)

Rous (*Stepping in front of platform*) Lost his wife! Aye! Can't ye see? Look at home, look at your own wives! What's to save them? Ye'll have the same in all your houses before long!

Lewis Aye, aye!

Henry Rous Right! George, right!

(*There are murmurs of assent*)

Rous It's not us that's blind, it's Roberts. How long will ye put up with 'im!

Henry Rous, Bulgin, Davies Give 'im the chuck!

(*The cry is taken up*)

Evans (*Fiercely*) Kick a man that's down? Down?

Henry Rous Stop his jaw there!

(**Evans** *throws up his arm at a threat from* **Bulgin**. *The bargeman, who has lighted the lantern, holds it high above his head*)

Rous (*Springing on to the platform*) What brought him down then, but 'is own black obstinacy? Are ye going' to follow a man that can't see better than that where e's goin'?

Evans He's lost 'is wife.

Rous An' whose fault's that but his own? 'Ave done with 'im, I say, before he's killed your own wives and mothers.

Davies Down 'im!

Henry Rous He's finished!

Brown We've had enough of 'im!

Blacksmith Too much!

(*The crowd takes up these cries, excepting only* **Evans, Jago,** *and* **Green**, *who is seen to argue mildly with the* **Blacksmith**)

Rous (*Above the hubbub*) We'll make terms with the Union, lads.

(*Cheers*)

Evans (*Fiercely*) Ye blacklegs!

Bulgin (*Savagely—squaring up to him*) Who are ye callin' blacklegs, Rat?

(**Evans** *throws up his fists, parries the blow, and returns it. They fight. The bargemen are seen holding up the lantern and enjoying the sight. Old* **Thomas** *steps forward and holds out his hands*)

Thomas Shame on your strife!

(*The* **Blacksmith, Brown, Lewis,** *and the* **Red-haired Youth** *pull* **Evans** *and* **Bulgin** *apart. The stage is almost dark*).

Act III

It is five o'clock. In the **Underwoods'** *drawing-room, which is artistically furnished,* **Enid** *is sitting on the sofa working at a baby's frock.* **Edgar**, *by a little spindle-legged table in the centre of the room, is fingering a china-box. His eyes are fixed on the double doors that lead into the dining-room.*

Edgar (*Putting down the china-box, and glancing at his watch*) Just on five, they're all in there waiting, except Frank. Where's he?

Enid He's had to go down to Gasgoyne's about a contract. Will you want him?

Edgar He can't help us. This is a directors' job. (*Motioning towards a single door half-hidden by a curtain*) Father in his room?

Enid Yes.

Edgar I wish he'd stay there, Enid. (**Enid** *looks up at him*) This is a beastly business, old girl.

(*He takes up the little box again and turns it over and over*)

Enid I went to the Roberts's this afternoon, Ted.

Edgar That wasn't very wise.

Enid He's simply killing his wife.

Edgar We are, you mean.

Enid (*Suddenly*) Roberts *ought* to give way!

Edgar There's a lot to be said on the men's side.

Enid I don't feel half so sympathetic with them as I did before I went. They just set up class feeling against you. Poor Annie was looking dreadfully bad—fire going out, and nothing fit for her to eat. (**Edgar** *walks to and fro*) But she would stand up for Roberts. When you see all this wretchedness going on and feel you can do nothing, you have to shut your eyes to the whole thing.

Edgar If you can.

Enid When I went I was all on their side, but as soon as I got there I began to feel quite different at once. People talk about sympathy with the working classes, they don't know what it means to try and put it into practice. It seems hopeless.

Edgar Ah! well.

Enid It's dreadful going on with the men in this state. I do hope Dad will make concessions.

Edgar He won't. (*Gloomily*) It's a sort of religion with him. Curse it! I know what's coming! He'll be voted down.

Enid They wouldn't dare!

Edgar They will—they're in a funk.

Enid (*Indignantly*) He'd never stand it!

Edgar (*With a shrug*) My dear girl, if you're beaten in a vote, you've got to stand it.

Enid Oh! (*She gets up in alarm*) But would he resign?

Edgar Of course! It goes to the roots of his beliefs.

Enid But he's so *wrapped up in this company*, Ted! There'd be nothing left for him! It'd be dreadful! (**Edgar** *shrugs his shoulders*) Oh, Ted, he's so old now! You mustn't let them!

Edgar (*Hiding his feelings in an outburst*) My sympathies in this strike are all on the side of the men.

Enid He's been Chairman for more than thirty years! He made the whole thing! And think of the bad times they've had, it's always been he who pulled them through. Oh, Ted, you must—

Edgar What is it you want? You said just now you hoped he'd make concessions. Now you want me to back him in not making them. This isn't a game, Enid!

Enid (*Hotly*) It isn't a game to *me* that the Dad's in danger of losing all he cares about in life. If he won't give way, and he's beaten, it'll simply break him down!

Edgar Didn't you say it was dreadful going on with the men in this state?

Enid But can't you see, Ted, Father'll never get over it! You must stop them somehow. The others are afraid of him. If you back him up—

Edgar (*Putting his hand to his head*) Against my convictions—against yours! The moment it begins to pinch one personally—

Enid It isn't personal, it's Dad!

Edgar Your family or yourself, and over goes the show!

Enid (*Resentfully*) If you don't take it seriously, I do.

Edgar I am as fond of him as you are; that's nothing to do with it.

Enid We can't tell about the men; it's all guess-work. But we know the Dad might have a stroke any day. D'you mean to say that he isn't more to you than—

Edgar Of course he is.

Enid I don't understand you then.

Edgar H'm!

Enid If it were for oneself it would be different, but for our own Father! You don't seem to realise.

Edgar I realise perfectly.

Enid It's your first duty to save him.

Edgar I wonder.

Enid (*Imploring*) Oh, Ted! It's the only interest he's got left; it'll be like a death-blow to him!

Edgar (*Restraining his emotion*) I know.

Enid Promise!

Edgar I'll do what I can.

(*He turns to the double doors. The curtained door is opened, and* **Anthony** *appears.* **Edgar** *opens the double doors, and passes through.* **Scantlebury**'s *voice is faintly heard:* 'Past five; we shall never get through—have to eat another dinner at that hotel!' *The doors are shut.* **Anthony** *walks forward*)

Anthony You've been seeing Roberts, I hear.

Enid Yes.

Anthony Do you know what trying to bridge such a gulf as this is like? (**Enid** *puts her work on the little table, and faces him*) Filling a sieve with sand!

Enid Don't!

Anthony You think with your gloved hands you can cure the trouble of the century.

(*He passes on*)

Enid Father! (**Anthony** *stops at the double doors*) I'm only thinking of you!

Anthony (*More softly*) I can take care of myself, my dear.

Enid Have you thought what'll happen if you're beaten—(*she points*) in there?

Anthony I don't mean to be.

Enid Oh! Father, don't give them a chance. You're not well; need you go to the meeting at all?

Anthony (*With a grim smile*) Cut and run?

Enid But they'll outvote you!

Anthony (*Putting his hand on the doors*) We shall see!

Enid I beg you, Dad! (**Anthony** *looks at her softly*) Won't you? (**Anthony** *shakes his head. He opens the doors. A buzz of voices comes in*)

Scantlebury Can you get dinner at that 6.30 train up?

Tench No, sir, I believe not, sir.

Wilder Well, I shall speak out; I've had enough of this.

Edgar (*Sharply*) What?

(*It ceases instantly.* **Anthony** *passes through, closing the doors behind him.* **Enid** *springs to them with a gesture of dismay. She puts her hand on the knob, and begins turning it; then goes to the fireplace, and taps her foot on the fender. Suddenly she rings the bell.* **Frost** *comes in by the door that leads into the hall*)

Frost Yes, M'm?

Enid When the men come, Frost, please show them in here; the hall's cold.

Frost I could put them in the pantry, M'm.

Enid No. I don't want to—to offend them; they're so touchy.

Frost Yes, M'm. (*Pause*) Excuse me, Mr Anthony's 'ad nothing to eat all day.

Enid I know, Frost.

Frost Nothin' but two whiskies and sodas, M'm.

Enid Oh! you oughtn't to have let him have those.

Frost (*Gravely*) Mr Anthony is a little difficult, M'm. It's not as if he were a younger man, an' knew what was good for 'im; he will have his own way.

Enid I suppose we all want that.

Frost Yes, M'm. (*Quietly*) Excuse me speakin' about the strike. I'm sure if the other gentlemen were to give up to Mr Anthony, and quietly let the men 'ave what they want, afterwards, that'd be the best way. I find that very useful with him at times, M'm. (**Enid** *shakes her head*) If he's crossed, it makes him violent (*with an air of discovery*), and I've noticed in my own case, when I'm violent I'm always sorry for it afterwards.

Enid (*With a smile*) Are you ever violent, Frost?

Frost Yes, M'm; oh! sometimes very violent.

Enid I've never seen you.

Frost (*Impersonally*) No, M'm; that is so. (**Enid** *fidgets towards the door's back*) (*With feeling*) Bein' with Mr Anthony, as you know, M'm, ever since I was fifteen, it worries me to see him crossed like this at his age. I've taken the liberty to speak to Mr Wanklin (*dropping his voice*)—seems to be the most sensible of the gentlemen—but 'e said to me: 'That's all very well, Frost, but this strike's a very serious thing,' 'e said. 'Serious for all parties, no doubt,' I said, 'but yumour 'im, sir,' I said, 'yumour 'im. It's like this, if a man comes to a stone wall, 'e doesn't drive 'is 'ead against it, 'e gets over it.' 'Yes,' 'e said, 'you'd better tell your master that.' (**Frost** *looks at his nails*) That's where it is, M'm. I said to Mr Anthony this morning: 'Is it worth it, sir?' 'Damn it,' he said to me, 'Frost! Mind your own business, or take a month's notice!' Beg pardon, M'm, for using such a word

Enid (*Moving to the double doors, and listening*) Do you know that man Roberts, Frost?

Frost Yes, M'm; that's to say, not to speak to. But to *look* at 'im you can tell what *he's* like.

Enid (*Stopping*) Yes?

Frost He's not one of these 'ere ordinary 'armless Socialists. 'E's violent; got a fire inside 'im. What I call 'personal'. A man may 'ave what opinion 'e likes, so long as 'e's not personal; when 'e's that 'e's *not* safe.

Enid I think that's what my Father feels about Roberts.

Frost No doubt, M'm, Mr Anthony has a feeling against him. (**Enid** *glances at him sharply, but finding him in perfect earnest, stands biting her lips, and looking at the double doors*) It's a regular right down struggle between the two. I've no patience with this Roberts; from what I 'ear he's just an ordinary workin' man like the rest of 'em. If he did invent a thing he's no worse off than 'undreds of others. My brother invented a new kind o' dumb waiter—nobody gave *him* anything for it, an' there it is, bein' used all over the place. (**Enid** *moves closer to the double doors*) There's a kind o' man that never forgives the world, because 'e wasn't born a gentleman. What I say is—no man that's a gentleman looks down on another man because 'e 'appens to be a class or two above 'im, no more than if 'e 'appens to be a class or two below.

Enid (*With slight impatience*) Yes, I know, Frost, of course. Will you please go in and ask if they'll have some tea; say I sent you.

Frost Yes, M'm

(*He opens the doors gently and goes in. There is a momentary sound of earnest, rather angry talk*)

Wilder I don't agree with you.

Wanklin We've had this over a dozen times.

Edgar (*Impatiently*) Well, what's the propostion?

Scantlebury Yes, what does your Father say? Tea? Not for me, not for me!

Wanklin What I understand the Chairman to say is this—

(**Frost** *re-enters, closing the door behind him*)

Enid (*Moving from the door*) Won't they have any tea, Frost?

(*She goes to the little table, and remains motionless, looking at the baby's frock. A parlourmaid enters from the hall*)

Parlourmaid A Miss Thomas, M'm.

Enid (*Raising her head*) Thomas? What Miss Thomas—d'you mean a—?

Parlourmaid Yes, M'm.

Enid (*Blankly*) Oh! Where is she?

Parlourmaid In the porch.

Enid I don't want—(*She hesitates*)

Frost Shall I dispose of her, M'm?

Enid I'll come out. No, show her in here, Ellen.

(*The* **Parlourmaid** *and* **Frost** *go out.* **Enid** *pursing her lips, sits at the little table, taking up the baby's frock. The* **Parlourmaid** *ushers in* **Madge Thomas** *and goes out;* **Madge** *stands by the door*)

Enid Come in. What is it? What have you come for, please?

Madge Brought a message from Mrs Roberts.

Enid A message? Yes.

Madge She asks you to look after her Mother.

Enid I don't understand.

Madge (*Sullenly*) That's the message.

Enid But—what—why?

Madge Annie Roberts is dead.

(*There is a silence*)

Enid (*Horrified*) But it's only a little more than an hour since I saw her.

Madge Of cold and hunger.

Enid (*Rising*) Oh! that's not true! the poor thing's heart—What makes you look at me like that? I tried to help her.

Madge (*With suppressed savagery*) I thought you'd like to know.

Enid (*Passionately*) It's so unjust! Can't you see that I want to help you all?

Madge I never harmed anyone that hadn't harmed me first.

Enid (*Coldly*) What harm have I done you? Why do you speak to me like that?

Madge (*With the bitterest intensity*) You come out of your comfort to spy on us! A week of hunger, that's what you want!

Enid (*Standing her ground*) Don't talk nonsense!

Madge I saw her die; her hands were blue with the cold.

Enid (*With a movement of grief*) Oh! why wouldn't she let me help her? It's such senseless pride!

Madge Pride's better than nothing to keep your body warm.

Enid (*Passionately*) I won't talk to you! How can you tell what I feel? It's not my fault that I was born better off than you.

Madge We don't want your money.

Enid You don't understand, and you don't want to; please to go away!

Madge (*Balefully*) You've killed her, for all your soft words, you and your father—

Enid (*With rage and emotion*) That's wicked! My father is suffering himself through this wretched strike.

Madge (*With sombre triumph*) Then tell him Mrs Roberts is dead! That'll make him better.

Enid Go away!

Madge When a person hurts us we get it back on them.

(*She makes a sudden and swift movement toward* **Enid**, *fixing her eyes on the child's frock lying across the little table.* **Enid** *snatches the frock up, as though it were the child itself. They stand a yard apart, crossing glances*)

Madge (*Pointing to the frock with a little smile*) Ah! You felt *that*! Lucky it's her mother—not her children—you've to look after, isn't it. *She* won't trouble you long!

Enid Go away!

Madge I've given you the message.

(*She turns and goes out into the hall.* **Enid**, *motionless till she has gone, sinks down at the table, bending her head over the frock, which she is still clutching to her. The double doors are opened, and* **Anthony** *comes slowly in; he passes his daughter, and lowers himself into an armchair. He is very flushed*)

Enid (*Hiding her emotion—anxiously*) What is it, Dad? (**Anthony** *makes a gesture, but does not speak*)

Who was it?

(**Anthony** *does not answer.* **Enid** *going to the double doors meets* **Edgar** *coming in. They speak together in low tones*)

What is it, Ted?

Edgar That fellow Wilder! Taken to personalities! He was downright insulting.

Enid What did he *say*?

Edgar Said, Father was too old and feeble to know what he was doing! The Dad's worth six of him!

Enid Of course he is.

(*They look at* **Anthony** *The doors open wider,* **Wanklin** *appears with* **Scantlebury**)

Scantlebury (*Sotto voce*) I don't like the look of this!

Wanklin (*Going forward*) Come, Chairman! Wilder sends you his apologies. A man can't do more.

(**Wilder** *followed by* **Tench**, *comes in, and goes to* **Anthony**)

Wilder (*Glumly*) I withdraw my words, sir. I'm sorry.

(**Anthony** *nods to him*)

Enid You haven't come to a decision, Mr Wanklin?

(**Wanklin** *shakes his head*)

Wanklin We're all here, Chairman; what do you say? Shall we get on with the business, or shall we go back to the other room?

Scantlebury Yes, yes; let's go on. We must settle something.

(*He turns from a small chair, and settles himself suddenly in the largest chair, with a sigh of comfort.*

Wilder *and* **Wanklin** *also sit; and* **Tench**, *drawing up a straight-backed chair close to his Chairman, sits on the edge of it with the minute-book and a stylographic pen*)

Enid (*Whispering*) I want to speak to you a minute, Ted.

(*They go out through the double doors*)

Wanklin Really, Chairman, it's no use soothing ourselves with a sense of false security. If this strike's not brought to an end before the General

Meeting, the shareholders will certainly haul us over the coals.

Scantlebury (*Stirring*) What—what's that?

Wanklin I know it for a fact.

Anthony Let them!

Wilder And get turned out?

Wanklin (**To Anthony**) I don't mind martyrdom for a policy in which I believe, but I object to being burnt for someone else's principles.

Scantlebury Very reasonable—you must see that, Chairman.

Anthony We owe it to other employers to stand firm.

Wanklin There's a limit to that.

Anthony You were all full of fight at the start.

Scantlebury (*With a sort of groan*) We thought the men would give in, but they—haven't!

Anthony They will!

Wilder (*Rising and pacing up and down*) I can't have my reputation as a man of business destroyed for the satisfaction of starving the men out. (*Almost in tears*) I can't have it! How can we meet the shareholders with things in the state they are?

Scantlebury Hear, hear—hear, hear!

Wilder (*Lashing himself*) If anyone expects me to say to them I've lost you fifty thousand pounds and sooner than put my pride in my pocket. I'll lose you another—(*Glancing at* **Anthony**) It's—it's unnatural! *I don't want to* go against you, sir—

Wanklin (*Persuasively*) Come, Chairman, we're *not* free agents. We're part of a machine. Our only business is to see the Company earns as much profit as it safely can. If you blame me for want of principle: I say that we're Trustees. Reason tells us we shall never get back in the saving of wages what we shall lose if we continue this struggle—really, Chairman, we *must* bring it to an end, on the best terms we can make.

Anthony No!

(*There is a pause of general dismay*)

Wilder It's a deadlock then. (*Letting his hands drop with a sort of despair*) Now I shall never get off to Spain!

Wanklin (*Retaining a trace of irony*) You hear the consequences of your victory, Chairman?

Wilder (*With a burst of feeling*) My wife's *ill*!

Scantlebury Dear, dear! You don't say so!

Wilder If I don't get her out of this cold, I won't answer for the consequences.

(*Through the double doors* **Edgar** *comes in looking very grave*)

Edgar (*To his father*) Have you heard this, sir? Mrs

Roberts is dead! (*Everyone stares at him, as if trying to gauge the importance of this news*) Enid saw her this afternoon, she had no coals, or food, or anything. It's enough!

(*There is a silence, everyone avoiding the other's eyes, except* **Anthony,** *who stares hard at his son*)

Scantlebury You don't suggest that we could have helped the poor thing?

Wilder (*Flustered*) The woman was in bad health, Nobody can say there's any responsibility on us. At least—not on me.

Edgar (*Hotly*) I say that we *are* responsible.

Anthony War is war!

Edgar Not on women!

Wanklin It not infrequently happens that women are the greatest sufferers.

Edgar If we knew that, all the more responsibility rests on us.

Anthony This is no matter for amateurs.

Edgar Call me what you like, sir. It's sickened me. We had no right to carry things to such a length.

Wilder I don't like this business a bit—that Radical rag will twist it to their own ends; see if they don't! They'll get up some cock-and bull story about the poor woman's dying from starvation. I wash my hands of it.

Edgar You can't. None of us can.

Scantlebury (*Striking his fist on the arm of his chair*) But I protest against this—

Edgar Protest as you like, Mr Scantlebury, it won't alter facts.

Anthony That's enough.

Edgar (*Facing him angrily*) No, sir. I tell you exactly what I think. If we pretend the men are not suffering, it's humbug; and if they're suffering, we know enough of human nature to know the women are suffering more, and as to the children—well—it's damnable! (**Scantlebury** *rises from his chair*) I don't say that we meant to be cruel, I don't say anything of the sort; but I do say it's criminal to shut our eyes to the facts. We employ these men, and we can't get out of it. I care so much about the men, but I'd sooner resign my position on the Board than go on starving women in this way.

(*All except* **Anthony** *are now upon their feet,* **Anthony** *sits grasping the arms of his chair and staring at his son*).

Scantlebury I don't—I don't like the way you're putting it, young sir.

Wanklin You're rather overshooting the mark.

Wilder I should think so indeed!

Edgar (*Losing control*) It's no use blinking things! If *you* want to have the death of women on your hands—*I* don't!

Scantlebury Now, now, young man!

Wilder On *our* hands? Not on *mine*, I won't have it!

Edgar We are five members of this Board; if we were four against it, why did we let it drift till it came to this? You know perfectly well why—because we hoped we should starve the men out. Well, all we've done is to starve one woman out!

Scantlebury (*Almost hysterically*) I protest, I protest! I'm a humane man—we're all humane men!

Edgar (*Scornfully*) There's nothing wrong with our *humanity*. It's our imaginations, Mr Scantlebury.

Wilder Nonsense! My imagination's as good as yours.

Edgar If so, it isn't good enough.

Wilder I foresaw this!

Edgar Then why didn't you put your foot down?

Wilder Much good that would have done.

(*He looks at* **Anthony**)

Edgar If you, and I, and each one of us here who say that our imaginations are so good—

Scantlebury (*Flurried*) I never said so.

Edgar (*Paying no attention*)—had put our feet down, the thing would have been ended long ago, and this poor woman's life wouldn't have been crushed out of her like this. For all we can tell there may be a dozen other starving women.

Scantlebury For God's sake, sir, don't use that word at a—at a Board meeting; it's—it's monstrous.

Edgar I *will* use it, Mr Scantlebury.

Scantlebury Then I shall not listen to you. I shall not listen! It's painful to me.

(*He covers his ears*)

Wanklin None of us are opposed to a settlement, except your father.

Edgar I'm certain that if the shareholders knew—

Wanklin I don't think you'll find their imaginations are any better than ours. Because a woman happens to have a weak heart—

Edgar A struggle like this finds out the weak spots in everybody. Any child knows that. If it hadn't been for this cut-throat policy, she needn't have died like this; and there wouldn't be all this misery that anyone who isn't a fool can see is going on.

(*Throughout the foregoing* **Anthony** *has eyed his son; he now moves as though to rise, but stops as* **Edgar**

speaks again)

I don't defend the men, or myself, or anybody.

Wanklin You may have to! A coroner's jury of disinterested sympathisers may say some very nasty things. We mustn't lose sight of our position.

Scantlebury (*Without uncovering his ears*) Coroner's jury! No, no, it's not a case for that?

Edgar I've had enough of cowardice.

Wanklin Cowardice is an unpleasant word, Mr Edgar Anthony. It will look very like cowardice if we suddenly concede the men's demands when a thing like this happens; we must be careful!

Wilder Of course we must. We've no knowledge of this matter, except a rumour. The proper course is to put the whole thing into the hands of Harness to settle for us; that's natural, that's what we *should* have come to any way.

Scantlebury (*With dignity*) Exactly! (*Turning to* **Edgar**) And as to you, young sir, I can't sufficiently express my—my distaste for the way you've treated the whole matter. You ought to withdraw! Talking of starvation, talking of cowardice! Considering what our views are! Except your own father—we're all agreed the only policy is—is one of goodwill—it's most irregular, it's most improper, and all I can say is it's—it's given me pain—

(*He places his hand on the centre of his stomach*)

Edgar (*Stubbornly*) I withdraw nothing.

(*He is about to say more when* **Scantlebury** *once more covers up his ears.* **Tench** *suddenly makes a demonstration with the minute-book. A sense of having been engaged in the unusual comes over all of them, and one by one they resume their seats.* **Edgar** *alone remains on his feet*)

Wilder (*With an air of trying to wipe something out*) I pay no attention to what young Mr Anthony has said. Coroner's Jury! The idea's preposterous. I—I move this amendment to the Chairman's Motion: That the dispute be placed at once in the hands of Mr. Simon Harness for settlement, on the lines indicated by him this morning. Anyone second that?

(**Tench** *writes in the book*)

Wanklin I do.

Wilder Very well, then; I ask the Chairman to put it to the Board.

Anthony (*With a great sigh—slowly*) We have been made the subject of an attack. (*Looking round at* **Wilder** *and* **Scantlebury** *with ironical contempt*) I take it on *my* shoulders. I am seventy-six years old. I have been Chairman of this Company since its inception two-and-thirty years ago. I have seen it pass through good and evil report. My connection with it began in the year that this young man was born. (**Edgar** *bows his head.* **Anthony** *gripping his chair, goes on*) I have had to do with 'men' for fifty years; I've always stood up to them; I have never been beaten yet. I have fought the men of this Company four times, and four times I have beaten them. It has been said that I am not the man I was. (*He looks at* **Wilder**) However that may be, I am man enough to stand to my guns.

(*His voice grows stronger. The double doors are opened.* **Enid** *slips in, followed by* **Underwood,** *who restrains her*)

The men have been treated justly, they have had fair wages, we have always been ready to listen to complaints. It has been said that times have changed; if they have, I have not changed with them. Neither will I. It has been said that masters and men are equal! Cant! There can only be one master in a house! Where two men meet the better man will rule. It has been said that Capital and Labour have the same interests. Cant! Their interests are as wide asunder as the poles. It has been said that the Board is only part of a machine. Cant! We *are* the machine; its brains and sinews; it is for us to lead and to determine what is to be done, and to do it without fear or favour. Fear of the men! Fear of the shareholders! Fear of our own shadows! Before I am like that, I hope to die. (*He pauses, and meeting his son's eyes, goes on*) There is only one way of treating 'men'—with *the iron hand.* This half-and-half business, the half-and-half manners of this generation has brought all this upon us. Sentiment and softness, and what this young man, no doubt, would call his social policy. You can't eat cake and have it! This middle-class sentiment, or socialism, or whatever it may be, is rotten. Masters are masters, men are men! Yield one demand, and they will make it six. They are (*he smiles grimly*) like Oliver Twist, asking for more. If I were in *their* place I should be the same. But I am not in their place. Mark my words: one fine morning, when you have given way here, and given way there—you will find you have parted with the ground beneath your feet, and are deep in the bog of bankruptcy; and with you, floundering in that bog, will be the very men you have given way to. I have been

An angry Anthony (Derek Smith) confronts the Board in the 1967 production at the Theatre Royal, Bristol

accused of being a domineering tyrant, thinking only of my pride—I am thinking of the future of this country, threatened with the black waters of confusion, threatened with mob government, threatened with what I cannot see. If by any conduct of mine I help to bring this on us, I shall be ashamed to look my fellows in the face.

(**Anthony** *stares before him, at what he cannot see, and there is perfect stillness.* **Frost** *comes in from the hall, and all but* **Anthony** *look round at him uneasily*)

Frost (*To his master*) The men are here, sir. (**Anthony** *makes a gesture of dismissal*) Shall I bring them in, sir?

Anthony Wait! (**Frost** *goes out,* **Anthony** *turns to face his son*) I come to the attack that has been made upon me.

(**Edgar,** *with a gesture of deprecation, remains motionless with his head a little bowed*) A woman has died. I am told that her blood is on my hands; I am told that on my hands is the starvation and the suffering of other women and children.

Edgar I said 'on *our* hands,' sir.

Anthony It is the same. (*His voice grows stronger and stronger, his feeling is more and more made manifest*) I am not aware that if my adversary suffer in a fair fight not sought by me, it is *my* fault. If I fall under *his* feet—as fall I may—I shall not complain. That will be *my* look-out—and this is —his. I cannot separate, as I would, these men from their women and children. A fair fight is a fair fight! Let them learn to think before they pick a quarrel!

Edgar (*In a low voice*) But is it a fair fight, Father?

Look at them, and look at us! They've only this one weapon!

Anthony (*Grimly*) And you're weak-kneed enough to teach them to use it! It seems the fashion nowadays for men to take their enemy's side. I have not learnt that art. Is it my fault that they quarrelled with their Union too?

Edgar There is such as a thing as Mercy.

Anthony And Justice comes before it.

Edgar What seems just to one man, sir, is injustice to another.

Anthony (*With suppressed passion*) You accuse me of injustice—of what amounts to inhumanity—of cruelty—

(**Edgar** *makes a gesture of horror—a general frightened movement*)

Wanklin Come, come, Chairman!

Anthony (*In a grim voice*) These are the words of my own son. They are the words of a generation that I don't understand; the words of a soft breed.

(*A general murmur. With a violent effort* **Anthony** *recovers his control*)

Edgar (*Quietly*) I said it of *myself*, too, Father.

(*A long look is exchanged between them, and* **Anthony** *puts out his hand with a gesture as if to sweep the personalities away; then places it against his brow, swaying as though from giddiness. There is a movement towards him. He waves them back*)

Anthony Before I put this amendment to the Board, I have one more word to say. (*He looks from face to face*) If it is carried, it means that we shall fail in what we set ourselves to do. It means that we shall fail in the duty that we owe to all Capital. It means that we shall fail in the duty that we owe ourselves. It means that we shall be open to constant attack to which we as constantly shall have to yield. Be under no misapprehension—run this time, and you will never make a stand again! You will have to fly like curs before the whips of your own men. If that is the lot you wish for, you will vote for this amendment.

(*He looks again from face to face, finally resting his gaze on* **Edgar**; *all sit with their eyes on the ground.* **Anthony** *makes a gesture, and* **Tench** *hands him the book. He reads*)

'Moved by Mr Wilder, and seconded by Mr Wanklin. "That the men's demands be placed at once in the hands of Mr Simon Harness for settlement on the lines indicated by him this morning." ' (*With sudden vigour*) Those in favour: Signify the same in the usual way!

(*For a minute no-one moves; then hastily, just as* **Anthony** *is about to speak,* **Wilder**'s *hand and* **Wanklin**'s *are held up, then* **Scantlebury**'s *and last* **Edgar**'s *who does not lift his head*) Contrary? (**Anthony** *lifts his own hand*) (*In a clear voice*). The amendment is carried. I resign my position on this board. (**Enid** *gasps, and there is a dead silence.* **Anthony** *sits motionless, his head slowly drooping; suddenly he heaves as though the whole of his life has risen up within him*) Fifty years! You have disgraced me, gentlemen. Bring in the men!

(*He sits motionless, staring before him. The Board draws hurriedly together, and forms a group.* **Tench** *in a frightened manner speaks into the hall.* **Underwood** *almost forces* **Enid** *from the room*)

Wilder (*Hurriedly*) What's to be said to them? Why isn't Harness here? Ought we to see the men before he comes? I don't—

Tench Will you come in, please?

(*Enter* **Thomas, Green, Bulgin** *and* **Rous**, *who file up in a row past the little table.* **Tench** *sits down and writes. All eyes are fixed on* **Anthony**, *who makes no sign*)

Wanklin (*Stepping up to the little table, with nervous cordiality*) Well, Thomas, how's it to be? What's the result of your meeting?

Rous Sim Harness has our answer. He'll tell you what it is. We're waiting for him. He'll speak for us.

Wanklin Is that so, Thomas?

Thomas (*Sullenly*) Yes. Roberts will not be coming, his wife is dead.

Scantlebury Yes, yes! Poor woman! Yes! Yes!

Frost (*Entering from the hall*) Mr Harness, sir!

(*As* **Harness** *enters he retires.* **Harness** *has a piece of paper in his hand. He bows to the Directors, nods towards the men, and takes his stand behind the little table in the very centre of the room*)

Harness Good evening, gentlemen.

(**Tench**, *with the paper he has been writing, joins him; they speak together in low tones*)

Wilder We've been waiting for you, Harness. Hope we shall come to some—

Frost (*Entering from the hall*) Roberts.

(*He goes.* **Roberts** *comes hastily in, and stands staring at* **Anthony**. *His face is drawn and old*).

Roberts Mr Anthony, I am afraid I am a little late. I would have been here in time but for something that—has happened. (*To the men*) Has anything been said?

Thomas No! But, man, what made ye come?

Roberts Ye told us this morning, gentlemen, to go away and reconsider our position. We have reconsidered it; we are here to bring you the men's answer. (*To* **Anthony**) Go ye back to London. We have nothing for you. By no jot or tittle do we abate our demands, nor will we until the whole of those demands are yielded.

(**Anthony** *looks at him but does not speak. There is a movement amongst the men as though they were bewildered*)

Harness Roberts!

Roberts (*Glancing fiercely at him, and back to* **Anthony**) Is that clear enough for ye? Is it short enough and to the point? Ye made a mistake to think that we would come to heel. Ye may break the body, but ye cannot break the spirit. Get back to London, the men have nothing for ye!

(*Pausing uneasily he takes a step towards the unmoving* **Anthony**)

Edgar We're all sorry for you, Roberts, but—

Roberts Keep your sorrow, young man. Let your Father speak!

Harness (*With the sheet of paper in his hand, speaking from behind the little table*) Roberts!

Roberts (*To* **Anthony**, *with passionate intensity*) Why don't ye answer?

Harness Roberts!

Roberts (*Turning sharply*) What is it?

Harness (*Gravely*) You're talking without the book; things have travelled past you.

(*He makes a sign to* **Tench** *who beckons the Directors. They quickly sign his copy of the terms*) Look at this, man! (*Holding up his sheet of paper.*) 'Demands conceded, *with the exception of those relating to the engineers and furnace men.* Double wages for Saturday's overtime. Night-shifts as they are.' These terms have been agreed. The men go back to work again to-morrow. The strike is at an end.

Roberts (*Reading the paper, and turning on the men. They shrink back from him, all but* **Rous**, *who stands his ground. With deadly stillness*) Ye have gone back on me? I stood by ye to the death; ye waited for *that* to throw me over!

(*The men answer, all speaking together*)

Rous It's a lie!

Thomas Ye were past endurance, man.

Green If ye'd listen to me—

Bulgin (*Under his breath*) Hold your jaw!

Roberts Ye waited for *that!*

Harness (*Taking the Directors' copy of the terms, and handing his own to* **Tench**) That's enough, men. You had better go.

(*The men shuffle slowly, awkwardly away*)

Wilder (*In a low, nervous voice*) There's nothing to stay for now, I suppose. (*He follows to the door*) I shall have a try for that train! Coming, Scantlebury?

Scantlebury (*Following with* **Wanklin**) Yes, yes; wait for me.

(*He stops as* **Roberts** *speaks*)

Roberts (*To* **Anthony**) But *ye* have not signed them terms! They can't make terms without their Chairman! Ye would never sign them terms!

(**Anthony** *looks at him without speaking*) Don't tell me ye have! for the love o'God! (*With passionate appeal*) I reckoned on ye!

Harness (*Holding out the Directors' copy of the terms*) The *Board* has signed!

(**Roberts** *looks dully at the signatures—dashes the paper from him, and covers up his eyes*).

Scantlebury (*Behind his hand to* **Tench**) Look after the Chairman! He's not well; he's not well—he had no lunch. If there's any fund started for the women and children, put me down for—for twenty pounds.

(*He goes out into the hall, in cumbrous haste; and* **Wanklin**, *who has been staring at* **Roberts** *and* **Anthony** *with twitchings of his face, follows.* **Edgar** *remains seated on the sofa, looking at the ground;* **Tench**, *returning to the bureau, writes in his minutebook.* **Harness** *stands by the little table, gravely watching* **Roberts**)

Roberts Then you're no longer Chairman of this Company! (*Breaking into half-mad laughter*) Ah! ha—ah, ha, ha! They've thrown ye over—thrown over their Chairman: Ah—ha—ha! (*With a sudden dreadful calm*) So—they've done us both down, Mr Anthony?

(**Enid**, *hurrying through the double doors, comes quickly to her father and bends over him*)

Harness (*Coming down and laying his hands on* **Roberts** *sleeve*) For shame, Roberts! Go home quietly, man; go home!

Roberts (*Tearing his arm away*) Home? (*Shrinking together—in a whisper*) Home!

Enid (*Quietly to her father*) Come away, dear! Come to your room!

(**Anthony** *rises with an effort. He turns to* **Roberts**, *who looks at him. They stand several seconds, gazing at each other fixedly;* **Anthony** *lifts his hand, as though to salute, but lets it fall. The expression of*

Roberts' *face changes from hostility to wonder. They bend their heads in token of respect.* **Anthony** *turns, and slowly walks towards the curtained door. Suddenly he sways as though about to fall, recovers himself and is assisted out by* **Enid** *and* **Edgar**, *who has hurried across the room.* **Roberts** *remains motionless for several seconds, staring intently after* **Anthony**, *then goes out into the hall)*

Tench (*Approaching* **Harness**) It's a great weight off my mind, Mr Harness! But what a painful scene, sir!

(*He wipes his brow.* **Harness**, *pale and resolute, regards with a grim half-smile the quavering* **Tench**) It's all been so violent! What did he mean by: 'Done us both down?' If he has lost his wife, poor fellow, he oughtn't to have spoken to the Chairman like that!

Harness A woman dead; and the two best men both broken!

(**Underwood** *enters suddenly*)

Tench (*Staring at* **Harness**—*suddenly excited*) D'you know, sir—these terms, they're the *very same* we drew up together, you and I, and put to both sides before the fight began? All this—all this—and—and what for?

Harness (*In a slow grim voice*) That's where the fun comes in!

(**Underwood** *without turning from the door makes a gesture of assent*)

George S. Kaufman & Moss Hart:
You Can't Take It With You

Many of us think of 'doing our own thing'. Why decide on an ambition, get a conventional job and pursue a career, grimly struggling until we achieve (or fail to achieve) our goal?

In *You Can't Take It With You* (1936) the Vanderhof family live an open, generous unambitious life. The entire play is set in the household living room, and live in it is just what they do. Everything happens there, as noted in the opening stage directions. Penny writes her plays in bursts, untroubled by a sense of deadlines for completion; Essie, her daughter, spends most of her time practising ballet and making superb candy, which the family all enjoy; her husband, Paul, and Mr de Pinna (a houseguest who has stayed on and on since goodness knows when) make fireworks in the cellar; Ed, Essie's husband, plays at being a printer in-between tinkling on the xylophone; Grandpa presides over the spirit of the household. They do not seem to have much money but they are relaxed and wonderfully happy, taking life as it comes.

Is this style of life possible (or desirable) in the 'real' world? Much between-the-wars American drama deals with characters who do not fit into their environment, either because they do not understand society or because they understand it well and do not like it. When the 'real' world intrudes into this play in the shape of a financier and his wife, federal agents and an inland revenue man, that world does not stand a chance against the Vanderhofs. Hart and Kaufman manipulate us so that, long before the end of the play, we regard the anarchic, likeable Vanderhofs as normal, and the world outside as bizarre, distorted in its values and utterly forgetful that 'you can't take it with you'. The play builds up to an exchange towards the end between the Wall Street financier and Grandpa:

Kirby A man can't give up his business.
Grandpa Why not? You've got all the money you need. You can't take it with you.
Kirby That's a very easy thing to say, Mr Vanderhof. But I have spent my entire life building up my business.

Characters in the play

Penelope Sycamore
Essie
Rheba
Paul Sycamore
Mr De Pinna
Ed
Donald
Martin Vanderhof
Alice
Henderson
Tony Kirby
Boris Kolenkhov
Gay Wellington
Mr Kirby
Mrs Kirby
Three Men
Olga

Grandpa And what's it got you? Same kind of mail every morning, same kind of deals, same kind of meetings, same dinners at night, same indigestion. . . .

I have a lot of fun. Time enough for everything—read, talk, visit the zoo now and then, practice my darts, even have time to notice when spring comes around. Don't see anybody I don't want to, don't have six hours of things I *have* to do every day before I get *one* hour to do what I like in—and I haven't taken bicarbonate of soda in thirty-five years. What's the matter with that?

Kirby The matter with that? Suppose we *all* did it? . . . And, it's a very dangerous philosophy, Mr Vanderhof. It's—it's un-American.

Act I,   Scene I

The home of **Martin Vanderhof**—*just around the corner from Columbia University, but don't go looking for it. The room we see is what is customarily described as a living room, but in this house the term* *is something of an understatement. The every-man-for-himself room would be more like it. For here meals are eaten, plays are written, snakes collected, ballet steps practiced, xylophones played, printing presses operated—if there were room enough there would probably be ice skating. In short, the brood presided over by* **Martin Vanderhof** *goes on about the business of living in the fullest sense of the word. From* **Grandpa Vanderhof** *down, they are individualists. This is a house where you do as you like, and no questions asked.*

At the moment, **Grandpa Vanderhof**'s *daughter,* **Mrs Penelope Sycamore**, *is doing what she likes more than anything else in the world. She is writing a play—her eleventh. Comfortably ensconced in what is affectionately known as Mother's Corner, she is pounding away on a typewriter perched precariously on a rickety card table. Also on the table is one of those plaster-paris skulls ordinarily used as an ash tray, but which serves* **Penelope** *as a candy jar. And, because* **Penny** *likes companionship, there are two kittens on the table, busily lapping at a saucer of milk.*

Penelope Vanderhof Sycamore *is a round little woman in her early fifties, comfortable looking, gentle, homey. One would not suspect that under that placid exterior there surges the Divine Urge—but it does, it does.*

After a moment her fingers lag on the keys; a thoughtful expression comes over her face. Abstractedly she takes a piece of candy out of the skull, pops it into her mouth. As always, it furnishes the needed inspiration—with a furious burst of speed she finishes a page and whips it out of the machine. Quite mechanically, she picks up one of the kittens, adds the sheet of paper to the pile underneath, replaces the kitten. As she goes back to work, **Essie Carmichael, Mrs Sycamore**'s *eldest daughter, comes in from the kitchen. A girl of about twenty-nine, very slight, a curious air of the pixie about her. She is wearing ballet slippers—in fact, she wears them throughout the play.*

Essie (*Enters U.R. as* **Penny** *crosses back with skull and fanning herself takes paper out of typewriter*) My, that kitchen's hot.

Penny (*Finishing a bit of typing*) What, Essie? (*Rises and crosses to R.a step*)

Essie (*Crossing to R. of table*) I say the kitchen's awful hot. That new candy I'm making—it just won't ever get cool.

Penny Do you have to make candy today, Essie? It's such a hot day.

Essie Well, I got all those new orders. Ed went out and got a bunch of new orders. (*Leg limbering exercise on chair*)

Penny My, if it keeps on I suppose you'll be opening up a store.

Essie That's what Ed was saying last night (*She leans body forward*), but I said No, I want to be a dancer. (*Points to C.*)

Penny (*Returning to her desk*) The only trouble with dancing is, it takes so long. You've been studying such a long time.

Essie (*Slowly drawing a leg up behind her as she talks*) Only—eight—years. After all, Mother, you've been writing plays for eight years. We started about the same time, didn't we?

Penny Yes, but you shouldn't count my first two years, because I was learning to type. (*At her desk*)

(*From the kitchen comes a colored maid named* **Rheba**—*a very black girl somewhere in her thirties. She carries eight napkins*)

Rheba (*As she enters*) I think the candy's *hardening up* now, Miss Essie. (*Puts napkins on U.S. chair of table*)

Essie Oh, thanks, Rheba. I'll bring some in, Mother—I want you to try it. (*She goes into kitchen U.R.*)

(**Penny** *returns to her work, sits—puts fresh paper in and types—as* **Rheba** *removes table centrepiece and goes to buffet*)

Rheba (*Taking a tablecloth from buffet drawer*) Finish the second act, Mrs Sycamore?

Penny Uh? What?

Rheba (*Returning to table, she throws tablecloth over back of a chair and removes table cover*) I said, did you finish the second act?

Penny (*Crosses to R. a step with script, papers, and pencil*) Oh, no, Rheba. I've just got Cynthia entering the monastery.

Rheba She was at the Kit Kat, wasn't she?

Penny (*Crosses to L. of table*) Well, she gets tired of the Kit Kat Club, and there's this monastery, so she goes there.

Rheba Do they let her in?

Penny Yes, I made it Visitors' Day, so of course anybody can come.

Rheba Oh. (*As she spreads tablecloth*)

Penny So she arrives on Visitors' Day, and—just stays.

Rheba You mean she stays all night?

Penny Oh, yes. She stays six years. (*Crosses to her desk and sits*)

Rheba Six years? (*Starting for kitchen*) My, I bet she busts that monastery wide open. (*She is gone*)

Penny (*Half to herself, as she types*) 'Six Years Later.' . . .

(**Paul Sycamore** *comes up from the cellar. Mid-fifties, but with a kind of youthful air. His quiet charm and mild manner are distinctly engaging. He is carrying a frying pan containing several small firecrackers. He is smoking a cigarette*)

Paul (*Turning back as he comes through door D.R.*) Mr De Pinna! (*A voice from below: 'Yah?'*) Mr De Pinna, will you bring up one of those new skyrockets, please? I want to show them to Mrs Sycamore. (*An answering 'Sure!' from cellar as he crosses toward* **Penny**, *who rises*) Look, Penny— what do you think of these little firecrackers we just made? We can sell them ten strings for a cent. Listen. (*He puts one down in the pan on table and lights it. It goes off with a good bang*) Nice, huh?

Penny Yes. Paul, dear, were you ever in a monastery?

Paul (*Puts half of firecrackers in pan, quite calmly as he crosses to her*) No, I wasn't. . . . Wait till you see the new rockets. Gold stars, then blue stars, and then bombs, and then a balloon. Mr De Pinna thought of the balloon.

(**De Pinna** *enters*)

Penny Sounds lovely. Did you do all that today? (*Crosses to desk chair*)

Paul Sure. We made up—Oh, here we are. (**De Pinna** *comes up from cellar. A bald-headed little man with a serious manner, carrying 2 good-sized skyrockets. He crosses to* **Paul. Paul** *takes one to show* **Penny**) Look, Penny. Costs us eighteen cents to make and we sell 'em for fifty. How many do you figure we can make before the Fourth of July, Mr De Pinna?

De Pinna Well, we've got two weeks yet—what day you going to take the stuff up to Mount Vernon?

Paul (*Picking up his pan and firecrackers*) About a week. You know, we're going to need a larger booth this year—got a lot of stuff made up. (**Paul** *starts R.*) Come on, we're not through yet.

(**De Pinna** *follows*)

De Pinna Look, Mr Sycamore, (*examining rocket in his hand*) I'm afraid the powder chamber is just a little bit close to the balloon.

Paul Well, we got the stars and the bombs in

between.

De Pinna But that don't give the balloon time enough. A balloon needs plenty of time.

Paul Come on—come on. Let's go down in the cellar and try it.

(*He exits D.R.*)

De Pinna (*Starting off*) All right.

Penny (*Rising and crossing two steps R.*) Mr De Pinna, if a girl you loved entered a monastery, what would you do?

De Pinna Oh I don't know, Mrs Sycamore . . . it's been so long.

(**Penny** *sits at her desk, as* **De Pinna** *exits D.R. She starts to type again as* **Rheba** *enters from kitchen bringing a pile of plates and salt and pepper shakers*)

Rheba (*Crossing down to table*) Miss Alice going to be home to dinner tonight, Mrs Sycamore? (*She puts pile of plates on table*)

Penny (*Deep in her thinking*) What? I don't know, Rheba. Maybe.

Rheba Well, I'll set a place for her, but she's only been home one night this week.

Penny Yes, I know.

Rheba (*She puts down a plate or two*) Miss Essie's making some mighty good candy today. She's doing something new with cocoanuts. (*More plates*)

Penny Uh-huh. That's nice.

Rheba Let's see . . . six and Mr De Pinna, and if Mr Kolenkhov comes that makes eight, don't it? (**Penny** *types. At which point, a whistling sound of a rocket followed by a series of explosions comes up from cellar.* **Penny** *and* **Rheba**, *however, don't even notice it.* **Rheba** *goes right on*) Yes, I'd better set for eight. (*Puts napkins from chair to table. Puts down one more plate, looks over her setting of the table, and starts off U.R.*)

Penny (*Rising*) Rheba, I think I'll put this play away for a while and go back to the war play.

(**Essie** *returns from kitchen carrying a plate of freshly made candy*)

Rheba Oh, I always liked that one—the war play. Boom, boom! (*She exits U.R.*)

Essie (*Crossing over to* **Penny**) They'll be better when they're harder, Mother, but try one—I want to know what you think.

Penny Oh, they look lovely. (*She takes one*) What do you call them?

Essie I think I'll call 'em Love Dreams. (*She places them on C. table*)

Penny Yes, that's nice. . . . (*Nibbling on one of the*

candies) I'm going back to my war play, Essie. What do you think?

Essie (*Dances back to buffet*) Oh, are you, Mother?

Penny (*Puts script down*) Yes, I sort of got myself into a monastery and I can't get out.

Essie (*Pointing her toe*) Oh, well, it'll come to you, Mother. Remember how you got out of that brothel. . . . (*She looks at snake solarium, a glass structure looking something like a goldfish aquarium, but containing, believe it or not, snakes*) The snakes look hungry. Did Rheba feed them?

(**Rheba** *enters U.R. carrying silverware*)

Penny (*As* **Rheba** *re-enters, puts silverware down on table. Sets two places*) I don't know. Rheba, did you feed the snakes yet?

Rheba No, Donald's coming and he always brings flies with him. (**Essie** *dances to R. of buffet*)

Penny Well, try to feed them before Grandpa gets home. You know how fussy he is about them. (*Crossing to desk, she picks up file box with kittens in it*)

Rheba (*Starts to go*) Yes'm.

Penny (*Crossing to* **Rheba**. *Handing her the kittens*) And here, take Groucho and Harpo into the kitchen with you. (**Rheba** *exits U.R.*) Believe I'll have another Love Dream. (*Sits at her desk*)

(**Paul** *emerges from cellar again*)

Paul (*Enters D.R. and crosses to* **Essie**) Mr De Pinna was right about the balloon. It was too close to the powder.

Essie (*Points to plate*) Want a Love Dream, Father? They're on the table.

Paul (*Starts for stairs*) No, thanks. I gotta wash.

Penny I'm going back to the war play, Paul.

Paul Oh, that's nice. We're putting some red stars after the bombs and *then* the balloon. That ought to do it. (*He goes up stairs*)

Essie (*Crossing down to back of chair L. of table*) You know, Mr Kolenkhov says I'm his most promising pupil.

Penny You'd think with forty monks and one girl that *something* would happen.

(**Ed Carmichael** *comes down stairs. A nondescript young man in his mid-thirties. He removes his coat as he crosses to xylophone*)

Ed Essie! Heh! Essie! (**Penny** *sits as music starts. He hums a snatch of melody as he heads for the far corner of the room—the xylophone corner. Arriving there, he picks up the sticks and continues the melody on the xylophone. Immediately* **Essie** *is up on her toes, performing intricate ballet steps to* **Ed**'s *accompaniment*)

Essie (*After a bar, rising on toes—dancing—to R. below table*) I like that, Ed. Did you write it? (**Penny** *types*)

Ed (*Pauses in his playing. Shakes his head*) No, Beethoven. (*Music continues*)

Essie (*Never coming down off her toes*) Lovely. Got a lot of *you* in it. . . . I made those new candies this afternoon, Ed. (*Dancing to the L.*) (**Penny** *puts scripts from U.S. end to D.S. end*)

Ed (*Playing away*) Yah?

Essie (*A series of leaping steps*) You can take 'em around tonight.

Ed All right. . . . Now, here's the finish. This is me. (*He works up to an elaborate crescendo, but* **Essie** *keeps pace with him, right to the finish, pirouetting to the last note*) How's that?

Essie That's fine. (**Penny** *picks up half of pile of scripts, D.S. end desk*) Remember it when Kolenkhov comes, will you?

Penny (*Who has been busy with her scripts*) Ed, dear. Why don't you and Essie have a baby? I was thinking about it just the other day.

(**Ed** *puts xylophone hammers down—comes down from alcove*)

Ed (*As* **Essie** *busies herself with her slippers*) I don't know—we could have one if you wanted us to. What about it, Essie? Do you want to have a baby?

Essie Oh, I don't care. I'm willing if Grandpa is. (*And off into kitchen*)

Ed (*Calling after her*) Let's ask him.

Penny (*Running through a pile of scripts*) Labor play, (**Ed** *works printing press with a bang*) religious play, (*Another bang.* **Rheba** *enters U.R. with silverware. Puts table cover from chair on buffet arm*) sex play—(*Still another bang*) I know it's here some place.

De Pinna (*Coming out of cellar D.R., bound for kitchen to wash up*) I was right about the balloon. It was too close to the powder.

Ed (*Who has crossed to his press*) Anything you want printed, Mr De Pinna? How about some more calling cards?

De Pinna No, thanks. I've still got the *first* thousand.

Ed Well, call on somebody, will you?

De Pinna All right! (*Exits U.R.*)

Ed (*Coming downstage—type stick in hand*) What have we got for dinner, Rheba? I'm ready to print the menu.

Rheba Let's see. Corn flakes, watermelon, some of

these candies Miss Essie made, and some kind of meat—I forget. (*Sets silverware*)

Ed I think I'll set it up in bold face Cheltenham tonight. (*Going to printing press U.R.*) You know, if I'm going to take those new candies around I'd better print up some descriptive matter after dinner.

Penny Do you think anybody reads those things, Ed—that you put in the candy boxes? . . . Oh, here's the war play. (*She pulls a script out of pile*) 'Poison Gas.' (*The doorbell rings. Changes tone*) I guess that's Donald. (**Rheba** *smiles and starts for hall door, U.L*) Look at Rheba smile.

Ed The boy friend, eh, Rheba?

(**Rheba** *is out of sight*)

Penny They're awfully cute, Donald and Rheba. Sort of like Porgy and Bess.

Donald (*Off stage*) Hello, Rheba.

Rheba Donald! (**Rheba** *having opened door,* **Donald** *now looms up in arch, straw hat in hand*)

Donald Evening, everybody!

Ed Hi, Donald! How've you been?

Donald (*Coming into room*) I'm pretty good, Mr Ed. How you been, Mrs Sycamore. (*He starts R.*)

Penny Very well, thank you. (*Rises*) Donald?

Donald Yes, ma'am?

Penny Were you ever in a monastery?

Donald No-o. I don't go no place much. I'm on relief. (*Reaching for bottle of flies in his pocket*)

Penny Ah, yes, of course. (*Sits*)

Donald (*Crossing to* **Rheba.** *Pulling a bottle out of side pocket*) Here's the flies, Rheba. Caught a big mess of them today.

Rheba (*Taking the jar*) You sure did. (**Rheba** *goes into the kitchen U.R.*) (**Donald** *crosses to L.*)

Donald I see you've been working, Mrs Sycamore.

Penny Yes, indeed, Donald.

Donald How's Grandpa?

Penny Just fine. He's over at Columbia this afternoon. The Commencement exercises.

Donald (*Crossing to table*) My . . . my. The years certainly do roll 'round. M-m-m. (*Takes a candy*)

Ed (*With his typesetting*) M—E—A—T. . . . What's he go there for all the time, Penny?

Penny I don't know, it's so handy—just around the corner.

(**Paul** *comes down stairs, an impressive looking tome under his arm*)

Paul Oh, Donald! Mr De Pinna and I are going to take the fireworks up to Mount Vernon next week. Do you think you could give us a hand?

Donald Yes, sir, only I can't take no money for it this year, because if the Government finds out I'm working they'll get sore.

Paul Oh! (**Donald** *drifts up to buffet and feeds bits of candy to the snakes*) Ed, I got a wonderful idea in the bathroom just now. I was reading Trotzky [sic]. It's yours, isn't it?

Ed (*Crossing down*) Yah, I left it there.

Penny *Who* is it?

Paul (*A step to* **Penny**) You know, Trotzky. The Russian Revolution. (*Showing her book*)

Penny Oh.

Paul (**Donald** *turns*) Anyhow, it struck me it was a great fireworks idea. Remember 'The Last Days of Pompeii'?

Penny Oh, yes. Palisades Park. (*With a gesture of her arms she loosely describes a couple of arcs, indicative of the eruption of Mt. Vesuvius*) That's where we met.

Paul Well, I'm going to do the Revolution! A full hour display.

Donald Say!

Penny Paul, that's wonderful!

Ed The red fire is the flag, huh?

Paul (*Crossing a step to R.*) Sure! And the Czar, and the Cossacks!

Donald And the freeing of the slaves?

Paul No, no, Donald—the Russian Revolution. (*The sound of the front door slamming. A second's pause, then* **Grandpa** *enters living room.* **Grandpa** *is about 75, a wiry little man whom the years have treated kindly. His face is youthful, despite the lines that sear it; his eyes are very much alive. He is a man who made his peace with the world long, long ago, and his whole attitude and manner are quietly persuasive of this*) Hello, Grandpa. (**Donald** *crosses to door U.R.* **Ed** *up to L. of xylophone.* **Paul** *sits above table*)

Grandpa (*Putting his hat on newel post and surveying the group*) Well, sir, you should have been there. That's all I can say—you should have been there.

Penny Was it a nice Commencement, Grandpa?

Grandpa Wonderful. They get better every year. (*He peers into snake solarium*) You don't know how lucky you are you're snakes. (*Crossing to alcove for his house coat*)

Ed Big class this year, Grandpa? How many were there?

Grandpa Oh, must have been two acres. *Everybody* graduated. (*Removes street coat*) Yes, sir. And much funnier speeches than they had last year.

(*Crossing down to his chair, putting on house coat*)

Donald (*Coming D.S.*) You want to listen to a good speech you go up and hear Father Divine.

Grandpa I'll wait—they'll have him at Columbia. (*Sits R. of table, as* **Donald** *crosses to R.*)

Penny Donald, will you tell Rheba Grandpa's home now and we won't wait for Miss Alice.

(**De Pinna** *enters from kitchen, rolling down his sleeves*)

Donald yes'm . . . (*As he exits through kitchen door U.R.*) Rheba, Grandpa's home . . . we can have dinner.

Paul We made a new skyrocket today, Grandpa. Wait till you see it.

De Pinna Evening, Grandpa.

Grandpa (*Starting to remove his shoes*) Evening, Mr De Pinna.

Paul Didn't we make a fine rocket today, Mr De Pinna?

De Pinna (*As he exits through cellar door D.R.*) We certainly did.

Paul Wonder why they don't have fireworks at Commencements?

Grandpa Don't make enough noise. You take a good Commencement orator and he'll drown out a whole carload of fireworks. (**Ed** *gets a new pair of hammers*) And say just as much, too.

Penny Don't the graduates ever say anything?

Grandpa No, they just sit there in cap and night-gown, get their diplomas, and then along about forty years from now they suddenly say, 'Where am I?'

Essie (**Essie** *enters from kitchen, carrying a plate of tomatoes for the evening meal*) Hello, Grandpa. Have a nice day?

Grandpa Hello-have-a-nice-day. Don't I even get kissed?

Essie (*Kissing him*) Excuse me, Grandpa.

Grandpa I'll take a tomato, too. (**Ed** *strikes three tentative notes on xylophone.* **Grandpa** *takes a tomato and sits with it in his hand, weighing it*) You know I could have used a couple of these this afternoon. . . .

Essie (*Offering plate to* **Paul**) Father?

(*Again* **Ed** *strikes the keys of his xylophone*)

Paul No, thanks.

(**Essie** *crosses to* **Penny**)

Essie Mother?

Penny No, thanks, dear.

Grandpa Play something, Ed.

Ed All right. (**Ed** *at once obliges on the xylophone.*

Immediately **Essie** *is up on her toes, drifting through the mazes of a toe dance, placing plate of tomatoes on the table as she dances*)

Essie (*After a moment of dancing 'The Dying Swan'*) There was a letter came for you, Grandpa. Did you get it?

Grandpa (*Cutting a tomato*) Letter for me? I don't know anybody.

Essie It was for you, though. Had your name on it.

Grandpa That's funny. Where is it?

Essie I don't know. Where's Grandpa's letter, Mother?

Penny (*Who has been deep in her work*) What, dear?

Essie (*Dancing dreamily away*) Where's that letter that came for Grandpa last week?

Penny I don't know. (*Then brightly*) I remember seeing the kittens on it.   (**Essie** *starts to floor*)

Grandpa Who was it from? Did you notice?

Essie Yes, it was on the outside.

Grandpa Well, who was it?

Essie (*First finishing the graceful flutterings of 'The Dying Swan'*) United States Government. (*The music ends*)

Grandpa Really? Wonder what *they* wanted.

Essie (*Rising and starting R.*) There was one before that, too, from the same people. There was a couple of them.

Grandpa Well, if any more come I wish you'd give them to me.

Essie (*Exits through kitchen door on her toes*) Yes, Grandpa.

Grandpa (*Rises—shoes in hand*) I think I'll go out to Westchester tomorrow and do a little snake-hunting. (*Starts up to alcove for slippers*) (**Ed** *looks over xylophone, figuring out tune*)

Paul (*Who has settled down with his book some time before this*) 'God is the State; the State is God.'

Grandpa What's that? (*Coming down—slippers in one hand, album in the other*)

Paul 'God is the State; the State is God.'

Grandpa Who says that?

Paul Trotsky.

Grandpa Well, that's all right—I thought *you* said it. (*Sits R. of table*)

Ed It's nice for printing, you know. Good and short. (*He reaches into type case*) G—O—D—space—I—S—space—T—H—E—space—

(*The sound of the outer door closing, and* **Alice Syca-more** *enters the room. A lovely, fresh young girl of about twenty-two. She is plainly* **Grandpa**'*s grand-daughter, but there is something that sets her apart* *from the rest of the family. For one thing, she is in daily contact with the world; in addition, she seems to have escaped the tinge of mild insanity that pervades the rest of them. But she is a Sycamore for all that, and her devotion and love for them are plainly apparent. At the moment she is in a small, nervous flutter, but she is doing her best to conceal it)*

Alice (*As she makes the rounds, kissing her mother, her father, her grandfather*) And so the beautiful princess came into the palace, and kissed her mother, and her father, and her grandfather—

Grandpa Hello, darling!

Alice Hi, Grandpa—and what do you think? They turned into the Sycamore family. Surprised? (*Removing her hat*) (**Ed** *gets another set of hammers*)

Essie (*Enters U.R. Examining* **Alice**'s *dress*) Oh, Alice, I like it.

Alice Do you?

Essie It's new, isn't it?

Penny Looks nice and summery.

Essie Where'd you get it?

Alice Oh, I took a walk during lunch hour.

Grandpa You've been taking a lot of walks lately. That's the second new dress this week.

Alice (*Takes off gloves*) I just like to brighten up the office once in a while. I'm known as the Kay Francis of Kirby & Co. . . . Well, what's new around here? In the way of plays, snakes, ballet dancing or fireworks. Dad, I'll bet you've been down in that cellar all day. (**Ed** *sees if hammers are straight*)

Paul Huh?

Penny I'm going back to the war play, Alice. (**Essie** *does dance step exercise*)

Alice Really, Mother? (*She takes her hat to the hatrack*) (**Ed** *strikes a note on xylophone*)

Essie Ed, play Alice that Beethoven thing you wrote.

(**Ed** *at xylophone. He plays.* **Essie** *is up on her toes*)

Grandpa You know, you can mail a letter all the way from Nicaragua now for two pesetos.

Paul Really?

Penny (*Reading from her script*) 'Kenneth! My virginity is a priceless thing to me.'

Alice Listen, people. . . . Listen. (*The music dies out. She gets a scattered sort of attention*) I'm not home to dinner. A young gentleman is calling for me. (**Ed** *fixes a xylophone hammer*)

Essie Really, who is it?

Penny Well, isn't that nice?

Alice I did everything possible to keep him from coming here but he's calling for me.

Penny Why don't you both stay to dinner?

Alice No, I want him to take you in easy doses. I've tried to prepare him a little, but don't make it any worse than you can help. Don't read him any plays, mother, and don't let a snake bite him. Grandpa, because I like him. And I wouldn't dance for him, Essie, because we're going to the Monte Carlo ballet tonight.

Grandpa Can't do *anything*. Who *is* he–President of the United States?

Alice (*Crossing to L. of C. table*) No, he's vice-president of Kirby & Co. Mr. Anthony Kirby, Jr.

Essie The boss's son?

Penny Well!

Alice (*A step to* **Penny**) The boss's son. Just like the movies.

Essie (*Crossing down*) That explains the new dresses.

Ed (*Comes down a step*) And not being home to dinner for three weeks.

Alice Why, Sherlock Holmes!

Penny (*Rises. All aglow, script in hand*) Are you going to marry him?

Alice Oh, of course. Tonight! Meanwhile I have to go up and put on my wedding dress. (**Penny** *laughs, crosses to desk*)

Essie Is he good-looking?

Alice (*Vainly consulting her watch. Starts U.S.*) Yes, in a word . . . Oh, dear! What time is it?

Penny (*Preoccupied with scripts*) I don't know. Anybody know what time it is?

Paul Mr De Pinna might know.

Ed It was about five o'clock a couple of hours ago.

Alice Oh, I ought to know better than to ask you people. . . . will you let me know the minute he comes, please?

Penny Of course, Alice.

Alice Yes, I know, but I mean the *minute* he comes.

Penny Why, of course.

(**Alice** *looks apprehensively from one to the other; then disappears up the stairs U.L.*)

Alice Well, be sure.

Penny Well, what do you think of that?

Grandpa She seems to like him, if you ask me.

Essie I should say so. She's got it bad.

(**Ed** *crosses into the room*)

Penny (*Crossing to R. a bit*) Wouldn't it be wonderful if she married him? We could have the wedding right in this room.

Paul Now, wait a minute, Penny. This is the first time he's ever called for the girl.

(**Essie** *stretching exercise*)

Penny You only called for me once.

Paul Young people are different nowadays.

Essie Oh, I don't know. Look at Ed and me. He came to dinner *once* and just stayed. (*Toe pointing*)

Penny Anyhow, I think it's wonderful. Don't you, Grandpa?

Grandpa She certainly seems happy about it.

Penny He must be crazy about her. Maybe he's the one who is taking her out every night. (*Door bell*) There he is! Never mind, Rheba, I'll answer it. (*She is fluttering to the door*) Now remember what Alice said, and be *very* nice to him.

Grandpa (*Rising*) All right—let's take a look at him.

(**Paul** *rises,* **Ed** *puts on his coat and comes into room. They all stand awaiting the stranger's appearance*)

Penny (*At the front door; milk and honey in her voice*) Well! Welcome to our little home!

Henderson How do you do?

Penny I'm Alice's mother. Do come right in! Here we are! (*She reappears in archway, piloting the stranger, holding his hand*) This is Grandpa, and that's Alice's father, and Alice's sister and her husband, Ed Carmichael. (*The family all give courteous little nods and smiles as they are introduced*) Well! Now give me your hat and make yourself at home. (**Penny** *takes his hat*)

The man I'm afraid you must be making a mistake. (*Reaching for his card*)

Penny How's that?

The man My card.

Penny (*Reading*) 'Wilbur C. Henderson. Internal Revenue Department.'

(**Paul** *and* **Grandpa** *exchange looks*)

Henderson That's right.

Grandpa What can we do for you?

Henderson Does a Mr Martin Vanderhof live here?

Grandpa Yes, sir. That's me.

Henderson (*Coming down to table*) Well, Mr Vanderhof, the Government wants to talk to you about a little matter of income tax.

Penny Income tax?

Henderson You mind if I sit down?

Grandpa No, no. Just go right ahead.

Henderson (*Settling himself in a chair L. of the table*) Thank you. (**Grandpa** *sits. From above stairs the voice of* **Alice** *floats down*)

Alice Mother! Is that Mr Kirby?

Penny (*Going to stairs*) No. No, it isn't, darling. It's—an internal something or other. (*To* **Henderson**) Pardon me.

De Pinna (*Entering from D.R. carrying a firecracker*) Mr Sycamore . . . oh, excuse me.

Paul What is it?

De Pinna (*Crossing to* **Paul**) These things are not going off. Look. (*He strikes a match*)

Paul Not here, Mr De Pinna. Grandpa's busy.

De Pinna Oh!

(*They start for hall*)

Paul Pardon me.

(*They start again for hall,* **De Pinna** *looking at* **Henderson** *until* **Paul** *and* **De Pinna** *exit*)

Henderson (*Pulling a sheaf of papers from his pocket*) Now, Mr Vanderhof, (*a quick look toward hall*) we've written you several letters about this, but have not had any reply. (**Penny** *sits in her desk chair*)

Grandpa Oh, that's what those letters were.

Essie (*Sitting on couch R.*) I told you they were from the Government.

Henderson According to our records, Mr Vanderhof, you have never paid an income tax.

Grandpa That's right.

Henderson Why not?

Grandpa I don't believe in it.

Henderson Well—you own property, don't you?

Grandpa Yes, sir.

Henderson And you receive a yearly income from it?

Grandpa I do.

Henderson Of—(*He consults his records*)—between three and four thousand dollars.

Grandpa About that.

Henderson You've been receiving it for years.

Grandpa I have. 1901, if you want the exact date.

Henderson Well, the Government is only concerned from 1914 on. That's when the income tax started. (*Pause*)

Grandpa Well?

Henderson Well—it seems, Mr Vanderhof, that you owe the Government twenty-four years' back income tax.

Ed (*Coming down as* **Essie** *joins him*) Wait a minute! You can't go back that far—that's outlawed.

Henderson (*Calmly regarding him*) M-m-m! What's *your* name?

Ed What difference does that make?

Henderson Ever file an income tax return?

Ed (*Turns to* **Essie**, **Essie** *steps in*) No, sir.

Henderson Ah! What was your income last year?

Ed Ah—twenty-eight dollars and fifty cents, wasn't it, Essie?

Essie Yes, sir.

Henderson If you please! (*Dismissing* **Ed** *and* **Essie**. *They drift U.S.*) Now, Mr Vanderhof, you know there's quite a penalty for not filing an income tax return.

Penny Penalty?

Grandpa Look, Mr Henderson, let me ask you something.

Henderson Well?

Grandpa Suppose I pay you this money—mind you, I don't say I'm going to pay it—but just for the sake of argument—what's the Government going to do with it?

Henderson How do you mean?

Grandpa Well, what do I get for my money? If I go into Macy's and buy something, there it *is*—I see it. What's the Government give me?

Henderson Why, the Government gives you everything. It protects you.

Grandpa What from?

Henderson Well—invasion. Foreigners that might come over here and take everything you've got.

Grandpa Oh, I don't think they're going to do that.

Henderson If you didn't pay an income tax, they would. How do you think the Government keeps up the Army and Navy? All those battleships. . . .

Grandpa Last time we used battleships was in the Spanish-American War, and what did we get out of it? Cuba—and we gave that back. I wouldn't mind paying if it were something sensible.

Henderson Sensible? Well, what about Congress, and the Supreme Court, and the President? We've got to pay *them*, don't we?

Grandpa Not with my money—no, sir.

Henderson (*Furious. Rises, picks up papers*) Now wait a minute! I'm not here to argue with you. (*Crossing L.*) All I know is that you haven't paid an income tax and you've got to pay it!

Grandpa They've got to show me.

Henderson (*Yelling*) We *don't* have to show you! I just told you! All those buildings down in Washington, (*To* **Penny**. *She nods*) and Interstate Commerce, and the Constitution!

Grandpa The Constitution was paid for long ago. And Interstate Commerce—what *is* Interstate Commerce, anyhow?

Henderson (*Business of look at* **Penny**—*at* **Ed**—*at* **Grandpa**. *With murderous calm, crosses and*

places his hands on table) There are forty-eight states—see? And if there weren't Interstate Commerce, nothing could go from one state to another. See?

Grandpa Why not? They got fences?

Henderson (*To* **Grandpa**) No, they haven't got fences. They've got *laws*! (*Crossing up to arch L.*) My God, I never came across anything like *this* before!

Grandpa Well, I might pay about seventy-five dollars, but that's all it's worth.

Henderson You'll pay every cent of it, like everybody else!

Ed (*Who has lost interest*) Listen, Essie—listen to this a minute.

(*The xylophone again;* **Essie** *goes into her dance*)

Henderson (*Going right ahead, battling against the music*) And let me tell you something else! You'll go to jail (**Penny** *rises*) if you don't pay, do you hear that? That's the law, and if you think you're bigger than the law, you've got another think coming. You're no better than anybody else, and the sooner you get that through your head, the better . . . you'll hear from the United States Government, that's all I can say. . . . (*The music has stopped. He is backing out of the room*)

Grandpa (*Quietly*) Look out for those snakes.

Henderson (*Jumping; exits off L.*) Jesus! (*An explosion from the hall. He exits through hall door*)

Ed How was that, Essie?

Essie Fine, Ed.

Paul (*Entering from hall with* **De Pinna**) How did that sound to you folks? (**Essie** *sits on couch*)

Grandpa I liked it.

Penny My goodness, he was mad, wasn't he?

Grandpa It's not his fault. It's just that the whole thing is so silly.

Penny He forgot his hat.

Grandpa Say, what size is that hat?

Penny Seven and an eighth.

Grandpa Just right for me.

De Pinna Who was that fellow, anyway? (*Door bell. As bell rings* **De Pinna** *makes for cellar door to get his coat*)

Penny This *must* be Mr Kirby.

Paul Better make sure this time.

Penny Yes, I will. (*She disappears U.L.*)

Essie (*Rises*) I hope he's good-looking.

(*The family is again standing awaiting the newcomer*)

Penny (*Heard at the door*) How do you do?

Man's Voice Good evening.

Penny (*Taking no chances*) Is this Mr Anthony Kirby, Jr.?

Tony (*Business.* **Paul** *affirms it.* **Ed** *and* **Essie** *come D.S.*) Yes. (**Grandpa** *rises*)

Penny (*Giving her all*) Well, Mr Kirby, come right in! We've been expecting you. Come right in! (*They come into sight;* **Penny** *expansively addresses the family*) This is *really* Mr Kirby! Now, I'm Alice's mother, and that's *Mr* Sycamore, and Alice's grandfather, and her sister Essie, and Essie's husband. (**De Pinna** *waves for recognition. There are a few mumbled greetings*) There! Now you know *all* of us, Mr Kirby. Give me your hat and make yourself right at home.

(**Tony Kirby** *comes a few steps into the room. He is a personable young man, not long out of Yale, and, as we will presently learn, even more recently out of Cambridge. Although he fits all the physical requirements of a boss's son, his face has something of the idealist in it. All in all, a very nice young man*)

Tony Thank you.

(*Again the voice of the vigilant* **Alice** *floats down from upstairs.* '*Is that Mr Kirby, Mother?*')

Penny (*Shouting up stairs*) Yes, Alice. It is. He's *lovely!*

Alice (*Aware of storm signals*) I'll be right down.

Penny (*Puts* **Tony**'s *hat on desk*) Do sit down, Mr Kirby.

Tony (**Paul** *places* **Tony**'s *chair*) Thank you. (*A glance at dinner table*) I hope I'm not keeping you from dinner?

Grandpa No, no. Have a tomato? (*He sits. Also* **Paul**)

Tony No, thank you.

Penny (*Producing candy-filled skull, crosses to* **Tony**) How about a piece of candy?

Tony (*Eyeing the container*) Ah—no, thanks. (**De Pinna** *again steps forward*)

Penny Oh, I forgot to introduce Mr De Pinna. This is Mr De Pinna, Mr Kirby. (*An exchange of 'How do you do's?'*)

De Pinna Wasn't I reading about your father in the newspaper the other day? Didn't he get indicted or something?

Tony (*Smiling*) Hardly that. He just testified before the Securities Commission.

De Pinna Oh.

Penny (*Sharply*) Yes, of course. I'm sure there was nothing crooked about it, Mr De Pinna. As a matter of fact—(*She is now addressing* **Tony**. *Drawing forward her desk chair, she sits*)—Alice has often told us what a lovely man your father is.

Tony (*Sitting L. of table*) Well, I know Father couldn't get along without Alice. She knows more about the business than any of us.

Essie You're awful young Mr Kirby, aren't you, to be vice-president of a big place like that?

Tony Well, you know what that means, vice-president. All I have is a desk with my name on it.

Penny Is that all? Don't you get any salary?

Tony (*With a laugh*) Well, a little. More than I'm worth, I'm afraid. (**De Pinna** *lights pipe*)

Penny Now you're just being modest.

Grandpa Sounds kind of dull to me—Wall Street. Do you like it?

Tony Well, the hours are short. And I haven't been there very long.

Grandpa Just out of college, huh?

Tony Well, I knocked around for a while first. Just sort of had fun.

Grandpa What did you do? Travel?

Tony For a while. Then I went to Cambridge for a year.

Grandpa (*Nodding*) England.

Tony That's right.

Grandpa Say, what's an English commencement like? Did you see any?

Tony Oh, very impressive.

Grandpa They are, huh?

Tony Anyhow, now the fun's over, and—I'm facing the world.

Penny Well, you've certainly got a good start, Mr Kirby. Vice-president, and a rich father.

Tony Well, that's hardly my fault.

Penny (*Brightly*) So now I suppose you're all ready to settle down and—get married.

Paul Come now, Penny, I'm sure Mr Kirby knows his own mind.

Penny I wasn't making up his mind for him—was I, Mr Kirby?

Tony That's quite all right, Mrs Sycamore.

Penny (*To the others*) You see?

Essie You mustn't rush him, Mother.

Penny Well, all I meant was he's bound to get married, (**Alice** *starts down stairs*) and suppose the wrong girl gets him?

(*The descending* **Alice** *mercifully comes to* **Tony**'s *rescue at this moment. Her voice is heard from stairs.* **Tony** *rises.*)

Alice Well, here I am, a vision in blue. (*She comes into the room—and very lovely indeed*) Apparently you've had time to get acquainted. (**Essie** *a step upstage.* **Tony** *rises. Also* **Paul**)

Penny (*Rises and pushes chair back*) Oh, yes, indeed. We were just having a delightful talk about love and marriage.

Alice Oh, dear. (*She turns to* **Tony**. **Rheba** *enters*) I'm sorry. I came down as fast as I could.

Tony I didn't mind in the least.

Rheba (*Enters U.R. bringing a platter of sliced watermelon*) Damn those flies in the kitchen. (**Alice** *looks at* **Penny** *and back to* **Tony**) Oh, Miss Alice, you look beautiful. Where you going?

Alice (*Making the best of it*) I'm going out, Rheba.

Rheba (*Noticing* **Tony**—*looks at him*) Stepping, huh? (*The door bell sounds.* **Rheba** *puts platter on table and crosses to hall door*)

Essie That must be Kolenkhov.

Alice (*Uneasily. She crosses to U.L.*) I think we'd better go, Tony.

Tony (*Crossing to desk*) All right.

(*Before they can escape, however,* **Donald** *emerges from kitchen U.R. bearing a tray*)

Donald Grandpa, you take cream on your corn flakes? I forget.

Grandpa Half and half, Donald.

(**Donald** *exits U.R. The voice of* **Boris Kolenkhov** *booms from outer door*)

Kolenkhov Ah, my little Rhebishka!

Grandpa Yes, that's Kolenkhov, all right.

Rheba (*With a scream of laughter*) Yessuh, Mr Kolenkhov!

Kolenkhov Good evening, everybody!

All Good evening.

(*He appears in archway, his great arm completely encircling the delighted* **Rheba**. **Mr Kolenkhov** *is one of* **Rheba**'*s pets, and if you like Russians he might be one of yours. He is enormous, hairy, loud, and very, very Russian. His appearance in the archway still further traps* **Alice** *and* **Tony**. **Rheba** *exits U.R.*)

Kolenkhov (*As he comes D.S.*) Grandpa, what do you think? I have had a letter from Russia! The Second Five-Year Plan is a failure! (*Throws hat on buffet. He lets out a laugh that shakes the rafters*)

Essie I practiced today, Mr Kolenkhov!

Kolenkhov (*With a deep Russian bow and a click of heels*) My Pavlowa!

Alice (*Crossing down*) Well, if you'll excuse us, Mr Kolenkhov. (**Penny** *hands* **Tony** *his hat*)

Kolenkhov My little Alice! (*He kisses her hand*) Never have I seen you look so magnificent.

Alice Thank you, Mr Kolenkhov. (**Kolenkhov** *steps back*) Tony, this is Mr Kolenkhov, Essie's dancing teacher. Mr Kirby.

Tony How do you do?

Kolenkhov How do you do? (*A click of the heels and a bow from* **Kolenkhov**)

Alice (*Determined, this time. A step down*) Will you pardon us, Mr Kolenkhov—we're going to the Monte Carlo Ballet.

Kolenkhov (*At the top of his tremendous voice*) The Monte Carlo Ballet! It *stinks*. (*Crossing U.C.*)

Alice (*Panicky now*) Yes. . . . Well—good-bye, everybody. Good-bye.

Tony Good-bye. I'm so glad to have met you all. (*A chorus of answering 'Good-byes' from the family. The young people are gone. The sound of hall door closing*)

De Pinna Good-bye.

Kolenkhov (*Still furious, crosses L.*) Monte Carlo Ballet!

Penny Isn't Mr Kirby lovely? . . . Come on, everybody! Dinner's ready! (**Paul** *indicates chair*)

Ed (*Pulling up chair from alcove*) I thought he was a nice fellow, didn't you? (*Gets another chair from hall*)

Essie (*Doing her toe steps*) Mm. (*Bending*) And so good-looking.

Penny And he had such nice manners. Did you notice, Paul? Did you notice his manners?

Paul I certainly did. You were getting pretty personal with him.

Penny Oh, now, Paul. . . . Anyhow, he's a very nice young man. (**De Pinna** *brings chair from alcove*)

De Pinna (*As he seats himself*) He looks like a cousin of mine. (**Essie** *bends*)

Kolenkhov Bakst! Diaghileff! *Then* you had the ballet!

Penny I think if they get married here I'll put the altar right where the snakes are. You wouldn't mind, Grandpa, would you?

Grandpa Not if the snakes don't.

Essie (*Crossing to chair back of table and sitting*) Oh, no, they'll want to get married in a church. His family and everything.

De Pinna I like a church wedding. ⎫
Ed Yes, of course they would. ⎬ (*Together*)
Kolenkhov Of course. ⎭

Grandpa (*Tapping on a plate for silence*) Quiet, everybody! Quiet! (*They are immediately silent. . . . Grace is about to be pronounced.* **Grandpa** *pauses a moment for her to bow then raises his eyes heavenward. He clears his throat* *and proceeds to say Grace*) Well, Sir, we've been getting along pretty good for quite a while now, and we're certainly much obliged. Remember, all we ask is to just go along and be happy in our own sort of way. Of course we want to keep our health but as far as anything else is concerned, we'll leave it to You. Thank You. (**Rheba** *to* **Kolenkhov.** *The heads come up as* **Rheba** *and* **Donald** *enter through kitchen door with steaming platters.*) So the Second Five-Year Plan is a failure, eh, Kolenkhov?

Kolenkhov Catastrophic! And wait until they try the Third Five-Year Plan!

Penny (*On the cue 'Thank You'*) Of course his family is going to want to come. Imagine. Alice marrying a Kirby!

Essie Think of that. Isn't it exciting?

Ed I'll play the wedding march on the xylophone.

Paul What have we got for dinner? I'm hungry.

CURTAIN

Scene 2

Late the same night. The house is in darkness save for a light in the hall. An accordion is heard off stage R., then suddenly a good loud BANG! from the cellar. Somewhere in the nether regions, one of the Sycamores is still at work.

As the accordion player finishes the song the sound of a key in the outer door. The voices of **Alice** *and* **Tony** *drift through.*

Alice (*Off stage*) I could see them dance every night of the week. I think they're marvellous.

Tony They are, aren't they? But of course just walking inside any theatre gives *me* a thrill.

Alice (*As they come into sight in hallway*) Well, it's been *so* lovely, Tony, I hate to have it over.

Tony Oh, is it over? Do I have to go right away?

Alice Not if you don't want to.

Tony I don't.

Alice Would you like a cold drink?

Tony Wonderful. (**Alice** *pauses to switch on lights*)

Alice I'll see what's in the icebox. Want to come along?

Tony I'd follow you to the ends of the earth.

Alice (*At door*) Oh just the kitchen is enough.

(*They exit through kitchen door. A pause, and the lights go on*)

Tony Why, I like it. You've done it very simply, haven't you?

Alice Yes, we didn't know whether to do it Empire or Neo-Grecian.

Tony So you settled for Frigidaire.

Alice Yes, it's so easy to live with. (*They return.* **Alice** *crosses to table. She is carrying two glasses.* **Tony,** *a bottle of ginger ale and a bottle opener*) Lucky you're not hungry, Mr K. An icebox full of corn flakes. That gives you a rough idea of the Sycamores. (**Tony** *follows down to table*)

Tony (*Working away with the opener*) Of course, why they make these bottle openers for Singer midgets I never did . . . (*As bottle opens*) All over my coat.

Alice (*As she hands him a glass*) I'll take mine in a glass, if you don't mind.

Tony (*Pouring*) There you are. A foaming beaker. (*Pours his own*)

Alice Anyhow, it's cold.

Tony (*As* **Alice** *sits R. of the table*) Now if you'll please be seated, I'd like to offer a toast.

Alice We are seated.

Tony Miss Sycamore (*He raises his glass on high*) . . . to you.

Alice Thank you, Mr Kirby. (*Lifting her own glass*) To you. (*She drinks and puts glass down*)

Tony You know something?

Alice What?

Tony (*Puts his glass down and sighs happily*) I wouldn't trade one minute of this evening for . . . all the rice in China.

Alice Really?

Tony Cross my heart.

Alice (*A little sigh of contentment. Then shyly*) Is there much rice in China?

Tony Terrific. Didn't you read 'The Good Earth'? (*She laughs. They are silent for a moment. He sighs and looks at his watch*) Well, I suppose I ought to go.

Alice Is it very late?

Tony (*Looks at his watch*) Very. (**Alice** *gives a little nod. Time doesn't matter*) I don't want to go.

Alice I don't want you to.

Tony All right, I won't. (*Sits L. of table. Silence again*) When do you get your vacation?

Alice Last two weeks in August.

Tony I might take mine then, too.

Alice Really?

Tony What are you going to do?

Alice I don't know. I hadn't thought much about it.

Tony Going away, do you think?

Alice I might not. I like the city in the summer time.

Tony I do too.

Alice But you always go up to Maine, don't you?

Tony That's right. (*Rises*) Oh—but I'm sure I *would* like the city in the summer time, if—Oh, you know what I mean, Alice. I'd love it if *you* were here.

Alice Well—it'd be nice if you were here, Tony. (*Rises and crosses to R.*)

Tony You know what you're saying, don't you?

Alice What?

Tony That you'd rather spend the summer with me than anybody else.

Alice (*Back to* **Tony**) Was I?

Tony (*Crossing few steps R.*) Well, if it's true about the summer, how would you feel about—the winter?

Alice (*Seeming to weigh the matter. Turns to* **Tony**) Yes, I'd—like that too.

Tony (*Tremulous*) Then there's spring and autumn. If you could—see your way clear about those, Miss Sycamore? (*Crossing to* **Alice**)

Alice (*Again a little pause*) I might.

Tony I guess that's the whole year. We haven't forgotten anything, have we?

Alice No.

Tony Well, then—(*Another pause; their eyes meet.* **Tony** *starts to embrace* **Alice**. *And at this moment,* **Penny** *is heard from stairway.* **Tony** *crosses to back of* **Grandpa**'s *chair*)

Penny (*Off stage*) Is that you, Alice? What time is it? (*She comes into room, wrapped in a bathrobe*) Oh! (*In sudden embarrassment*) Excuse me, Mr Kirby. I had no idea—that is, I—(*She senses the situation*)—I didn't mean to interrupt anything.

Tony Not at all, Mrs Sycamore.

Alice (*Quietly*) No, Mother.

Penny I just came down for a manuscript—(*fumbling at her desk*)—then you can go right ahead. Ah, here it is. 'Sex Takes a Holiday.' Well—good night, Tony.

Tony Good night, Mrs Sycamore.

Penny Oh, I think you can call me Penny, don't you, Alice? At least I hope so. (*With a little laugh she vanishes up stairs*) (**Tony** *turns back to* **Alice**. *Before* **Penny**'s *rippling laugh quite dies, BANG! from the cellar.* **Tony** *jumps*)

Tony What's that?

Alice (*Quietly. She crosses to below table*) It's all right, Tony. That's father.

Tony Oh—this time of night? (*Coming D.S.*)

Alice (*Ominously—turns to* **Tony**) *Any* time of night. Any time of *day*. (*She stands silent*) (*In the pause,*

Tony *gazes at her fondly*)

Tony (*Crossing to* **Alice**) You know, you're more beautiful, more lovely, more adorable than anyone else in the whole world.

Alice (*As he starts to embrace her, she backs away*) Don't, Tony.

Tony What? (*As* **Alice** *shakes her head*) My dear, just because your mother . . . all mothers are like that, Alice, and Penny's a darling. You see I'm even calling her Penny.

Alice I don't mean that. (*She faces him squarely—crosses to* **Tony**) Look, Tony, this is something I should have said a long time ago, but I didn't have the courage. (*Turns away*) I let myself be swept away because . . . I loved you so.

Tony (*Crosses to* **Alice**) Darling!

Alice No, wait, Tony. I want to make it clear to you. Listen, you're of a different world . . . a whole different kind of people. Oh I don't mean money or socially . . . that's too silly. But your family and mine . . . it just wouldn't work, Tony. It just wouldn't work. (**Alice** *crosses to R. below* **Tony**)

(*The sound of the outer door closing*)

Ed (*Heard in hallway off stage*) All right, have it your way. (*At the sound of the voice,* **Tony** *crosses to L.*) She can't dance. That's why they pay her all that money . . . because she can't dance. (**Alice** *takes a few steps to R.*)

Essie (*Still not in sight*) Well, I don't call that dancing what she does. (*She appears in archway followed by* **Ed**) Oh, hello! How was the ballet? (*Throwing her hat on desk*)

Alice It was fine, Essie.

Tony Wonderful.

Ed (*Following into room after* **Essie**) Hello there.

Tony Hello.

Essie Look, what do you people think? Ed and I just saw Fred Astaire and Ginger Rogers. Do you think she can dance, Mr Kirby? (*Crossing over to* **Tony**)

Tony Why yes. I always thought so.

Essie What does she *do* anyhow? (*Crossing to* **Tony**) Now look, you're Fred Astaire, and I'm Ginger Rogers. (*Puts herself close to* **Tony**)

Alice Essie, please!

Essie I only want to use him for a minute. Now look, Mr Kirby . . . (*Putting her arms around* **Tony**'s *neck*)

Alice Essie, you're just as good as Ginger Rogers. We all agree.

Essie You see, Ed?

Ed (*Crossing to arch. Backing up*) Yeh. . . . Come on, Essie . . . we're butting in here.

Essie Oh they've been together all evening. . . . (*Crosses up to arch*) Good night, Mr Kirby. Good night, Alice.

Tony Good night, Mrs Carmichael.

Ed Good night. Essie, did you ask Grandpa about us having a baby? (*Crossing up to stairs*)

Essie Oh yes—he said to go right ahead.

(*They are out of sight up stairs*)

Alice (*Crossing L. to below table*) You see, Tony? That's what it would be like.

Tony (*Crossing over to* **Alice**) Oh I didn't mind that. Anyhow, we're not going to live with your family. It's just you and I.

Alice No it isn't . . . it's never quite that. I love them, Tony . . . I love them deeply. Some people could break away, but I couldn't. I know they do rather strange things. . . . But they're gay and they're fun and . . . I don't know . . . there's a kind of nobility about them.

Tony Alice, you talk as though only you could understand them. That's not true. Why every family has got curious little traits. What of it? My father raises orchids at ten thousand dollars a bulb. (**Alice** *crosses up R. to back of chair*) Is that sensible? My mother believes in spiritualism. That's just as bad as your mother writing plays, isn't it?

Alice It goes deeper, Tony. Your mother believes in spiritualism because it's fashionable, and your father raises orchids because he can afford to. My mother writes plays because eight years ago a typewriter was delivered here by mistake. (*She crosses to R.*)

Tony Darling, what of it?

Alice (*Crossing back to chair*) And—and look at Grandpa. Thirty-five years ago he just quit business one day. He started up to his office in the elevator and came right down again. He just stopped. He could have been a rich man, (*sitting R. of table*) but he said it took too much time. So for thirty-five years, he's just collected snakes, and gone to circuses and commencements. It never occurs to any of them. . . .

(**Grandpa** *comes down stairs*)

Grandpa (*Pausing in doorway*) Hello there, children!

Tony (*Turns to* **Grandpa**) Good evening, Mr Vanderhof.

Alice Hello, Grandpa.

Grandpa (*Coming into the room*) How's the weather? Looks like a nice summer evening.

Alice Yes, it's lovely, Grandpa.

Grandpa (*Starting up*) Well, I'm off. Good-bye, Mr Kirby . . . I've got a date with the policeman on the corner.

Tony (*Crossing U.S.*) Policeman?

Grandpa We've got a standing date—twelve-thirty every night. Known him since he was a little boy. He's really a doctor, but after he graduated, he came to me and said he didn't want to be a doctor—he had always wanted to be a policeman. So I said, 'You go ahead and be a policeman, if that's what you want to be,' and that's what he did. . . . How do you like my new hat?

Tony It's very nice, Mr Vanderhof.

Grandpa (*Regarding hat*) Yeh, I like it. The Government gave it to me. (*Exits U.L.*)

Donald (*Entering from kitchen U.R. with an accordion slung over his shoulder*) Oh, excuse me. I didn't know you folks was in here.

Alice (*Resigned*) It's all right, Donald.

Donald Rheba kind of fancied some candy and I . . . Oh, there it is. (*Crossing to buffet*) You all don't want it, do you?

Alice No, Donald.

Donald (*Crossing to R.*) Thanks. . . . Did you have a nice evening?

Alice Yes, Donald.

Donald (*Edging over another step*) Nice dinner?

Alice Yes, Donald.

Donald (*Another step to the R.*) Was the ballet nice?

Alice Yes, Donald.

Donald That's nice. (*He exits through kitchen door R.*)

Alice (*Rising*) Now! Now, do you see what I mean? Could you explain Donald to your father? Could you explain Grandpa? You couldn't, Tony, you couldn't! I love you, Tony, but I love them too! And it's no use, Tony! It's no use! (*Crosses R. She is weeping now in spite of herself*)

Tony (*Takes her hands, quietly says*) There's only one thing you've said that matters, that makes any sense at all. You love me.

Alice But, Tony, I know so well. . . .

Tony But, darling, don't you think other people have had the same problem? Everybody's got a family.

Alice (*Through her tears*) But not like mine.

Tony That doesn't stop people who love each other . . . Darling! Darling, won't you trust me and go on loving me, and forget everything else?

Alice How can I?

Tony Because nothing can keep us apart. You know that. You must know it. They want you to be happy, don't they? They *must*.

Alice Of course they do. But they can't change, Tony. I wouldn't want them to change.

Tony (*Releases her hands*) They won't have to change. They're charming, lovable people, just as they are. Everything will work out . . . you're worrying about something that may never come up.

Alice Oh, Tony, am I?

Tony All that matters right now is that we love each other. That's so, isn't it?

Alice (*Whispering*) Yes.

Tony Well, then! (*They embrace, sigh and kiss*)

Alice (*In his arms*) Tony, Tony!

Tony (*As they break*) Now! I'd like to see a little gayety around here. Young gentleman calling, and getting engaged and everything.

Alice (*Smiling up into his face*) What do I say?

Tony Well, first you thank the young man for getting engaged to you.

Alice (*Crossing to below table*) Thank you, Mr Kirby, for getting engaged to me.

Tony (*Following her*) And then you tell him what it was about him that first took your girlish heart.

Alice (*Leaning against table*) The back of your head.

Tony Huh?

Alice Uh-huh. It wasn't your charm, and it wasn't your money . . . it was the back of your head. I just liked it.

Tony What happened when I turned around?

Alice Oh, I got used to it after a while.

Tony (*Tenderly*) Oh, Alice, think of it. We're pretty lucky, aren't we?

Alice I know that *I* am. I'm the luckiest girl in the world.

Tony I'm not exactly unlucky myself. (*Holding her in his arms; kiss; sigh*) Oh, dear, I guess I ought to . . . (*Backing away. He looks at his watch*) Good night, darling. Until tomorrow.

Alice (*Crosses to* **Tony**—*they kiss*) Good night.

Tony Isn't it wonderful we work in the same office? Otherwise I'd be hanging around *here* all day.

Alice (*Starts with* **Tony** *for the hall*) Won't it be funny in the office tomorrow—seeing each other and just going on as though nothing had happened?

Tony Thank God I'm vice-president. (*Turns up*) I can dictate to you all day (*Accordion*) 'Dear Miss

Sycamore: I love you, I love you, I love you.' (*They embrace*)

Alice Oh, darling! You're such a fool.

Tony (*An arm about her as he starts toward hallway U.L.*) Why don't you meet me in the drugstore in the morning—before you go up to the office? I'll have millions of things to say to you. (*Picks up his hat as they head for the door*)

Alice (*Off stage*) All right.

Tony And then lunch, and then dinner tomorrow night.

Alice Oh, Tony! What will people say?

Tony It's got to come out sometime. In fact, if you know a good housetop, I'd like to do a little shouting. (*She laughs—a happy little ripple. They are out of sight in hallway by this time; their voices become inaudible*)

(**Paul**, *at this point, decides to call it a day down in the cellar. He comes through door, followed by* **De Pinna**. *He is carrying a small metal container, filled with powder*)

Paul (*Crossing to table C.*) Yes, sir, Mr De Pinna, we did a good night's work.

De Pinna (*Following*) That's what. Five hundred Black Panthers, three hundred Willow Trees, and eight dozen Junior Kiddie Bombers. (**Alice** *comes back from hallway, still under the spell of her love*)

Paul Pretty good! . . . Why, hello, Alice. You just come in?

Alice (*Softly; leans against wall*) No. No, I've been home quite a while.

Paul Have a nice evening?

Alice (*Almost singing it*) I had a beautiful evening, Father.

Paul Say, I'd like you to take a look at this new red fire. Will you turn out the lights, Mr De Pinna? I want Alice to get the full effect.

(**De Pinna** *goes up to switch*)

Alice (*Who hasn't heard a word*) What, Father?

Paul Take a look at this new red fire. It's beautiful. (**De Pinna** *switches lights out;* **Paul** *touches a match to the powder. The red fire blazes, shedding a soft glow over the room*) There! What do you think of it? Isn't it beautiful?

Alice (*Radiant; her face aglow, her voice soft*) Yes. Oh, Father, everything's beautiful, it's the most beautiful red fire in the world! (*She rushes to him and throws her arms about him, almost unable to bear her own happiness*)

CURTAIN

Act II

As curtain rises, **Grandpa** is seated R. of the table, **Paul** above table, and a newcomer, **Gay Wellington**, is seated L. of table. **Penny** stands with one of her scripts at L. of table and **Ed** is standing to R. of table. **Donald** stands back of **Gay Wellington** holding tray of used dinner dishes. **Gay** is drinking as curtain rises. **Ed** stands R. holding type stick.

Gay All right, I said to him, you can take your old job . . . (*She drinks*)

Penny I'm ready to read you the new play, Miss Wellington, any time you are.

Gay (*Pours*) Just a minute, dearie. Just a minute. (*Drinks again*) (**Ed** preoccupied with type stick)

Penny The only thing is—I hope you won't mind my mentioning this, but—you don't drink when you're acting, do you, Miss Wellington? I'm just asking, of course.

Gay (*Crossing to* **Penny**) I'm glad you brought it up. Once a play opens, I never touch a drop. Minute I enter a stage door, the bottle gets put away until intermission.

(**Rheba** enters U.R. and crosses down to table carrying a tray)

Grandpa Have you been on the stage a long time, Miss Wellington?

Gay All my life. I've played everything. Ever see 'Peg o' My Heart'?

Grandpa Yes.

Gay I saw it too. Good show. . . . My! Hot night, ain't it?

Donald You want me to open the window, Miss Wellington?

Gay No, the Hell with the weather. . . . Say, he's cute.

(**Rheba**, clearing table at this moment, throws **Gay** a black look, bangs a glass on her tray and exits U.R.)

Donald (*Starting off after* **Rheba**) She's just acting, Rheba, that's all; she don't mean anything. (*Exits U.R.*)

Penny (*Making the best of it, crossing over to her desk*) Well, any time you're ready, we'll go up to my room and start. I thought I'd read the play up in my room. (*Crosses up to stairs*) (**Ed** drifts up to xylophone)

Gay (*Circling U.S.—takes glass from table*) All right, dearie, I'm ready. (*Suddenly her gaze becomes transfixed. She shakes her head as though to dislodge the image, then looks again and receives verification. Puts gin bottle and glass on table*) When I see snakes, it's time to lay down. (*She makes for couch R.*) (**Essie** starts downstairs)

Penny (*Crossing back of table to couch*) Oh dear! Oh dear! Oh, but those are real, Miss Wellington! (**Donald** enters up R. bearing a tray. **Paul** rises) They're Grandpa's. Those are real! (**Gay** has passed right out cold) Oh, dear! I hope she is not going to—Miss Wellington!

Ed (*Crossing up to hand press*) She's out like a light.

Paul (*Crossing U.S. a step*) Better let her sleep it off.

Donald Rheba, Miss Wellington just passed out. (*Exits U.R.*)

Rheba (*Off stage*) Good.

Penny Do you think she'll be all right?

Grandpa Yes, but I wouldn't cast her in the religious play.

Penny Well, I suppose I'll just have to wait.

(**Ed** bangs the hand press. **Essie** crosses down to chair L. of table)

Grandpa Next time you meet an actress on the top of a bus, Penny, I think I'd *send* her the play instead of bringing her home to read it.

(*Another bang.* **Penny** covers **Gay** with couch cover)

Essie Ed, I wish you'd stop printing and take those 'Love Dreams' around. You've got to get back in time to play for me when Kolenkhov comes. (*A bang of the hand press again*)

Grandpa Kolenkhov coming tonight? (*Goes to bookcase for stamp album and returns to table*)

Essie (*Executing a few toe steps*) Yes, tomorrow night's his night, but I had to change it on account of Alice.

Grandpa Oh! . . . Big doings around here tomorrow night, huh?

Penny (*Crossing to desk*) Isn't it exciting? You know I'm so nervous—you'd think it was me he was engaged to instead of Alice. (*Sitting in desk chair. Takes script and pencil*) (**Grandpa** busies himself with album)

Essie (*Doing leg exercise. She is L. of table*) What do you think they'll *be* like—his mother and father? . . . Ed, what are you doing now?

Ed (*Coming down*) Penny, did you see the new mask I made last night? (*He reveals a new side of his character by suddenly holding a homemade mask before his face*) Guess who it is?

Penny Don't tell me now, Ed. Wait a minute. . . . Helen of Troy?

Ed (*Disappointed*) It's Mrs Roosevelt. (**Essie** *on toes.* **Ed** *puts mask down and exits into kitchen*) (**Paul**, *meanwhile, comes D.R. from buffet with a steel-like contraption in his hand. It's a Meccano set model of the Queen Mary. He puts it down on floor and proceeds to sit down beside it*)

Paul You know the nice thing about these Meccano sets, you can make so many different things with them. Last week it was the Empire State Building.

Grandpa What is it this week?

Paul Queen Mary.

Grandpa Hasn't got the right hat on.

(**De Pinna** *enters from R. of hall.* **Penny** *sits.* **Ed** *comes in from kitchen bringing a pile of candy boxes beautifully wrapped and tied together for purposes of delivery. He crosses to U.C.*)

Ed . . . Look, Mr De Pinna—would you open the door and see if there's a man standing in front of the house?

De Pinna Why, what for?

Ed Well, the last two days, when I've been out delivering candy, I think a man's been following me.

Essie Ed, you're crazy.

Ed No, I'm not. He follows me, and he stands and watches the house.

De Pinna Really? (*Striding out*) I'll take a look and see.

Grandpa I don't see what anybody would follow *you* for, Ed.

Penny Well, there's a lot of kidnapping going on, Grandpa.

Grandpa Yes, but not of Ed.

Ed (*As* **De Pinna** *returns from hall U.L.*) Well? Did you see him?

De Pinna There's nobody out there at all.

Ed You're sure?

De Pinna Positive. I just saw him walk away.

(**Paul** *puts the model back on the buffet*)

Ed You see?

Essie Oh, it might have been anybody, walking along the street. Ed, will you hurry and get back? (**Paul** *starts D.R.*)

Ed (*Picking up his boxes U.C.*) Oh, all right. (*Exits U.L.*)

De Pinna (*Crossing to R. below table*) Want to go down now, Mr Sycamore, and finish packing up the fireworks?

Paul Yeh, we've got to take the stuff up to Mt Vernon in the morning. (**Paul** *and* **De Pinna** *exit D.R.*)

(*The voice of* **Alice**, *happily singing, is heard as she descends stairs*)

Alice (*As she comes into the room, finishing song*) Mother, may I borrow some paper? I'm making out a list for Rheba tomorrow night.

Penny Yes, dear. (*Drunken mutter from* **Gay**) Here's some.

Alice (*Crossing to table. As she sights* **Gay**) Why, what happened to your actress friend? Is she giving a performance?

Penny No, she's not acting, Alice. She's really drunk. (**Essie** *dances to R. of* **Grandpa**'s *chair*)

Alice Essie, dear, you're going to give Rheba the kitchen all day tomorrow, aren't you? Because she'll need it.

Essie Of course, Alice. I'm going to start some Love Dreams now, so I'll be 'way ahead. (*She goes into kitchen U.R.*)

Alice Thanks, dear. . . . (*Crossing to* **Penny**) Look, Mother, I'm coming home at three o'clock tomorrow. Will you have everything down in the cellar by that time? The typewriter, and the snakes, and the xylophone, and the printing press . . .

Grandpa And Miss Wellington.

Alice And Miss Wellington. That'll give me time to arrange the table, and fix the flowers.

Grandpa The Kirbys are certainly going to get the wrong impression of this house.

Alice You'll do all that, won't you, Mother?

Penny Of course, dear. . . . (*Turns*)

Alice . . . And I think we'd better have cocktails ready by seven-fifteen, in case they happen to come a little early. . . . I wonder if I ought to let Rheba cook the dinner. What do you think, Grandpa?

Grandpa Now, Alice, I wouldn't worry. From what I've seen of the boy I'm sure the Kirbys are very nice people, and if everything isn't so elaborate tomorrow night, it's all right too.

Alice (*Crossing to back of table*) Darling, I'm not trying to impress them, or pretend we're anything that we aren't. I just want everything to—to go off well.

Grandpa (*Putting his hand over* **Alice**'s) No reason why it shouldn't, Alice.

Penny We're all going to do everything we can to make it a nice party.

Alice (*Crossing to L.*) Oh, my darlings, I love you. You're the most wonderful family in the world, and I'm the happiest girl in the world. I didn't know anyone could be so happy. Why, this past week has been like—floating. He's so wonderful, Grandpa. (*Crossing to back of table*) Why, just seeing him—you don't know what it does to me.

Grandpa Just seeing him. Just seeing him for lunch, and dinner, and until four o'clock in the morning, and at nine o'clock *next* morning you're at the office again and there he is. Just seeing him, huh?

Alice I don't care! I'm in love! (*Kisses **Grandpa** and starts for U.R. She swings open kitchen door*) Rheba! Rheba! (*She goes into kitchen*)

Grandpa Nice, isn't it? Nice to see her so happy.

Penny (*Rises—crosses to table*) Yes, I remember when I was engaged to Paul—how happy I was. And you know, I still feel that way.

Grandpa I know. . . . Nice the way Ed and Essie get along too, isn't it?

Penny And Donald and Rheba, even though they're *not* married. . . . Do you suppose Mr De Pinna will every marry anyone, Grandpa?

Grandpa (*A gesture toward couch*) Well, there's Miss Wellington.

Penny Oh, dear, I *wish* she'd wake up. If we're going to read the play tonight—

(**De Pinna** *comes up from cellar, D.R., bringing along a rather large-sized unframed painting*)

De Pinna Mrs Sycamore, look what I found! (*He turns canvas around, revealing a portrait of a somewhat lumpy and largely naked discus thrower*) Remember? (*He props picture on chair above table*)

Penny (*Backs away*) Why, of course. It's my painting of you as The Discus Thrower. Look, Grandpa.

Grandpa I remember it. Say, you've gotten a little bald, haven't you, Mr De Pinna?

De Pinna (*Running a hand over his completely hairless head*) Is it very noticeable? Well, there's still some right here.

Penny Well, it was a long time ago—just before I stopped painting. Let me see—that's eight years.

De Pinna Too bad you never finished it, Mrs Sycamore. (*Crosses D.R.*)

Penny (*Looking back at picture*) I always meant to finish it, Mr De Pinna, but I just started to write a play one day and that was that. I never painted again.

Grandpa Just as well, too. *I* was going to have to strip next.

De Pinna (*Meditatively*) My goodness, who would have thought, that day I came to deliver the ice, that I was going to stay here for eight years?

Grandpa The milkman was here for five, just ahead of you.

De Pinna Say, why did he leave, anyhow? I forget.

Grandpa He didn't leave. He died.

De Pinna Oh, yes. (*Crossing R.*)

Penny He was such a nice man. Remember the funeral, Grandpa? We never knew his name and it was kind of hard to get a certificate.

Grandpa What was the name we finally made up for him?

Penny Martin Vanderhof. We gave him *your* name.

Grandpa Oh, yes, I remember. (*Rises and goes up to alcove*) (**De Pinna** *lights pipe*)

Penny It was a lovely thought, because otherwise he never would have got all those flowers.

Grandpa (*Coming down*) Certainly was. And it didn't hurt *me* any. Not bothered with mail any more, and I haven't had a telephone call from that day to this. (*Business of catching fly on painting and feeding it to snakes. Returns to his chair; sits, reads paper*)

Penny Yes, it was really a wonderful idea.

De Pinna (*Points to picture*) I wish you'd finish that sometime, Mrs Sycamore. I'd kind of like to have it.

Penny You know what, Mr De Pinna? I think I'll do some work on it. Right tonight.

De Pinna Say! Will you? (*Door bell*)

Penny (*Peering at the prostrate **Gay***) I don't think she's going to wake up anyhow. . . . Look, Mr De Pinna! You go down in the cellar—(**Rheba** *enters U.R., crosses to hall door*)—and put on your costume. And bring up the easel. (**De Pinna** *starts R.*) Is it still down there?

De Pinna (*Excited*) I think so! (*He exits D.R.*)

Penny (*Crossing to stairs*) Now, where did I put my palette and brushes?

(*The voice of **Kolenkhov** is heard at door, booming as usual*)

Kolenkhov Rhebishka! My little Rhebishka!

Rheba (*Delighted, as usual*) Yassuh, Mr Kolenkhov!

Penny (*As she goes up stairs*) Hello, Mr Kolenkhov. Essie's in the kitchen.

Kolenkhov Madame Sycamore, I greet you! (*His great arm again encircling **Rheba**, he drags her protestingly into room*) Tell me, Grandpa—what should I do about Rhebishka! I keep telling her she would make a great toe dancer—(*Breaking away, she laughs*)—but she laughs only!

Rheba (*Starts off for U.R.*) No, suh! I couldn't get up on my toes, Mr Kolenkhov! I got corns! (*She goes into kitchen*)

Kolenkhov (*Calling after her*) Rhebishka, you could wear diamonds! (*Throws his hat on buffet*) A great girl, Grandpa. (*Suddenly he sights portrait of* **De Pinna**) What is that?

Grandpa It's a picture of Mr De Pinna. Penny painted it.

Kolenkhov (*Summing it up*) It stinks. (*Sits L. of table*)

Grandpa I know. (*He indicates figure on couch*) How do you like that?

Kolenkhov (*Half rising. Peering over*) What is *that*?

Grandpa She's an actress. Friend of Penny's. (**Gay** *mutters*)

Kolenkhov She is drunk—no?

Grandpa She is drunk—yes. . . . How are *you*, Kolenkhov?

Kolenkhov Magnificent! Life is chasing around inside of me, like a squirrel.

Grandpa 'Tis, huh? . . . What's new in Russia? Any more letters from your friend in Moscow?

Kolenkhov (*Nods*) I have just heard from him. I saved for you the stamp.

Grandpa Thanks, Kolenkhov.

Kolenkhov They have sent him to Siberia.

Grandpa They have, eh? How's he like it?

Kolenkhov He has escaped. He has escaped and gone back to Moscow. He will get them yet if they do not get him. The Soviet Government! I could take the whole Soviet Government and—grrah! (*He crushes Stalin and all in one great paw, just as* **Essie** *comes in from kitchen U.R.* **Kolenkhov** *rises*)

Essie I'm sorry I'm late, Mr Kolenkhov. I'll get into my dancing clothes right away.

Kolenkhov (*Crossing up to stairs*) Tonight you will really work, Pavlowa. (*As* **Essie** *goes up stairs*) Tonight we will take something new.

Grandpa Essie making any progress, Kolenkhov?

Kolenkhov (*First making elaborately sure that* **Essie** *is gone, then in a voice that would carry to Long Island*) Confidentially, she stinks! (*Lights cigarette*)

Grandpa Well, as long as she's having fun . . .

(**Donald** *ambles in from kitchen, chuckling, carrying tray. He crosses down to table*)

Donald You sure do tickle Rheba, Mr Kolenkhov. She's laughing her head off out there. (*Gathers up remaining cups, bottle and glass*)

Kolenkhov (*Sits L. of table*) She is a great woman. . . . Donald, what do you think of the Soviet Government?

Donald (*Puzzled*) The what, Mr Kolenkhov?

Kolenkhov (*Gesture*) I withdraw the question. What do you think of *this* Government?

Donald Oh, I like it fine. I'm on relief, you know.

Kolenkhov Oh, yes. And you like it?

Donald Yassuh, it's fine. (*Starts to go R.*) Only thing is you got to go round to the place every week to get it, and sometimes you got to stand in line pretty near half an hour. Government ought to be run better than that—don't you think, Grandpa?

Grandpa (*As he fishes envelope out of his pocket. Opens letter*) Government ought to stop sending me letters. Want me to be at the United States Marshal's office Tuesday morning at ten o'clock. Look at that. (*Throws letter to* **Kolenkhov**)

Kolenkhov (*Peering at letter*) Ah! Income tax! They have got you, Grandpa.

Grandpa (*Puts letter back in pocket*) Mm. I'm supposed to give 'em a lot of money so as to keep Donald on relief.

Donald You don't say, Grandpa? *You going* to pay it from now on?

Grandpa That's what they want.

Donald You mean I can come right *here* and get it instead of standing in that line?

Grandpa No, Donald, I'm afraid you will have to waste a full half hour of your time every week.

Donald Well, I don't like it. It breaks up my week. (*Exits U.R.*)

Kolenkhov He should have been in Russia when the Revolution came. Then he would have stood in line . . . a bread line. Ah, Grandpa, what they have done to Russia. Think of it! The Grand Duchess Olga Katrina, a cousin of the Czar, she is a waitress in Childs' Restaurant! I ordered baked beans from her, only yesterday. It broke my heart. A crazy world, Grandpa.

Grandpa Oh, the world's not so crazy, Kolenkhov. It's the people *in* it. Life's pretty simple if you just relax.

Kolenkhov (*Rising, crosses U.C.*) How can you relax in times like these?

Grandpa Well, if they'd relax there wouldn't *be* times like these. That's just my point. Life is kind of beautiful if you let it come to you. (*Crossing to buffet for his target and darts*) But the trouble is, people forget that. I know I did. I was right in the thick of it . . . fighting, and scratching and clawing. Regular jungle. One day it just kind of struck me, I wasn't having any fun. (**Grandpa**, *having hung his target on cellar door, returns to table*)

Kolenkhov So you did what?

Grandpa (*Standing below the table*) Just relaxed. Thirty-five years ago, that was. And I've been a happy man ever since. (*Throws a dart and sits*)

Alice (*Entering from kitchen*) Good evening, Mr Kolenkhov.

Kolenkhov (*Crossing up to* **Alice** *C., he bows low over her hand*) Ah, Miss Alice! I have not seen you to present my congratulations.

Alice Thank you.

Kolenkhov May you be very happy and have many children. That is my prayer for you.

Alice That's quite a thought. (*She exits up stairs, humming a fragment of song*)

Kolenkhov (*Crossing down*) Ah, love! Love is all that is left in the world, Grandpa.

Grandpa Yes, but there is plenty of that.

Kolenkhov And soon Stalin will take that away, too, I tell you, Grandpa. . . .

(**Penny** *enters down stairs. She has on an artist's smock over her dress, a flowing black tie, and a large blue velvet tam-o'-shanter, worn at a rakish angle. She carries a palette and an assortment of paints and brushes*)

Penny Seems so nice to get into my art things again. They still look all right, don't they, Grandpa?

Grandpa Yes, indeed.

Kolenkhov You are a breath of Paris, Madame Sycamore.

(**Donald** *enters U.R., table cover over his arm*)

Penny Oh, thank you, Mr Kolenkhov.

Donald I didn't know you was working for the WPA.

Penny Oh, no, Donald. You see, I used to paint all the time—(*The outer door slams and* **Ed** *comes in*)

Ed (*In considerable excitement*) It happened again! There was a fellow following me every place I went!

Penny Nonsense, Ed. It's your imagination.

Ed No, it isn't. It happens every time I go out to deliver candy.

Grandpa Maybe he wants a piece of candy.

Ed It's all right for you *to laugh*, Grandpa, but he keeps following me.

Kolenkhov (*Somberly*) You do not know what following is. In Russia *everybody* is followed. I was followed right out of Russia.

Penny Of course. You see, Ed—the whole thing is just imagination.

(**De Pinna** *comes up from cellar, ready for posing. He is carrying Roman toga, headband and sandals.*

Taking off coat as he goes up to alcove)

Ed (*Crosses to L. of alcove*) Well, maybe. (*Takes off coat*)

(**Donald** *removes napkins and tablecloth and spreads table cover. Puts cover on U.S. chair*)

Penny (**Penny**'s *easel, a discus, and a small platform for posing purposes and Racing Form*) Ah, here we are!

De Pinna (*Crosses to D.L., places easel*) Where do you want this? Over there?

Penny (*Putting portrait on the easel*) Put it here, Mr De Pinna. (**De Pinna** *strikes a pose on the model stand*)

Kolenkhov Ed, for tonight's lesson we use the first movement of Scheherazade.

Ed Okay.

Penny (*Studying* **De Pinna**'s *figure*) Mr De Pinna, has something happened to your figure during these eight years?

De Pinna (*Pulling in his stomach*) No, I don't think it's any different. (*With a sudden snort,* **Gay** *comes to.* **De Pinna** *breaks pose and looks at* **Gay**)

Penny (*Crossing to below table. Immediately alert*) Yes, Miss Wellington? Yes? (*For answer,* **Gay** *peers first at* **Penny**, *then at* **De Pinna**.

Gay Wo-o-o! (*And with that she goes right back to sleep*)

Penny (*Exchanges look with* **De Pinna** *and then returns to her painting*) Oh, dear.

(**Essie** *comes tripping down stairs—very much the ballet dancer. She is in full costume—ballet skirt, tight white satin bodice, a garland of roses in her hair*)

Essie (*Crossing to xylophone*) Sorry, Mr Kolenkhov. I couldn't find my slippers.

Kolenkhov (*Coming down. Having previously removed his coat, he now takes off his shirt, displaying an enormous hairy chest beneath his undershirt*) We have a hot night for it, my Pavlowa, but art is only achieved through perspiration. (*Back to alcove*)

Penny Why, that's wonderful, Mr Kolenkhov. Did you hear that, Grandpa—art is only achieved through perspiration.

Grandpa (**Essie** *fixes slippers during this*) Yes, but it helps if you've got a little talent with it. (*He takes up a handful of feathered darts*) Only made two bull's-eyes last night. Got to do better than that. (*He hurls a dart at board, then his eye travels to* **Gay**, *whose posterior offers an even easier target. Looks to* **Penny** *for approval. Then returns to his game and hurls one more dart and sits. Reads his* *paper*) (**Ed** *strikes a few notes*)

Kolenkhov You are ready? We begin! (*With a gesture he orders the music started; under* **Kolenkhov**'s *critical eye* **Essie** *begins the mazes of the dance. Meanwhile* **De Pinna**'s *free hand now holds a copy of Racing Form, the total effect being a trifle un-Grecian*) Now! Pirouette! Pirouette! (**Essie** *hesitates*) Come, come! You can do that! It's eight years now! (**Essie** *pirouettes*) At last! Entre chat! Entre chat! (**Donald** *crosses U.R.* **Essie** *leaps into the air, her feet twirling.* **Kolenkhov** *turns to* **Grandpa**) No, Grandpa, you cannot relax with Stalin in Russia. The Czar relaxed, and what happened to *him?*

Grandpa He was too late!

Essie (*Still leaping away*) Mr Kolenkhov! Mr Kolenkhov!

Kolenkhov If he had not relaxed the Grand Duchess Olga Katrina would not be selling baked beans today.

Essie (*Imploringly*) Mr Kolenkhov!

Kolenkhov I'm sorry. We go back to the pirouette.

Penny Could you pull in your stomach, Mr De Pinna? (*Door bell*) That's right.

Kolenkhov A little freer. A little freer with the hands. The whole body must work. Ed, help us with the music. (**Rheba** *enters U.R. Crosses to hall door*) The music must be free, too. (*By way of guiding* **Ed**, **Kolenkhov** *hums the music at the pace that it should go. He is even pirouetting a bit himself*) (*From the front door comes the murmur of voices, not quite audible over the music. Then the stunned figure of* **Rheba** *comes into archway, her eyes popping*)

Rheba (*Heavy whisper*) Mrs Sycamore . . . Mrs Sycamore.

Penny What, Rheba?

(**Rheba** *edges over R. With a gesture that has a grim foreboding in it, motions toward the still invisible reason for her panic. There is a second's pause, and then the reason is revealed in all its horror. The* **Kirby**s, *in full evening dress, stand in archway. All three of them,* **Mr** *and* **Mrs Kirby**, *and* **Tony**. **De Pinna** *rushes to cellar door carrying his model stand with him.* **Kolenkhov** *runs to alcove to squirm into his shirt and coat.* **Essie** *makes for alcove, also.* **Ed** *pushes xylophone in place and hastily dons his coat.* **Rheba** *crosses to buffet.* **Donald** *comes D.R. still carrying soiled dinner linen.* **Penny** *utters a stifled gasp; she puts the painting against wall with the easel. Then removes her smock and tam.* **Grandpa**, *alone*

of them all, rises to the situation. With a kind of old world grace, he puts down his newspaper and makes the guests welcome)

Tony Good evening.

Grandpa (*Rising and crossing to back of table*) How do you do?

Kirby (*Uncertainly*) How do you do?

Tony Are we too early?

Grandpa No, no. Come right in. It's perfectly all right—we're glad to see you. (*His eyes still on the* **Kirbys**, *he gives* **Donald** *a good push toward kitchen, by way of a hint*) (**Donald** *goes, promptly, with a quick little stunned whistle that sums up his feelings.* **Rheba** *looking back exits U.R.*)

Penny Why—yes. Only—we thought it was to be tomorrow night.

Mrs Kirby Tomorrow night!

Kirby What!

Grandpa Now, it's perfectly all right. Just make yourselves at home. (*Crossing to back of table. Placing chair*)

Kirby Tony, how could you possibly—

Tony I—I don't know. I thought—

Mrs Kirby Really, Tony! This is most embarrassing.

Grandpa Not at all. Why, we weren't doing a thing.

Penny No, no. Just a quiet evening at home.

Grandpa That's all. . . . Now don't let it bother you. This is Alice's mother, Mrs Sycamore.

Penny How do you do.

Grandpa . . . Alice's sister, Mrs Carmichael . . . Mr Carmichael . . . Mr Kolenkhov. (**Kolenkhov** *comes down, bows and discovers his shirt tail exposed. Thrusts it into his trousers. At this point* **De Pinna** *takes an anticipatory step forward, and* **Grandpa** *is practically compelled to perform the introduction. Crossing to* **De Pinna**) And—Mr De Pinna.

The Kirbys How do you do?

De Pinna Don't mind my costume. I'll take it right off.

Grandpa Mr De Pinna, would you tell Mr Sycamore to come right up? Tell him that Mr and Mrs Kirby are here.

Penny (*Her voice a heavy whisper*) And be sure to put his pants on.

De Pinna (*Whispering right back*) All right. . . . Excuse me. (*He vanishes—discus, Racing Form, and all—D.R.*) (*At this point* **Penny** *hastily throws a couch cover over* **Gay**. **Penny** *pushes* **Gay**'s *posterior with her knee.* **Grandpa**, *crossing R. places chair*)

Mrs Kirby (*Crossing to* **Grandpa**'s *chair*) Thank you.

Penny (*Crossing to arch U.L.*) I'll tell Alice that you're—(*She is at foot of stairs*) Alice! Alice, dear! (**Kirby** *comes D.L. The voice of* **Alice** *from above, 'What is it?'*) Alice, will you come down, dear? We've got a surprise for you. (*She comes back into the room, summoning all her charm*) Well!

Grandpa Mrs Kirby, may I take your wrap? (*Removes it*)

Mrs Kirby Well—thank you. If you're perfectly sure (*She turns*) that we're not—(*Suddenly she sees snakes and lets out a scream*)

Grandpa Oh, don't be alarmed, Mrs Kirby. They're perfectly harmless.

Mrs Kirby Thank you. (*She sinks into a chair, weakly*)

Grandpa Ed, take 'em into the kitchen.

(**Tony** *takes his father's hat to hall and returns to the room.* **Ed** *at once obeys. Takes snake solarium to kitchen*)

Penny (*Putting Japanese bowl C. of buffet*) Of course we're so used to them around the house—

Mrs Kirby I'm sorry to trouble you, but snakes happen to be—

Kirby I feel very uncomfortable about this. Tony, how could you have done such a thing?

Tony I'm sorry, Dad. I thought it was tonight.

Kirby It was very careless of you. *Very!*

Penny Oh, now, anybody can get mixed up, Mr Kirby.

Grandpa Penny, how about some dinner for these folks? They've come for dinner, you know.

Mrs Kirby Oh, please don't bother. (**Ed** *enters U.R.*) We're really not hungry at all.

Penny (*Crosses to* **Ed**) But it's not a bit of bother. Ed!— (*Her voice drops to a loud whisper*) Ed, tell Donald to run down to the A. and P. and get half a dozen bottles of beer, and—ah—some canned salmon—(*Her voice comes up again*) Do you like canned salmon, Mr Kirby?

Kirby (*A step in to R.*) Please don't trouble, Mrs Sycamore. I have a little indigestion, anyway.

Penny Oh, I'm sorry. . . . How about you, Mrs Kirby? Do you like canned salmon?

Mrs Kirby (*You just know that she hates it*) Oh, I'm very fond of it.

Penny You can have frankfurters if you'd rather.

Mrs Kirby (*Regally*) Either one will do.

Penny (*To* **Ed** *again*) Well, make it frankfurters and some canned corn, and Campbell's Soup—(**Ed** crosses U.R. to door, **Penny** *following*) Got that, Ed?

Ed (*Going out kitchen door U.R.*) Okay!

Penny (*Calling after him*) And tell him to hurry! (**Penny** *again addresses the* **Kirbys**. *Comes down R.*) The A. and P. is just at the corner, and frankfurters don't take *any* time to boil.

Grandpa (*As* **Paul** *comes through cellar door D.R.*) And this is Alice's father, *Mr* Sycamore. Mr and Mrs Kirby.

The Kirbys How do you do?

Paul I hope you'll forgive my appearance.

(**Alice** *starts down stairs*)

Penny This is Mr Sycamore's busiest time of the year. Just before the Fourth of July he always—

(*And then* **Alice** *comes down. She is a step into the room before she realizes what has happened; then she fairly freezes in her tracks*)

Alice (*At arch*) Oh!

Tony (*Crossing up to her*) Darling, I'm the most dull-witted person in the world. I thought it was tonight.

Alice (*Staggered*) Why, Tony, I thought you—(*To the* **Kirbys**. *Coming D.L. of table*) I'm so sorry—I can't imagine—why, I wasn't—have you all met each other?

Kirby Yes, indeed.

Mrs Kirby How do you do, Alice?

Alice (*Not even yet in control of herself*) How do you do, Mrs Kirby? I'm afraid I'm not very—presentable.

Tony (*Crossing down to* **Alice**) Darling, you look lovely.

Kirby (*A step toward* **Alice**) Of course she does. Don't let this upset you, my dear—we've all just met each other a night sooner, that's all.

Mrs Kirby Of course.

Alice But I was planning such a nice party tomorrow night. . . .

Kirby (*Being the good fellow*) Well, we'll come again tomorrow night.

Tony There you are, Alice. Am I forgiven?

Alice I guess so. It's just that I—We'd better see about getting you some dinner.

Penny Oh, that's all done, Alice. (**Donald**, *hat in hand, comes through kitchen door; hurries across room and out front way. He is followed into room by* **Ed**, *who joins the family circle.* **Grandpa** *crosses to back of table*) That's all been attended to.

(*Door slams on* **Donald**'s *exit*)

Alice (*Sensing that* **Donald** *is on way to round up a* *meal crosses over to* **Penny**) But Mother—what did you send out for? Because Mr Kirby suffers from indigestion—he can only eat certain things.

Kirby (*Crossing to L. of table*) Oh, it's all right. It's all right.

Tony Of course it is, darling.

Penny I asked him what he wanted, Alice.

Alice (*Doubtfully*) Yes, but—

Kirby Now, now, it's not as serious as all that. Just because I have a little indigestion.

Kolenkhov (*Coming down to R. of table*) Perhaps it is not indigestion at all, Mr Kirby. Perhaps you have stomach ulcers.

Alice Don't be absurd, Mr Kolenkhov!

Grandpa You mustn't mind Mr Kolenkhov, Mr Kirby. He's a Russian, and Russians are inclined to look on the dark side.

Kolenkhov All right, I am a Russian. But a friend of mine, a Russian, *died* from stomach ulcers.

Kirby Really, I—

Alice (*Desperately*) Please, Mr Kolenkhov! Mr Kirby has indigestion and that's all. (**Paul** *drifts up to R. of buffet*)

Kolenkhov (*With a Russian shrug*) All right, let him wait. (*Crossing over to R.*)

Grandpa Do sit down, Mr Kirby. Make yourself comfortable.

Kirby Thank you. (*He sits L. of table*)

Penny (*Sitting above table*) Well—(*She sighs; a pause, a general shifting*) (**Paul** *drifts U.R.* **Alice** *joins* **Tony** *L.*)

Grandpa (*Coming D.S. Leaping into the breach*) Tell me, Mr Kirby, how do you find business conditions? Are we pretty well out of the depression?

Kirby What? . . . Yes, I think so. Of course, it all depends.

Grandpa But you figure that things are going to keep on improving?

Kirby Broadly speaking, yes. As a matter of fact, industry is now operating at sixty-four per cent of full capacity, as against eighty-two per cent in 1925. (**Gay** *rises*) Of course, in 1929—

Gay (*She weaves unsteadily across room singing: 'There was a young lady from Wheeling who had a remarkable feeling.'* **Alice** *crosses D.L. The imposing figure of* **Kirby** *intrigues* **Gay**). Wo-o-o – (*She pinches his cheeks and with that lunges on her way up stairs*)

Penny She—ah—

(*The* **Kirbys**, *of course, are considerably astounded*

by this exhibition. The **Sycamores** *have watched it with varying degrees of frozen horror.* **Alice** *in particular is speechless; it is* **Grandpa** *who comes to her rescue*)

Grandpa (*Crossing to back of table*) That may seem a little strange to you people, but she's not quite accountable for her actions. A friend of Mrs Sycamore's. She came to dinner and was overcome by the heat. (*Sits above table*)

Penny Yes, some people feel it, you know, more than others. Perhaps I'd better see if she's all right. Excuse me please? (*She goes hastily up stairs*)

Alice (*Crossing to L. of table*) It *is* awfully hot. (*A fractional pause*) You usually escape all this hot weather, don't you, Mrs Kirby? Up in Maine?

Mrs Kirby (*On the frigid side*) As a rule. I had to come down this week, however, for the Flower Show.

Tony Mother wouldn't miss that for the world. That blue ribbon is the high spot of her year.

Essie (*Crossing down to R. of table*) I won a ribbon at a Flower Show once. For raising onions. Remember, Alice?

Alice (*Quickly*) That was a Garden Show, Essie.

Essie (*Crosses to couch*) Oh, yes. (**Penny** *comes bustling down stairs again U.L. Comes D.L.* **Kirby** *rises*)

Penny I think she'll be all right now. . . . Has Donald come back yet?

Alice No, he hasn't.

Penny Well, he'll be right back, and it won't take any time at all. I'm afraid you must be starved.

Kirby (*Going U.C.*) Oh, no. Quite all right. (*He sees* **Paul**'s *Meccano boat model*) Hello! What's this? I didn't know there were little children in the house.

Paul Oh, no. That's mine.

Kirby Really? Well, I suppose every man has his hobby. Or do you use this as a model of some kind?

Paul No, I just play with it.

Kirby I see.

Tony Maybe you'd be better off if *you* had a hobby like that, Dad. Instead of raising orchids.

Kirby (*Crossing down to back of table. Indulgently*) Yes, I wouldn't be surprised. (**Penny** *sits L. of table.* **Alice** *comes down R.*)

Alice (*Leaping on this as a safe topic*) Oh, *do* tell us about your orchids, Mr Kirby. (**Kirby** *crosses up to alcove.* **Alice** *addresses others*) You know, they take six years before they blossom, don't they? Think of that!

Kirby (*Addressing* **Grandpa** *and* **Penny**. *Warming to his subject*) Oh, some of them take longer than that. I've got one coming along now that I've waited *ten* years for. (**Essie** *sits*) Of course during that time they require the most scrupulous care. (*The sound of hall door closing and* **Donald** *suddenly bulges through U.L. archway, his arms full. The tops of beer bottles and two or three large cucumbers peep over the tops of the huge paper bag*) I remember a bulb that I was very fond of—

Alice (*Crossing up to* **Donald**) Donald!

Penny (*Rising and going to* **Donald**) Ah, here we are! Did you get everything, Donald?

Donald Yes'm. Only they didn't have any frankfurters, so I got pickled pig's feet. (*Exits U.R.*)

(**Kirby** *blanches at the very idea. He crosses to L. below the table.* **Ed** *sits U.S. end of couch*)

Alice (*Following* **Donald** *to kitchen door. Taking command*) Never mind, Donald—just bring everything into the kitchen. (*She turns at kitchen door*) Mr Kirby, please tell them *all* about the orchids—I know they'd love to hear it. And— excuse me. (*She goes U.R.*) (**Penny** *crosses, looks off into kitchen, and comes down R. of table*)

Grandpa Kind of an expensive hobby, isn't it, Mr Kirby—raising orchids?

Kirby (*Sits L. of table*) Yes, it is, but I feel that if a hobby gives one sufficient pleasure, it's never expensive.

Grandpa That's very true. (**Paul**, **Essie** *and* **Ed** *are sitting on the couch.* **Tony** *is at the desk*)

Kirby You see, I need something to relieve the daily nerve strain. After a week in Wall Street I'd go crazy if I didn't have something like that. Lot of men I know have yachts—just for that very reason.

Grandpa (*Mildly*) Why don't they give up Wall Street?

Kirby How's that?

Grandpa I was just joking.

Mrs Kirby I think it's necessary for everyone to have a hobby. Of course, it's more to me than a hobby, but my great solace is—spiritualism.

Penny Spiritualism? Now, Mrs Kirby, everybody knows that's a fake.

Mrs Kirby (*Freezing*) To me, Mrs Sycamore, spiritualism is—well—I would rather not discuss it, Mrs Sycamore. (*she looks at* **Kirby**. *He rises*)

Paul (*Rising from couch and crossing to* **Penny**)

Remember, Penny, you've got one or two hobbies of your own.

Penny Yes, but not silly ones.

Grandpa (*With a little cough*) I don't think it matters what the hobby is—the important thing is to have one.

Kolenkhov (*Crossing over back of table to D.L. in front of desk*) To be ideal, a hobby should improve the body as well as the mind. The Romans were a great people! Why? What was their hobby? Wrestling. In wrestling you have to think quick with the mind and act quick with the body.

Kirby Yes, but I'm afraid wrestling is not very practical for most of us. (*He gives a deprecating little laugh*) I wouldn't make a very good showing as a wrestler.

Kolenkhov You could be a *great* wrestler. You are built for it. Look! (*With a startlingly quick movement* **Kolenkhov** *grabs* **Kirby**'s *arms, knocks his legs from under him with a quick movement of a foot, and presto!* **Kirby** *is flat on his whatsis. Not only that, but instantaneously* **Kolenkhov** *is on top of him.* **Mrs Kirby** *rises. Just at this moment* **Alice** *re-enters the room—naturally, she stands petrified. Then rushes immediately to the rescue,* **Tony** *and* **Ed** *arriving at the scene of battle first. Amidst the general confusion they help* **Kirby** *to his feet*)

Alice Mr Kirby! Are you—hurt?

Tony Are you all right, Father?

Kirby (*Pulling himself together*) I—I—uh—(*He blinks, uncertainly*) Where are my glasses?

Alice Here they are, Mr Kirby. . . . Oh, Mr Kirby, they're broken. (**Paul** *turns to* **Penny**)

Kolenkhov (*Full of apology*) Oh, I am sorry. But when you wrestle again, Mr Kirby, you will of course not wear glasses!

Kirby (*Coldly furious*) I do not intend to wrestle again, Mr Kolenkhov. (*He draws himself up, stiffly, and in return gets a sharp pain in the back. He gives a little gasp*)

Tony (*He assists his father to chair L. of table*) Better sit down, Father.

Alice (*Crossing to* **Kolenkhov**) Mr Kolenkhov, how could you do such a thing? Why didn't somebody stop him? (**Kolenkhov** *turns U.S.*)

Mrs Kirby (*Rises*) I think, if you don't mind, perhaps we had better be going. (*Gathers wraps*) (**Grandpa** *rises*)

Tony Mother!

Alice (*Close to tears*) Oh, Mrs Kirby—please! Please don't go! Mr Kirby—please! I—I've ordered some scrambled eggs for you, and—plain salad—Oh, please don't go!

Kolenkhov (*Comes D.L.*) I am sorry if I did something wrong. And I apologize. (*Crosses U.L.*)

Alice I can't tell you how sorry I am, Mr Kirby. If I'd been here—

Kirby (*From a great height*) That's quite all right.

Tony Of course it is. It's all right, Alice. (*To Mrs Kirby*) We're not going. (*Arm around Alice*)

(*A moment's silence—no one knows quite what to say. Then Mrs Kirby looks at Kirby and sits. Then Kirby sits. Finally Grandpa sits*)

Penny (*Brightly*) Well! That was exciting for a minute, wasn't it?

Grandpa (*Quickly*) You were talking about your orchids, Mr Kirby. Do you raise many different varieties?

Kirby (*Still unbending*) I'm afraid I've quite forgotten about my orchids. (*More silence, and everyone very uncomfortable*)

Alice I'm—awfully sorry, Mr Kirby.

Kolenkhov (*Coming D.L. Exploding*) What did I do that was so terrible? I threw him on the floor! Did it kill him?

Alice Please, Mr Kolenkhov. (*An annoyed gesture from Kolenkhov. He sits in desk chair. Another general pause*)

Penny I'm sure dinner won't be any time at all now. (*Crosses U.R., looks off into kitchen. A pained smile from Mrs Kirby*)

Essie (*Coming D.S.R.*) Would you like some candy while you're waiting, Mr Kirby? I've got some freshly made.

Kirby My doctor does not permit me to eat candy. Thank you.

Essie But these are nothing, Mr Kirby. Just cocoanut and marshmallow and fudge.

Alice Don't, Essie.

Essie Well—(*Crosses to couch. They sit there again*) (*Then Rheba appears in kitchen doorway, beckoning violently to Alice*)

Rheba (*In a loud whisper*) Miss Alice! Miss Alice!

Alice Excuse me. (*Starts U.R.*) What is it, Rheba? (*Quickly flies to Rheba's side*)

Rheba The eggs done fell down the sink.

Alice (*Desperately*) Make some more! Quick!

Rheba I ain't got any.

Alice Send Donald out for some!

Rheba (*Disappearing U.R.*) All right.

Alice (*Calling after her*) Tell him to hurry! (*She turns back to the Kirbys*) I'm so sorry. There'll be a little delay, but everything will be ready in just a minute. (*At this moment Donald fairly shoots out of kitchen door and across living room, beating the Olympic record for all time. SLAM on Donald's exit. He exits through hall door U.L. Penny tries to ease situation with a gay little laugh. It doesn't quite come off, however*) 'Woosh!'

Tony I've certainly put you people to a lot of trouble, with my stupidity.

Grandpa Not at all, Tony.

Penny (*Coming down R. of table*) Look! Why don't we all play a game of some sort while we're waiting?

Tony Oh, that'd be fine.

Alice Mother, I don't think Mr and Mrs Kirby—

Kolenkhov (*Rising from desk chair*) I have an idea. I know a wonderful trick with a glass of water. (*He reaches for a full glass that stands on desk. Crosses to Kirby and holds it over Kirby's head*)

Alice (*Quickly*) No, Mr Kolenkhov.

Grandpa (*Rises, shaking his head*) No-o, Mr Kolenkhov. (*Sits*) (*A shrug and Kolenkhov returns glass to desk*)

Penny But I'm sure Mr and Mrs Kirby would love this game. It's perfectly harmless.

Alice Please, Mother . . .

Kirby I'm not very good at games, Mrs Sycamore.

Penny (*Crossing below table to the desk*) Oh, but *any* fool could play this game, Mr Kirby. All you do is write your name on a piece of paper—(*Getting pads and pencils*) (**Tony** *helps* **Kolenkhov** *and himself to pads and pencils*)

Alice But, mother, Mr Kirby doesn't want—

Penny Oh, he'll love it! (*Going right on distributing pencils, pads*) Here you are, Mr Kirby. Write your name on this piece of paper. And Mrs Kirby, you do the same on this one. (**Paul**, **Essie** *and* **Ed** *sit on couch.* **Essie** *takes pencils,* **Ed** *pads*)

Alice Mother, what *is* this game?

Penny (*Crossing back of table to L.* **Kolenkhov** *sits at desk*) I used to play it at school. It's called Forget-Me-Not. Here you are, Grandpa. Now, I'm going to call out five words—just anything at all—and as I say each word, you're to put down the first thing that comes into your mind. Is that clear? For instance, if I say 'grass,' you might put down 'green'—just whatever you think of, see? Or if I call out 'chair,' you might put down 'table.' It shows the reactions people have to different things. You see how simple it is, Mr Kirby?

Tony Come on, Father! Be a sport!

Kirby (*Stiffly*) Very well. I shall be happy to play it.
Penny You see, Alice? He *does* want to play.
Alice (*Uneasily*) Well—
Penny Now, then! Are we ready?
Kolenkhov Ready!
Penny Now, remember—you must play fair. Put down the first thing that comes into your mind.
Kirby (*Pencil poised*) I understand.
Penny Everybody ready? . . . The first word is 'potatoes.' (*She repeats it*) 'Potatoes.' . . . Ready for the next one? . . . 'Bathroom.' (**Alice** *shifts rather uneasily*)
Alice Mother! (*But seeing that no one else seems to mind, she relaxes again*)
Penny Bathroom!—Got that?
Kolenkhov Go ahead.
Penny All ready? . . . 'Lust.'
Alice Mother, this is not exactly what you—
Penny Nonsense, Alice—that word's all right.
Alice Mother, it's *not* all right.
Mrs Kirby (*Unexpectedly*) Oh, I don't know. (*To* **Alice**) It seems to me that's a perfectly fair word.
Penny (*To* **Alice**) You see? Now, you mustn't interrupt the game. (**Alice** *drifts U.S.*)
Kirby May I have that last word again, please?
Penny 'Lust,' Mr Kirby.
Kirby (*Writing*) I've got it.
Grandpa This is quite a game, isn't it?
Penny Sssh, Grandpa. . . . All ready? . . . 'Honeymoon.' (**Essie** *snickers a little, which is all it takes to start* **Penny** *off. Then she suddenly remembers herself*) Now, Essie! . . . All right. The last word is 'Sex.'
Alice (*Under her breath*) Mother! (*Crossing to buffet*)
Penny Everybody got 'sex'? . . . All right—(*She takes* **Tony**'s *and* **Kolenkhov**'s *papers*) now give me all the papers. May I have your paper, Mr Kirby? (*Crosses back of table to R. gathering the pads*) (*Three at table tear off sheets.* **Ed** *hands three pads to* **Penny**)
Grandpa What happens now?
Penny Oh, this is the best part. Now I read out your reactions. (*Coming D.R.*)
Kirby I see. It's really quite an interesting game.
Penny I knew you'd like it. I'll read your paper first, Mr Kirby. (*To the others*) I'm going to read Mr Kirby's paper first. Listen, everybody! This is Mr Kirby. . . . 'Potatoes—steak.' That's very good. See how they go together? Steak and potatoes?
Kirby (*Modestly, but obviously pleased with himself*)

I just happened to think of it. (**Alice** *turns front*)
Penny It's *very* good. . . . 'Bathroom—toothpaste.' Well! 'Lust—unlawful.' Isn't that nice? 'Honeymoon—trip.' Yes. (*Giggle*) And 'sex—male.' Oh yes, of course . . . you are. That's really a wonderful paper, Mr Kirby.
Kirby (*Taking a curtain call*) Thank you. . . . It's more than just a game, you know. It's sort of an experiment in psychology, isn't it?
Penny Yes, it is—it shows just how your *mind* works. Now we'll see how *Mrs* Kirby's mind works. . . . Ready? . . . This is *Mrs* Kirby. . . . 'Potatoes—starch.' I know just what you mean, Mrs Kirby. M-m—oh dear! . . . 'Bathroom—Mr Kirby.'
Kirby What's that?
Penny 'Bathroom—Mr Kirby.'
Kirby (*Turning to his wife*) I don't quite *follow that*, my dear.
Mrs Kirby I don't know—I just thought of you in connection with it. After all, you *are* in there a good deal, Anthony. Bathing, and shaving—well, you *do* take a long time.
Kirby Indeed? I hadn't realized that I was being selfish in the matter. . . . Go on, Mrs Sycamore.
Alice (*Worried. Comes down to* **Kirby**) I think it's a very silly game and we ought to stop it.
Mrs Kirby Yes.
Kirby No, no. Please go on, Mrs Sycamore. (**Alice** *crosses up*)
Penny Where was I? . . . Oh, yes . . . . 'Lust—human.'
Kirby Human? (*Thin-lipped*) Really! Miriam!
Mrs Kirby I just meant, Anthony, that lust is after all a—human emotion.
Kirby I don't agree with you, Miriam. Lust is *not* a *human* emotion. It is depraved.
Mrs Kirby Very well, Anthony. I'm wrong.
Alice (*Crossing down to L. of* **Kirby**) Really, it's the most pointless game. Suppose we play Twenty Questions?
Mrs Kirby Yes.
Kirby (*Raises hand.* **Alice** *goes U.S.*) No, I find *this* game rather interesting. Will you go on, Mrs Sycamore? What was the next word?
Penny (*Reluctantly*) Honeymoon.
Kirby Oh, yes. And what was Mrs Kirby's answer?
Penny Ah—'Honeymoon—dull.'
Kirby (*Murderously calm*) Did you say—dull?
Mrs Kirby What I meant, Anthony, was that Hot Springs was not very gay that season. All those old people sitting on the porch all afternoon, and—

nothing to do at night. (*Realizes she has gone too far*)

Kirby That was not your reaction at the time, as I recall it.

Tony (*Crosses in a step*) Father, this is only a *game*.

Kirby A very illuminating game. Go on, Mrs Sycamore!

Penny (*Brightly, having taken a look ahead*) This one's all right, Mr Kirby. 'Sex—Wall Street.'

Kirby Wall Street? What do you mean by that, Miriam?

Mrs Kirby (*Nervously*) I don't know what I meant, Anthony. Nothing.

Kirby But you must have meant something, Miriam, or you wouldn't have put it down.

Mrs Kirby It was just the first thing that came into my head, that's all.

Kirby But what does it mean? 'Sex—Wall Street.'

Mrs Kirby (*Annoyed*) Oh, I don't know what it means, Anthony. It's just that you're always talking about Wall Street, even when—(*She catches herself*) I don't know what I meant. . . . Would you mind terribly, Alice, if we didn't stay for dinner? (*Rises.* **Grandpa** *and* **Kolenkhov** *rise. Also* **Essie**, **Ed** *and* **Paul**) I'm afraid this game has given me a headache.

Alice (*Quietly*) I understand, Mrs Kirby.

Kirby (*Rises. Clearing his throat*) Yes, possibly we'd better postpone the dinner, if you don't mind. (**Kolenkhov** *drifts U.C.*)

Penny But you're coming tomorrow night, aren't you?

Mrs Kirby (*Quickly*) I'm afraid we have an engagement tomorrow night. (*Wrap is half on shoulders*)

Kirby Perhaps we'd better postpone the whole affair a little while. The hot weather and—ah—

Tony (*Smouldering*) I think we're being very ungracious, Father. Of *course* we'll stay to dinner—tonight.

Mrs Kirby (*Unyielding*) I have a very bad headache, Tony.

Kirby (*To* **Tony**) Come, come, Tony, I'm sure everyone understands. (**Kolenkhov** *continues drifting down to back of the table*)

Tony (*Flaring*) Well, *I* don't. I think we ought to stay.

Alice (*Very low. She comes down to* **Tony**) No, Tony.

Tony What?

Alice We were fools, Tony, ever to think it would work. It won't. Mr Kirby, I won't be at the office

tomorrow. I—won't be there at all any more. (*Crosses D.L. below desk*)

Tony (*Follows her. Puts his arm around her*) Alice, what are you talking about?

Kirby (*To* **Alice**) I'm sorry, my dear—very sorry. . . . Are you ready, Miriam?

Mrs Kirby (*with enormous dignity. She crosses over to* **Kirby**) Yes, Anthony.

Tony Darling, you mustn't mind this.

Kirby Oh—it's been very nice to have met you all. (*With* **Mrs Kirby**, *he goes as far as the archway*)

Mrs Kirby Yes, lovely.

Kirby Are you coming, Tony?

Tony No, Father. I'm not.

Kirby (*Crossing up to arch with* **Mrs Kirby**) I see. . . . Your mother and I will be waiting for you at home. . . . Good night.

Penny and **Essie** Good night.

(*Before the* **Kirby**s *can take more than a step toward the door, however, a new* **Figure** *looms up in the archway. It is a quiet and competent-looking individual with a steely eye, and two more just like him loom up behind him*)

The Man (*Very quietly*) Stay right where you are, everybody. (*There is a little scream from* **Mrs Kirby**, *an exclamation from* **Penny**) Don't move.

Penny Oh, good heavens!

Kirby (*Speaks on cue 'Don't move'*) How dare you? Why, what does this mean?

Grandpa What is all this?

Kirby I demand an explanation!

The Man Keep your mouth shut, you! (**Penny** *turns to* **Paul**. **Ed** *backs up as G-Man crosses R. He advances slowly into the room, looking the group over. Then he turns to one of his men*) Which one is it?

Third Man (*Goes over and puts a hand on* **Ed**'s *shoulder and brings him D.R.* **Essie** *follows*) This is him.

Ed Heh! What are you doing?

Essie Ed!

Ed (*Terrified*) Why, what do you mean?

Alice (*Crossing to* **Grandpa**) Grandpa, what is it?

Kirby This is an outrage!

The Man Shut up! (*He turns to* **Ed**) What's your name?

Ed Edward—Carmichael. I haven't done anything.

The Man. You haven't, huh?

Grandpa (*Not at all scared*) This seems rather high-handed to me. What's it all about?

The Man Department of Justice.

Penny Oh, my goodness! J-men!

Essie Ed, what have you done?

Ed I haven't done anything.

Grandpa What's the boy done, Officer?

Alice What is it? What's it all about?

The Man (*Taking his time, and surveying the room*) That door lead to the cellar?

Penny Yes it does.

Paul Yes.

The Man (*Ordering a man to investigate*) Mac . . . (**Third G-Man** *exits D.R.*) . . . Jim!

Jim Yes, sir.

The Man Take a look *upstairs* and see what you find.

Jim Okay. (**Jim** *exits upstairs*)

Ed (*Panicky*) I haven't done anything.

The Man Come here, you! (*He takes some slips of paper out of his pocket*) Ever see these before?

Ed (*Gulping*) They're my—circulars.

The Man You print this stuff, huh?

Ed Yes, sir.

The Man And you put 'em into boxes of candy to get 'em into people's homes.

Essie The Love Dreams!

Ed But I didn't mean anything—

The Man You didn't, huh? (*He reads circulars*) 'Dynamite the Capitol!' 'Dynamite the White House!' 'Dynamite the Supreme Court!' 'God is the State; the State is God!'

Ed But I didn't mean that. I just like to print. Don't I, Grandpa? (**Donald** *enters U.L.*)

Grandpa (*Waves* **Ed** *and* **Essie** *U.S.*) Now, Officer, the Government's in no danger from Ed. Printing is just his hobby, that's all. He prints anything.

The Man He does, eh?

Penny I never heard of such nonsense.

Kirby I refuse to stay here and—

(**De Pinna**, *at this point, is shoved through cellar door by* **Mac**, *protesting as he comes*)

De Pinna Hey, let me get my pipe, will you? Let me get my pipe!

Mac Shut up, you! . . . We were right, Chief. They've got enough gunpowder down there to blow up the whole city.

Paul But we only use that—

The Man Keep still! . . . Everybody in this house is under arrest.

Kirby What's that?

Mrs Kirby Oh, good heavens!

Grandpa Now look here, Officer—this is all nonsense.

De Pinna You'd better let me get my pipe. I left it—

The Man Shut up, all of you!

Kolenkhov It seems to me, Officer—

The Man Shut up! (*From the stairs comes sound of drunken singing—'There was a young lady,' etc.* **Gay**, *wrapped in* **Penny**'s *negligee, is being carried down stairway by a somewhat bewildered G-man*)

Jim Keep still, you! Stop that! Stop it!

The Man Who's that?

Grandpa That is my mother! (*He sits*)

Kolenkhov The fireworks! The fireworks! (*And then we hear from the cellar. A whole year's supply of fireworks just goes off*)

Rheba (*Enters U.R.*) Donald! Donald!

(**Mrs Kirby**'s *scream is just a little louder than the explosion*)

Kirby Miriam! Miriam! Are you all right? Are you all right?

Tony (*Dashing to his mother*) It's all right! Mother! There's no danger.

Alice Grandpa! Grandpa! (*Crosses to* **Grandpa**)

Grandpa (*Ever so quietly*) Well, well, well!

De Pinna (*Wrenching himself loose from the G-man*) Let go of me! I've got to go down there!

Paul Good lord! (*With* **De Pinna**, *he dashes into the cellar*)

Penny My manuscripts! I've got to save my manuscripts! (*She dashes to her desk*)

Ed My xylophone! How will I get the xylophone out?

Essie Mr Kolenkhov! Mr Kolenkhov!

Kolenkhov Do not worry! Do not worry!

Donald (*Rushing toward the kitchen*) It's all right, Rheba, it's all right!

The G-Man (*Vainly trying to keep order*) Line up, you people! Line up, all of you!

(*And* **Gay** *just keeps singing*)

CURTAIN

Act III

The following day. **Rheba** *is in the midst of setting table for dinner, pausing occasionally in her labors to listen to the Edwin C Hill of the moment—***Donald**. *With intense interest and concentration, he is reading aloud from a newspaper.*

Donald '. . . for appearance in the West Side Court this morning. After spending the night in jail, the defendants, thirteen in all, were brought before Judge Callahan and given suspended sentences for manufacturing fireworks without a permit.'

Rheba (*Puts plate down*) Yah. Kept me in the same cell with a strip teaser from a burlesque show.

Donald I was in the cell with Mr Kirby. My, he was mad!

Rheba (*Sets knife and fork*) Mrs Kirby and the strip teaser—they were fighting *all night*.

Donald Whole lot about *Mr* Kirby here. (**Rheba** *places napkins. Reading again*) 'Anthony W Kirby, head of Kirby & Co., 62 Wall Street, who was among those apprehended, declared he was in no way interested in the manufacture of fireworks, but refused to state why he was on the premises at the time of the raid. Mr Kirby is a member of the Union Club, the Racquet Club, the Harvard Club, and the National Geographic Society.' My, he certainly is a joiner!

Rheba (*Pushes in chair above table*) All them rich men are Elks or something.

Donald (*Looking up from his paper*) I suppose, after all this, Mr Tony ain't ever going to marry Miss Alice, huh?

Rheba No, suh, and it's too bad, too. Miss Alice sure *loves* that boy.

Donald Ever notice how white folks always getting themselves in trouble?

Rheba Yassuh, I'm glad I'm colored.

Donald Me, too.

Rheba (*She sighs heavily. Turns chair L. in*) I don't know what I'm going to do with all that food out in the kitchen. Ain't going to be no party tonight, that's sure.

Donald Ain't we going to eat it anyhow?

Rheba (*Gets salad plates from buffet*) Well, I'm cooking it, but I don't think anybody going to have an appetite.

Donald *I'm* hungry.

Rheba (*Setting salad forks*) Well, *they ain't*. They're all so broke up about Miss Alice.

Donald What's she want to go 'way for? Where's she going?

Rheba (*Puts half of salad plates D.S. of table*) I don't know—mountains some place. And she's *going*, all right, no matter what they say. I know Miss Alice when she gets that look in her eye.

Donald Too bad, ain't it?

Rheba Sure is.

(**De Pinna** *comes up from cellar, bearing earmarks of the previous day's catastrophe. There is a small bandage around his head and over one eye, and another round his R. hand. He also limps slightly*)

De Pinna Not even a balloon left. Look. (*Pointing to exploded firecracker he is holding*)

Rheba How's your hand, Mr De Pinna? Better?

De Pinna Yes, it's better. (*A step toward kitchen*) Is there some more olive oil out there?

Rheba (*Nods*) It's in the salad bowl.

De Pinna Thanks. (*Crosses to R. He goes out kitchen door as* **Penny** *comes down stairs. It is a new and rather subdued* **Penny**. **Donald** *rises.* **Rheba** *turns to her*)

Penny (*With a sigh*) Well, she's going. Nothing anybody said could change her.

Rheba She ain't going to stay away long, is she, Mrs Sycamore?

Penny I don't know, Rheba. She won't say.

Rheba My, going to be lonesome around here without her. (*She goes into kitchen U.R.*)

Donald How *you* feel, Mrs Sycamore?

Penny Oh, I'm all right, Donald. Just kind of upset. (*She is at her desk*) Perhaps if I do some work maybe I'll feel better. (*Sits at her desk*)

Donald Well, I won't bother you then, Mrs Sycamore. (*He goes into kitchen U.R.*) (**Penny** *leans back and sits staring straight ahead.* **Paul** *comes slowly down stairs; stands surveying room a moment; sighs*)

Paul (*Coming D.S.*) She's going, Penny.

Penny Yes. (*She is quiet for a moment; then she starts to weep, softly*)

Paul (*Going to her*) Now, now, Penny.

Penny I can't help it, Paul. Somehow I feel it's our fault.

Paul It's mine more than yours, Penny. All these years I've just been—going along, enjoying myself, when maybe I should have been thinking more about Alice.

Penny Don't say that, Paul. You've been a wonderful father. And husband, too.

Paul (*Crossing to L. of table*) No, I haven't. Maybe if I'd gone ahead and been an architect—I don't know—something Alice could have been proud of. I felt that all last night, looking at Mr Kirby.

Penny But we've been so happy, Paul.

Paul I know, but maybe that's not enough. I used to think it was, but—I'm kind of all mixed up now.

Penny (*After a pause*) What time is she going?

Paul Pretty soon. Train leaves at half past seven.

Penny Oh, if only she'd see Tony. I'm sure he could persuade her.

Paul But she won't, Penny. He's been trying all day.

Penny Where is he now?

Paul (*Crossing below table to R.*) I don't know—I suppose walking around the block again. Anyhow, she won't talk to him.

Penny Maybe Tony can catch her as she's leaving.

Paul It won't help, Penny.

Penny No, I don't suppose so. . . . I feel so sorry for Tony, too. (**Grandpa** *comes down stairs L. unsmiling, but not too depressed by the situation.* **Penny,** *anxiously, rises*) Well?—Grandpa?

Grandpa Now, Penny, let the girl alone.

Penny But, Grandpa—

Grandpa (*Crossing back of table to chair R.*) Suppose she *goes* to the Adirondacks? She'll be back. You can take just so much Adirondacks, and then you come home.

Penny (*Sits desk chair*) Oh, but it's all so terrible, Grandpa.

Grandpa In a way, but it has its bright side, too. (*Sits R. of table*)

Paul How do you mean?

Grandpa Well, Mr Kirby getting into the patrol wagon, for one thing, and the expression on his face when he and Donald had to take a bath together. I'll never forget that if I live to be a hundred, and I warn you people I intend to. If I can have things like that going on.

Penny (*Rises—crosses to L. of table*) Oh, it was even worse with Mrs Kirby. When the matron stripped her. There was a burlesque dancer there and she kept singing a strip song while Mrs Kirby undressed. (*She goes back to desk*)

Grandpa I'll bet you Bar Harbor is going to seem pretty dull to the Kirbys this summer. (*With a determined step,* **Alice** *comes swiftly down stairs. Over her arm she carries a couple of dresses. Looking neither to R. nor L., she heads for kitchen*) Need any help, Alice? (**Ed** *starts down stairs carrying suitcase and hatbox*)

Alice (*In a strained voice*) No thanks, Grandpa. I'm just going to press these.

Penny Alice, dear—

Grandpa Now, Penny. (**Ed** *has appeared in hallway with a hatbox, etc.,* **Essie** *behind him*)

Ed (*Puts bags in hall*) I'll bring the big bag down as soon as you're ready, Alice.

Alice Thank you.

Essie Do you want to take some candy along for the train, Alice?

Alice No, thanks, Essie.

Penny (*Crossing step to R.*) Really, Alice, you could be just as alone here as you could in the mountains. You could stay right in your room all the time.

Alice (*Quietly*) No, Mother, I want to be by myself—away from everybody. (*She includes the whole group. Crosses down to table—picks up a dart*) I love you all—you know that. But I just have to go away for a while. I'll be all right. . . . Father, did you phone for a cab?

Paul No, I didn't know you wanted one.

Penny Oh, I told Mr De Pinna to tell you, Paul. Didn't he tell you?

Ed Oh, he told *me*, but I forgot.

Alice (*The final straw*) Oh, I wish I lived in a family that didn't always forget *every*thing. That—that behaved the way *other* people's families do. I'm sick of corn flakes, and—Donald, and—oh—(*Unconsciously, in her impatience, is surprised to find dart suddenly in her hand*)—everything! (*She dashes dart to floor*) Why can't we be like other people? Roast beef, and two green vegetables, and—doilies on the table and—a place you could bring your friends to—without—(*Unable to control herself further, she bursts out of room, into kitchen U.R.*)

Essie I'll—see if I can do anything. (*She goes into kitchen U.R.*) (*The others look at each other for a moment, helplessly.* **Penny,** *with a sigh, drops into her chair again.* **Paul** *drifts R.* **Grandpa** *mechanically picks up dart from floor; smooths out the feathers, sits.* **Ed** *crosses to xylophone with a futile gesture, runs his hammer idly over xylophone keys. He stops quickly as every head turns to look at him. The sound of the door opening, and* **Tony** *appears in archway. A worried and disheveled* **Tony**)

Penny (*Rises quickly*) Tony, talk to her! She's in the kitchen.

Tony Thanks. (*He goes immediately into kitchen. The family, galvanized, listen intently. Almost immediately* **Alice** *emerges from kitchen again, followed by* **Tony.** *She crosses living-room and starts quickly up stairs*) Alice, won't you listen to me? Please!

Alice (*Not stopping*) Tony, it's no use.

Tony (*Following her*) Alice, you're not being fair. At least let me talk to you. (*They are both gone—*

up the stairs) (**Essie** *comes out of kitchen*)

Essie Where'd they go?

(**Ed** *with a gesture, indicates upstairs region*)

Ed Upstairs.

Essie (*Looking upstairs*) She walked right out the minute he came in. (**Penny** *sits at desk.* **Essie** *sits L. of table as* **De Pinna** *also emerges from kitchen U.R.*)

De Pinna (*Crossing down to* **Grandpa**) Knocked the olive oil right out of my hand. I'm going to smell kind of fishy.

Grandpa How're you feeling, Mr De Pinna? Hand still hurting you?

De Pinna No, it's better.

Paul Everything burnt up, huh? Downstairs?

De Pinna (*Nodding, sadly*) Everything. And my Roman costume, too.

Grandpa (*To* **Penny**) M-m-m. I told you there was a bright side to everything. All except my twenty-three years' back income tax. (*He pulls an envelope out of his pocket*) I get another letter every day.

De Pinna Say, what are you going to do about that, Grandpa?

Grandpa Well, I had a kind of idea yesterday. It may not work, (**Kolenkhov** *starts on from U.L. door*) but I'm trying it, anyhow.

De Pinna (*Eagerly*) What is it?

(*Suddenly* **Kolenkhov** *appears in the arch U.L.*)

Kolenkhov Good evening, everybody!

Penny Why, Mr Kolenkhov!

Grandpa Hello, Kolenkhov.

Kolenkhov Forgive me. The door was open.

Grandpa Come on in.

Kolenkhov (*Comes into room*) You will excuse my coming today. I realize you are—upset.

Penny That's all right, Mr Kolenkhov.

Essie I don't think I can take a lesson, Mr Kolenkhov. I don't feel up to it.

Kolenkhov (*Uncertainly*) Well, I—ah—

Penny Oh, but do stay to dinner, Mr Kolenkhov. We've got all the food out there, and somebody's got to eat it.

Kolenkhov I will be happy to, Madame Sycamore.

Penny Fine.

Kolenkhov Thank you. . . . Now, I wonder if I know you well enough to ask of you a great favour.

Penny Why, of course, Mr Kolenkhov. What is it?

Kolenkhov (*Comes D.S.*) You have heard me talk about my friend, the Grand Duchess Olga Katrina.

Penny Yes?

Kolenkhov She is a great woman, the Grand Duchess. (*To group*) Her cousin was the Czar of Russia, and today she is a waitress in Childs' Restaurant, Times Square.

Penny Yes, I know. If there's anything at all that we can do, Mr Kolenkhov . . .

Kolenkhov I tell you. The Grand Duchess Olga Katrina has not had a good meal since before the Revolution.

Grandpa She must be hungry.

Kolenkhov And today the Grand Duchess not only has her day off—Thursday—but it is also the anniversary of Peter the Great. A remarkable man!

Penny (*Rises*) Mr Kolenkhov, if you mean you'd like the Grand Duchess to come to dinner, why, we'd be honored.

Essie (*Rises*) Oh, yes!

Kolenkhov (*With a bow*) In the name of the Grand Duchess, I thank you. (*Starts for door*)

Penny I can hardly wait to meet her. Where is she now?

Kolenkhov She is outside in the street, waiting. I bring her in. (*And he goes out U.L.* **De Pinna** *rushes to the cellar door for his coat off stage*)

Penny (*Feverishly*) Ed, straighten your tie. Essie, your dress. How do I look? All right?

(**Kolenkhov** *appears in hallway and stands at rigid attention*)

Grandpa You know, if this keeps on I want to live to be a hundred and *fifty*.

Kolenkhov (*His voice booming*) The Grand Duchess Olga Katrina! (*And* **Grand Duchess Olga Katrina**, *wheat cakes and maple syrup out of her life for the day, sweeps into the room. She wears a dinner gown that has seen better days, and the whole is surmounted by an extremely tacky-looking evening wrap, trimmed with bits of ancient and moth-eaten fur. But once a Grand Duchess, always a Grand Duchess. She rises above everything—Childs, evening wrap, and all*) Your Highness, permit me to present Madame Sycamore—(**Penny**, *having seen a movie or two in her time, knows just what to do. She curtsies right to the floor, and catches hold of a chair just in time*) Madame Carmichael—(**Essie** *does a curtsy that begins where all others leave off. Starting on her toes, she merges 'The Dying Swan' with an extremely elaborate genuflection*) Grandpa—

Grandpa (*With a little bow*) Madame.

Kolenkhov Mr Carmichael, Mr Sycamore, and Mr

De Pinna.

(**Paul** and **Ed** *content themselves with courteous little bows, but not so the social-minded* **De Pinna**. *He curtsies to the floor—and stays there for a moment*)

Grandpa All right now, Mr De Pinna.

(**De Pinna** *gets to his feet again.* **Essie** *crosses down to chair L. of table*)

Penny Will you be seated, Your Highness?

Grand Duchess (*Sits L. of table*) Thank you. You are most kind. (**Grandpa** *sits*)

Penny (**Essie** *sits above table*) We are honored to receive you, Your Highness. (*Backing away*)

Grand Duchess I am most happy to be here. How soon is dinner? (*To* **Penny**)

Penny (*A little startled*) Oh, it'll be quite soon, Your Highness—very soon.

Grand Duchess I do not mean to be rude, but I must be back at the restaurant by eight o'clock. I am substituting for another waitress.

Kolenkhov I will make sure you are on time, Your Highness.

Grand Duchess Thank you, Kolenkhov.

De Pinna You know, Highness, I think you *waited on me* in Childs' once. The Seventy-second Street place?

Grand Duchess No, no. That was my sister.

Kolenkhov The Grand Duchess Natasha.

Grand Duchess *I* work in Times Square.

De Pinna Oh!

Grandpa Quite a lot of your folks living over here now, aren't there?

Grand Duchess (*To* **Grandpa**) Oh, yes—many. (*Front*) My uncle, the Grand Duke Sergei—he is an *elevator man* at Macy's. A very nice man. (*To* **Grandpa**) Then there is my cousin, Prince Alexis. He will not speak to the rest of us because he works at Hattie Carnegie. He is in ladies' underwear.

Kolenkhov When he was selling hot dogs at Coney Island he was willing to talk to you.

Grand Duchess Ah, Kolenkhov, our time is coming. My sister, Natasha, is studying to be a manicurist, Uncle Sergei they have promised to make floor-walker, and next month I get transferred to the *Fifth Avenue* Childs'. From there it is only a step to *Schraffts'*, and (*To* **Grandpa**) then we will see what Prince Alexis says!

Grandpa (*Nodding*) I think you've got him.

Grand Duchess You are telling *me*? (*She laughs in a triumphant Russian laugh, in which* **Kolenkhov** *joins*)

Penny Your Highness—did you know the Czar? Personally, I mean.

Grand Duchess Of course—he was my cousin. It was terrible, what happened, but perhaps it was for the best. Where could he get a job now?

Kolenkhov Pravda, Pravda. That is true.

Grand Duchess (*Philosophically*) And poor relations are poor relations. It is the same in every family. My cousin, the King of Sweden—he was very nice to us for about ten years. Every once in a while he would send a money order. But then he said, (*To* **Grandpa**) I just cannot go on. I am not doing so well myself. I do not blame him.

Penny No, of course not. . . . Would you excuse me for just a moment? (*She goes to foot of stairs and stands peering up anxiously, hoping for news of* **Alice**)

De Pinna (*The historian at heart. Crosses in a step*) Tell me, Grand Duchess, is it true what they say about Rasputin?

Grand Duchess Everyone wants to know about Rasputin. . . . Yes, my dear sir, it is true. And how.

De Pinna You don't say?

Kolenkhov Your Highness, we have to watch the time.

Grand Duchess Yes, I must not be late. The manager does not like me. He is a Communist. (*To* **Penny**)

Penny We'll hurry things up. Essie, why don't you go out in the kitchen and see if you can help Rheba? (**De Pinna** *crossing D.R.* **Paul** *drifts U.S.*)

Grand Duchess (*Rising.* **Essie** *and* **Grandpa** *also rise,* **Ed** *backs U.S.*) I will help, too. I am a very good cook.

Penny Oh, but Your Highness! Not on your day off!

Grand Duchess I do not mind. (*Front turn*) Where is your kitchen? (**Kolenkhov** *takes her wrap to hatrack*)

Essie Right through here, but you're the guest of honor, Your Highness.

Grand Duchess But I love to cook! Come, Kolenkhov! (*Beckons to* **Kolenkhov**) If they have got sour cream and pot-cheese I will make you some blintzes! (*And sweeps through kitchen door*)

Kolenkhov Ah! Blintzes! . . . Come, Pavlowa! We show you something! (*With* **Essie**, *he goes into the kitchen*)

De Pinna Say! The Duchess is all right, isn't she? Hey, Duchess! Can I help? (*And into the kitchen*)

Ed Gee! She's got a wonderful face for a mask, hasn't she?

Penny Really, she's a very nice woman, you know. Considering she's a Grand Duchess.

Grandpa Wonderful what some people go through, isn't it? And still keep kind of gay, too.

Penny M-m. She made me forget about everything for a minute. (*She returns to stairs and stands listening*)

Paul I'd better call that cab, I suppose.

Penny No, wait, Paul. Here they are. Maybe Tony has—(*She stops as* **Alice**'s *step is heard on stair. She enters—dressed for traveling.* **Tony** *looms up behind her*)

Alice (*Crossing to above table*) Ed, will you go up and bring my bag down?

Tony (*Quickly*) Don't you do it, Ed! (**Ed** *hesitates, uncertain*)

Alice Ed, please!

Tony (*A moment's pause; then he gives up*) All right, Ed. Bring it down. (**Ed** *goes up stairs*) Do you know that you've got the stubbornest daughter in all forty-eight states? (*The doorbell rings*)

Alice That must be the cab. (*She goes to door*) (**Tony** *crosses to U.C.* **Paul** *crosses to R.*)

Grandpa If it is, it's certainly wonderful service. (*To the considerable surprise of everyone, the voice of* **Kirby** *is heard at the front door.* **Grandpa** *rises, goes to back of his chair*)

Kirby Is Tony here, Alice?

Alice (*At R. of arch*) Yes. Yes, he is. Come in, Mr Kirby. (**Kirby** *comes in*)

Grandpa How do you do?

Kirby (*Uncomfortably*) Ah—good evening.

Penny Good evening.

Kirby Forgive my intruding. . . . Tony, I want you to come home with me. Your mother is very upset.

Tony (*He looks at* **Alice**) Very well, Father. . . . Good-bye, Alice.

Alice (*Very low*) Good-bye, Tony.

Kirby (*Trying to ease the situation*) I need hardly say that this is as painful to Mrs Kirby and myself as it is to you people. I—I'm sorry, but I'm sure you understand.

Grandpa (*Coming down to table*) Well, yes—and in a way, no. Now, I'm not the kind of person tries to run other people's lives, but the fact is, Mr Kirby, I don't think these two young people have got as much sense as—ah—you and I have.

Alice (*Tense*) Grandpa, will you please not do this?

Grandpa (*Disarmingly*) I'm just talking to Mr Kirby. A cat can look at a king, can't he? (**Alice**, *with no*

further words, takes up phone and dials. There is finality in her every movement)

Penny You—you want me to do that for you, Alice?

Alice No, thanks, Mother.

Paul (*Looks at* **Penny**) You've got quite a while before the train goes, Alice.

Alice (*Into phone*) Will you send a cab to 761 Claremont, right away, please? . . . That's right. Thank you. (*She hangs up. Starts R.*)

Paul Alice!

Alice (*Embrace*) Father!

Kirby Are you ready, Tony?

Grandpa Mr Kirby, I suppose after last night you think this family is kind of crazy?

Kirby No, I would not say that, although I am not accustomed to going out to dinner and spending the night in jail.

Grandpa Well, you've got to remember, Mr Kirby, you came on the wrong night. Now tonight, I'll bet you, nothing'll happen at all. Maybe. (*Coming down R. of his chair*)

Kirby (*Crossing to table*) Mr Vanderhof, it was not merely last night that convinced Mrs Kirby and myself that this engagement would be unwise.

Tony Father, I can handle my own affairs. (*He crosses to* **Alice** *stage R.*) Alice, for the last time, will you marry me?

Alice No, Tony. I know exactly what your father means, and he's right.

Tony No, he's *not*, Alice.

Grandpa (*Crosses to them*) Alice, you're in love with this boy, and you're not marrying him because we're the kind of people we are.

Alice Grandpa—

Grandpa I know. You think the two families wouldn't get along. Well, maybe they wouldn't—but who says they're right and we're wrong?

Alice I didn't say that, Grandpa. I only feel—

Grandpa Well, what *I* feel is that Tony's too nice a boy to wake up twenty years from now with nothing in his life but stocks and bonds. (**Alice** *and* **Tony** *drift upstage*)

Kirby How's that?

Grandpa (*Turning to* **Kirby** *and crossing to below table*) Yes. Mixed up and unhappy, the way you are.

Kirby (*Outraged*) I beg your pardon, Mr Vanderhof. I am a very happy man. (**Alice** *crosses to printing press*)

Grandpa Are you?

Kirby Certainly I am.

Grandpa (*Sits*) I don't think so. What do you think you get your indigestion from? Happiness? No, sir. You get it because most of your time is spent in doing things you don't want to do.

Kirby I don't do anything I don't want to do.

Grandpa Yes, you do. You said last night that at the end of a week in Wall Street you're pretty near crazy. Why do you keep on doing it?

Kirby Why do I keep on—why, that's my *business*. A man can't give up his business.

Grandpa Why not? You've got all the money you need. You can't take it with you.

Kirby That's a very easy thing to say, Mr Vanderhof. But I have spent my entire life building up my business.

Grandpa And what's it got you? Same kind of mail every morning, same kind of deals, same kind of meetings, same dinners at night, same indigestion. Where does the fun come in? Don't you think there ought to be something *more*, Mr Kirby? You must have wanted more than that when you started out. We haven't got too much time, you know—any of us.

Kirby What do you expect me to do? Live the way *you* do? Do nothing?

Grandpa Well, I have a lot of fun. Time enough for everything—read, talk, visit the zoo now and then, practice my darts, even have time to notice when spring comes around. Don't see anybody I don't want to, don't have six hours of things I *have* to do every day before I get *one* hour to do what I like in—and I haven't taken bicarbonate of soda in thirty-five years. What's the matter with that?

Kirby The matter with that? Suppose we *all* did it? A fine world we'd have, everybody going to *zoos*. Don't be ridiculous, Mr Vanderhof. Who would do the work?

Grandpa There's always people that like to work— you can't *stop* them. Inventions, and they fly the ocean. There're always people to go down to Wall Street, too—because they *like* it. But from what I've seen of you I don't think you're one of them. I think you're missing something.

Kirby (*Crossing toward* **Penny**) I am not aware of missing anything.

Grandpa I wasn't either, till I quit. I used to get down to that office nine o'clock sharp no matter how I felt. Lay awake nights for fear I wouldn't get that contract. Used to worry about the world, too. Got all worked up about whether Cleveland or Blaine was going to be elected President— seemed awful important at the time, but who cares now? What I'm trying to say, Mr Kirby, is that I've had thirty-five years that nobody can take away from me, no matter what they do to the world. See?

Kirby (*Crossing to table*) Yes, I do see. And it's a very dangerous philosophy, Mr Vanderhof. It's— it's un-American. And it's exactly why I'm opposed to this marriage. (**Alice** *turns*) I don't want Tony to come under its influence.

Tony (*Crossing down from buffet. A gleam in his eye*) What's the matter with it, Father?

Kirby Matter with it? Why, it's—it's downright Communism, that's what it is. (*Crosses L.*)

Tony You didn't always think so.

Kirby I most certainly did. What are you talking about?

Tony I'll tell you what I'm talking about. You didn't always think so, because there was a time when you wanted to be a trapeze artist. (**Alice** *comes down*)

Kirby Why—why, don't be an idiot, Tony.

Tony Oh, yes, you did. I came across those letters you wrote to Grandfather. Do you remember those?

Kirby NO! . . . (*Turns away*) How dared you read those letters? How dared you?

Penny Why, isn't that wonderful? Did you wear tights, Mr Kirby?

Kirby Certainly not! The whole thing is absurd. I was fourteen years old at the time.

Tony (*Crosses a step*) Yes, but at *eighteen* you wanted to be a saxophone player, didn't you?

Kirby Tony!

Tony And at twenty-one you ran away from home because Grandfather wanted you to go into the business. It's all down there in black and white. You didn't always think so. (*Crosses U.S. to R.*) (**Alice** *turns*)

Grandpa Well, well, well!

Kirby I may have had silly notions in my youth, but thank God my father knocked them out of me. I went into the business and forgot about them.

Tony (*Crossing back to* **Kirby**) Not altogether, Father. There's still a saxophone in the back of your clothes closet.

Grandpa There is?

Kirby (*Quietly*) That's enough, Tony. We'll discuss this later.

Tony No, I want to talk about it *now*. I think Mr

Vanderhof is right—dead right. I'm never going back to that office. I've always hated it, and I'm not going on with it. And I'll tell you something else. (**Ed** *starts down the stairs and crosses down to* **Penny**) I didn't make a mistake last night. I knew it was the wrong night. I brought you here on purpose.

Alice Tony!

Penny Well, for heaven's—

Tony Because I wanted to wake you up. I wanted you to see a real family—as they really *were*. A family that loved and understood each other. You don't understand *me*. You've never had time. Well, I'm not going to make *your* mistake. I'm clearing out.

Kirby Clearing out? What do you mean?

Tony I mean I'm not going to be pushed into the business just because I'm your son. I'm getting out while there's still time.

Kirby But, Tony, what are you going to do?

Tony I don't know. Maybe I'll be a bricklayer, but at least I'll be doing something *I want to do*. (*Door bell*)

Penny That must be the cab.

Grandpa (*Rises and crosses a step to the R.*) Ask him to wait a minute, Ed. (**Ed** *exits hall door U.L.*)

Alice Grandpa!

Grandpa Do you mind, Alice? (**Alice** *goes to alcove—press—back to group.* **Grandpa** *rises, crosses up to* **Tony**) You know, Mr Kirby, Tony is going through just what you and I did when we were his age. I think if you listen hard enough you can hear yourself saying the same things to *your* father twenty-five years ago. We all did it. And we were right. How many of us would be willing to settle when we're young for what we eventually get? All those plans we make . . . what happens to them? It's only a handful of the lucky ones that can look back and say that they even came close. (**Alice** *turns.* **Grandpa** *has hit home.* **Kirby** *turns slowly to look at his son, as though seeing him for the first time.* **Grandpa** *continues*) So . . . before they clean out that closet, Mr Kirby, I think I'd get in a few good hours on that saxophone. (*Comes down to his chair*) (**Ed** *returns U.L. A slight pause after* **Kirby**'s *business.* **Grand Duchess,** *an apron over her evening dress, comes in from kitchen U.R.*)

Grand Duchess I beg your pardon, but before I make the blintzes, how many will there be for dinner?

Grandpa Your Highness, may I present Mr Anthony Kirby, and Mr Kirby, Jr? The Grand Duchess Olga Katrina.

Kirby How's that?

Grand Duchess How do you do? Before I make the blintzes, how many will there be to dinner?

Grandpa Oh, I'd made quite a stack of them, Your Highness. Can't ever tell.

Grand Duchess Good! The Czar always said to me, Olga, do not be stingy with the blintzes. (*She returns to kitchen U.R. leaving a somewhat stunned* **Kirby** *behind her*) (**Grandpa** *laughs, crosses D.R.*)

Kirby Ah . . . who did you say that was, Mr Vanderhof?

Grandpa (*Very offhand. Comes down to below table*) The Grand Duchess Olga Katrina. She's cooking the dinner.

Kirby Oh!

Grandpa And speaking of dinner, Mr Kirby, why don't you and Tony both stay?

Penny Oh, please do, Mr Kirby. We've got all that stuff we were going to have last night. I mean tonight.

Grandpa (*Sits R. of table*) Looks like a pretty good dinner, Mr Kirby, and'll kind of give us a chance to get acquainted. Why not stay?

Tony How about it, Father? Are we staying for dinner?

Kirby (*Shifting*) Why, if you'd care to, Tony, I'd like to, very much.

Tony (*Crossing up to* **Alice**) Now if Alice will send away that cab, Mr Vanderhof . . .

Grandpa How about it, Alice? Going to be a nice crowd. (**Alice** *starts down*) Don't you think you ought to stay for dinner? (**Alice** *is hesitant*)

Kirby I'm staying, Alice. The families ought to get to know each other, don't you think?

Alice Mr Kirby . . . Tony . . . oh, Tony!

Tony Darling. (*They embrace*)

Alice (*Crossing down and kissing* **Grandpa**) Grandpa, you're wonderful!

Grandpa I've been telling you that for years.

Essie (*Entering from kitchen U.R., carrying letter and butter dish. She crosses down to* **Grandpa**) Grandpa, here's a letter for you. It was in the icebox.

Grandpa Let me see. (*Looking at envelope*) The Government again.

Essie How do you do, Mr Kirby?

Kirby How do you do?

Tony (*Crossing to R. with* **Alice**) Won't you step into the office, Miss Sycamore? I'd like to do a little dictating.

Ed I'd better tell that cab. (*Exits U.L.*)

Grandpa Well, well, well! (**Ed** *enters U.L.*)

Penny (*Crossing to table*) What is it, Grandpa?

Grandpa The United States Government apologizes. I don't owe 'em a nickel; it seems I died eight years ago. (**Ed** *crosses to C. of buffet*)

Essie Why, what do they mean, Grandpa?

Grandpa Remember Charlie, the milkman? Buried under my name?

Penny Yes.

Grandpa Well, I just told them they made a mistake and I was Martin Vanderhof, Jr. So they're very sorry and I may even get a refund. (**Ed** *crosses to xylophone*)

Alice Why, Grandpa, you're an old crook. (*She crosses up to alcove with* **Tony**)

Grandpa Sure!

Kirby (*Interested*) Pardon me, how did you say you escaped the income tax, Mr Vanderhof?

Kolenkhov (*Bursting through kitchen door, bringing a chair with him*) Tonight, my friends, you are going to eat . . . (*He stops short as he catches sight of* **Kirby**)

Kirby (*Heartily*) Hello, there!

Kolenkhov (*Stunned*) How do you do?

Kirby Fine! Fine! Glad to see you!

Kolenkhov (*To* **Grandpa**) What has happened?

Grandpa He's relaxing. (**Ed** *strikes keys of xylophone*) That's right, play something, Ed. **Ed** *starts to play*. **Essie** *is immediately up on her toes as* **Kolenkhov** *goes up to xylophone and sings 'Goody-Goody!'* **Penny** *applauds*. **Kirby** *joins group at xylophone*)

Grand Duchess (*Entering from kitchen*) Everything will be ready in a minute. You can sit down.

Penny (*Pulling her desk chair over*) Come on, everybody. Dinner! (*They start to pull up chairs*) Come on, Mr Kirby! (**De Pinna** *enters from kitchen*)

Kirby (*Still interested in xylophone*) Yes, yes, I'm coming.

Penny Essie, stop dancing and come to dinner. (**Essie** *brings a chair from hall, dances to table*)

Kolenkhov You will like Russian food, Mr Kirby.

Penny But you must be careful of your indigestion.

Kirby Nonsense! I haven't any indigestion.

Tony Well, Miss Sycamore, how was your trip to the Adirondacks?

Alice Shut your face, Mr Kirby.

Kolenkhov In Russia when they sit down to dinner . . .

Grandpa (*Tapping on his plate*) Quiet! everybody! Quiet! (*Immediately the talk ceases. All heads are lowered as* **Grandpa** *starts to say Grace*) Well, Sir, here we are again. We want to say thanks once more for everything You've done for us. Things seem to be going along fine. Alice is going to marry Tony, and it looks as if they're going to be very happy. Of course the fireworks blew up, but that was Mr De Pinna's fault, (**De Pinna** *raises his head*) not Yours. We've all got our health and as far as anything else is concerned we'll leave it to You. Thank You. (*The heads come up again.* **Rheba** *and* **Donald** *in fresh uniforms come through kitchen door with a goose on a large platter and a huge stack of blintzes*)

Kolenkhov Grandpa, I have heard from my friend in Siberia. (*Curtain starts down*) He has escaped again!

Grandpa Save the stamp for me!

Penny (*On the cue '. . . friend in Siberia'*) Mr Kirby, do you like roast goose? We have roast goose for dinner.

Kirby Like it? Why, it's my favourite dish.

Essie Mr Kirby, I'm going to dance for you later. I've got a new mazurka.

Ed I've written some special music for it.

De Pinna Tell me, Mr Kirby . . . what do you think of The Securities Commission?

Paul Mr De Pinna, we've got to start thinking about next year's fireworks.

Alice Well, here goes the Adirondacks.

Tony And a very good thing, too.

CURTAIN

Alan Ayckbourn: *Mother Figure*

Superficially, *Mother Figure* (1976) is a comic play about a mother who can only utter baby talk. However, as with much twentieth-century drama, comedy is used to underline the pathos—terror, even—of the situation.

In various ways, some obvious, some hinted at, Lucy has withdrawn from the world into a single role of 'mother figure'. Any mother in the audience will recognise the despair which at certain times must overtake the most balanced of mums. Any women's-libber will be outraged at Lucy's plight, and at Terry's reaction to it:

Terry . . . Take me, I'm home on the nose six o'clock every night. That's the way she wants it. Who am I. . .? (*Pause*) Yes, I think I could quite envy your husband sometimes. Getting about a bit. I mean, when you think about it, it's more natural. For a man. His natural way of life. Right back to the primitive. Woman stays in the cave, man the hunter goes off roaming at will. Mind you, I think the idea originally was he went off hunting for food. Different sort of game these days, eh?
Rosemary (*hissing*) Terry!
Terry Be after something quite different these days, eh? (*He nods and winks*)
Lucy Now don't get silly, Terry.
Terry What? Ah—beg your pardon.

One of Ayckbourn's favourite motifs is male insensitivity towards women. Contact only with children has led Lucy into treating everybody as children. Rosemary and Terry are overwhelmed by this 'mother figure': Rosemary is crushed; Terry reacts with a spasm of male chauvinism. All this will make the audience laugh, but at the same time think: 'What am I laughing at? This isn't funny, it's tragic.' Just as Lucy does not allow her husband's telephone call to get through to her, so Rosemary and Terry are failing to communicate meaningfully with one another, and when Lucy treats them like children they quickly fall into bickering in the manner of children. Again, this is funny; until we realise that we are not witnessing children falling out, but a broken-down marriage.

Characters in the play

Lucy
Rosemary
Terry
Harry

Lucy's *sitting-room. It is a suburban room, fairly untidy, with evidence of small children. There are two doors—one to the kitchen and back door, one to the bedrooms and front door.*

(**Lucy** *hurries in from the bedrooms on her way to the kitchen. She is untidy, unmade-up, in dressing-gown and slippers*)
Lucy (*calling behind her*) Nicholas! Stay in your own bed and leave Sarah alone.
(*The telephone rings.* **Lucy** *goes out to the kitchen, returning at once with a glass of water*)
    All right, Jamie, darling. Mummy's coming with a dinkie . . . (*As she passes the telephone, she lifts the receiver off the rest and almost immediately replaces it*) Mummy's coming, Jamie, Mummy's coming.
(**Lucy** *goes off to the bedroom with the glass. The front door chimes sound. A pause, then they sound again.* **Lucy** *returns from the bedrooms*)
    Sarah! You're a naughty, naughty girl. I told you not to play with Jamie's syrup. That's for Jamie's toothipegs. . .
(*The door chimes sound again.* **Lucy** *ignores these and goes off to the kitchen. She returns almost at once with a toilet roll, hauling off handfuls of it as she goes to perform some giant mopping-up operation*)
    Nicholas, if you're not in bed by the time I come up, I shall smack your botty.
(*There are two rings on the back door bell.* **Lucy** *goes off to the bedroom. A pause.* **Rosemary**, *a rather frail, mousey-looking woman, comes in from the kitchen*)
Rosemary (*calling timidly*) Woo-hoo!

(*Lucy returns from the bedroom*)

Lucy (*calling as before*) Now go to sleep. At once. (*Seeing Rosemary*) Oh.

Rosemary Hallo. I thought you must be in.

Lucy (*puzzled*) Hallo?

Rosemary I thought you were in.

Lucy Yes.

Rosemary You are.

Lucy Yes.

Rosemary Hallo.

Lucy Hallo. (*A slight pause*) Who are you?

Rosemary Next door.

Lucy What?

Rosemary From next door. Mrs Oates. Rosemary. Do you remember?

Lucy (*vaguely*) Oh, yes. Hallo.

Rosemary Hallo. I did ring both bells but nobody seemed. . .

Lucy No. I don't take much notice of bells.

Rosemary Oh.

Lucy I've rather got my hands full.

Rosemary Oh yes. With the children, you mean? How are they?

Lucy Fine.

Rosemary All well?

Lucy Yes.

Rosemary Good. It's three you've got, isn't it?

Lucy Yes.

Rosemary Still, I expect it's time well spent.

Lucy I haven't much option.

Rosemary No.

Lucy Well.

Rosemary Oh, don't let me—if you want to get on. . .

Lucy No.

Rosemary I mean, if you were going to bed.

Lucy Bed?

Rosemary (*indicating Lucy's attire*) Well. . .

Lucy Oh, no. I didn't get dressed today, that's all.

Rosemary Oh. Not ill?

Lucy No.

Rosemary Oh.

Lucy I just wasn't going anywhere.

Rosemary Oh, well. . .

Lucy I haven't been anywhere for weeks.

Rosemary That's a shame.

Lucy I don't think I've got dressed for weeks, either.

Rosemary Ah. No, well, I must say we haven't seen you. Not that we've been looking but we haven't seen you.

Lucy No. Do you want to sit down?

Rosemary Oh, thank you. Just for a minute.

Lucy If you can find somewhere. (*She moves the odd toy*)

Rosemary (*sitting*) Yes, we were wondering if you were alright, actually. My husband and I—Terry, that's my husband—he was remarking that we hadn't seen you for a bit.

Lucy No.

Rosemary We heard the children, of course. Not to complain of, mind you, but we heard them but we didn't see you.

Lucy No. (*She picks up various toys during the following and puts them in the play-pen*)

Rosemary Or your husband.

Lucy No.

Rosemary But then I said to Terry, if they need us they've only to ask. They know where we are. If they want to keep themselves to themselves, that's all right by us. I mean, that's why they put up that great big fence so they could keep themselves to themselves. And that's all right by us.

Lucy Good.

Rosemary And then ten minutes, ago, we got this phone call.

Lucy Phone call?

Rosemary Yes. Terry answered it—that's my husband—and they say will you accept a transfer charge call from a public phone box in Middlesborough and Terry says, hallo, that's funny, he says, who do we know in Middlesborough and I said, not a soul and he says, well, that's funny. Terry says, well who is it? How do we know we know him? If we don't know him, we don't want to waste money talking to him but if we do, it might be an emergency and we won't sleep a wink. And the operator says, well suit yourself, take it or leave it, it's all the same to me. So we took it and it was your husband.

Lucy Harry?

Rosemary Harry, yes. Mr Compton.

Lucy What did he want?

Rosemary Well—you. He was worried. He's been ringing you for days. He's had the line checked but there's been no reply.

Lucy Oh.

Rosemary Has it not been ringing?

Lucy Possibly. I don't take much notice of bells. (*She goes to listen for the children*)

Rosemary Oh. Anyway, he sounded very worried. So I said I'd pop round and make sure. I took his number in case you wanted to. . .

(**Lucy** *is clearly not listening*)
    Are you all right?
Lucy Yes, I was listening for Nicholas.
Rosemary Oh. That's the baby?
Lucy No.
Rosemary (*warmly*) Ah.
Lucy I'm sorry. I'm being very rude. It's just I haven't—spoken to anyone for days. My husband isn't home much.
Rosemary Oh, I quite understand. Would you like his number?
Lucy What?
Rosemary Your husband's telephone number in Middlesborough. Would you like it? He said he'd hang on. It's from a hotel.
Lucy No.
Rosemary Oh.
Lucy Whatever he has to say to me, he can say to my face or not at all.
Rosemary Ah. (*Laying a slip of paper gingerly on the coffee-table*) Well, it's there.
Lucy Would you care for a drink or something?
Rosemary A drink? Oh—well—what's the time? Well—I don't know if I should. Half past—oh yes, well—why not? Yes, please. Why not? A little one.
Lucy Orange or lemon?
Rosemary I beg your pardon?
Lucy Orange juice or lemon juice? Or you can have milk.
Rosemary Oh, I see. I thought you meant. . .
Lucy Come on. Orange or lemon? I'm waiting.
Rosemary Is there a possibility of some coffee?
Lucy No.
Rosemary Oh.
Lucy It'll keep you awake. I'll get you an orange, it's better for you.
Rosemary Oh. . .
Lucy (*as she goes*) Sit still. Don't run around. I won't be a minute.
(**Lucy** *goes out into the kitchen.* **Rosemary** *sits nervously. She rises after a second, looks guiltily towards the kitchen and sits again. The door chimes sound.* **Rosemary** *looks towards the kitchen. There is no sign of* **Lucy**. *The door chimes sound again.* **Rosemary** *gets up hesitantly*)
Rosemary (*calling*) Mrs—er. . .
Lucy (*off, in the kitchen*) Wait, wait, wait! I'm coming. . .
(*The door chimes sound again.* **Rosemary** *runs off to the front door.* **Lucy** *returns from the kitchen with*

a glass of orange juice)
    Here we are, Rosemary, I . . . (*She looks round the empty room, annoyed. Calling*) Rosemary! It's on the table.
(**Lucy** *puts the orange juice on the coffee-table and goes out to the kitchen again.* **Rosemary** *returns from the hall with* **Terry**, *a rather pudgy man in shirt sleeves*)
Rosemary (*sotto voce*). Come in a minute.
Terry I'm watching the telly.
Rosemary Just for a minute.
Terry I wondered where you'd got to. I mean, all you had to do was give her the number. . .
Rosemary I want you to meet her. See what you think. I don't think she's well.
Terry How do you mean?
Rosemary She just seems. . .
Terry Is she ill?
Rosemary I don't know. . .
Terry Well, either she's ill or she isn't.
Rosemary Ssh.
(**Lucy** *returns from the kitchen with a plate of biscuits*)
Lucy Here are are now. (*Seeing* **Terry**) Oh.
Terry Evening.
Lucy Hallo.
Rosemary My husband.
Lucy Terry, isn't it?
Terry Yes.
Lucy That's a nice name, isn't it? (*Pointing to the sofa*) Sit down there then. Have you got your orange juice, Rosemary?
(**Terry** *sits*)
Rosemary Yes, thank you. (*She picks up the glass of orange juice and sits*)
Terry Orange juice?
Rosemary Yes.
Terry Why are you doing drinking that?
Rosemary I like orange juice.
Lucy Now, here's some very special choccy bics but you mustn't eat them all. I'm going to trust you. (*She starts tidying up again*)
Rosemary (*still humouring her*) Lovely. (*She mouths 'say something' to* **Terry**)
Terry Yes. Well, how are you keeping then—er, sorry, I'm forgetting. Lesley, isn't it?
Lucy Mrs Compton.
Terry Yes. Mrs Compton. How are you?
Lucy I'm very well, thank you, Terry. Nice of you to ask.
Terry And what about Har—Mr Compton?

Lucy Very well. When I last saw him. Rosemary dear, try not to make all that noise when you drink.

Rosemary Sorry.

Terry Yes, we were saying that your husband's job obviously takes him round and about a lot.

Lucy Yes. (*She starts folding nappies*)

Terry Doesn't get home as much as he'd like, I expect.

Lucy I've no idea.

Terry But then it takes all sorts. Take me, I'm home on the nose six o'clock every night. That's the way she wants it. Who am I. . .? (*Pause*) Yes, I think I could quite envy your husband, sometimes. Getting about a bit. I mean, when you think about it, it's more natural. For a man. His natural way of life. Right back to the primitive. Woman stays in the cave, man the hunter goes off roving at will. Mind you, I think the idea originally was he went off hunting for food. Different sort of game these days, eh?

Rosemary (*hissing*) Terry!

Terry Be after something quite different these days, eh? (*He nods and winks*)

Lucy Now don't get silly, Terry.

Terry What? Ah—beg your pardon.

(*A pause,* **Terry** *munches a biscuit.* **Rosemary** *sips her orange juice*)

Rosemary Very pleasant orange juice.

Lucy Full of vitamin C.

Terry No, I didn't want to give you the wrong impression there. But seriously, I was saying to Rosie here, you can't put a man in a cage. You try to do that, you've lost him. See my point?

Lucy That can apply to women, too, surely?

Rosemary Yes, quite right.

Terry What do you mean, quite right?

Rosemary Well. . .

Terry You're happy enough at home, aren't you?

Rosemary Yes, but—yes—but. . .

Terry Well then, that's what I'm saying. You're the woman, you're happy enough at home looking after that. I'm the man, I have to be out and about.

Rosemary I don't know about that. You'd never go out at all unless I pushed you.

Terry What do you mean? I'm out all day.

Rosemary Only because you have to be. You wouldn't be if you didn't have to be. When you don't, you come in, sit down, watch the television and go to bed.

Terry I have to relax.

Rosemary You're always relaxing.

Terry Don't deny me relaxing.

Rosemary I don't.

Terry Yes, you do, you just said. . .

Lucy Now, don't quarrel. I won't have any quarrelling.

Terry Eh?

Rosemary Sorry.

Lucy Would you like an orange drink as well, Terry? Is that what it is?

Terry Er . . . Oh no—I don't go in for that sort of drink much, if you know what I mean. (*He winks then reaches for a biscuit*) I'll have another one of these though, if you don't mind?

Lucy Just a minute, how many have you had?

Terry This is my second. It's only my second.

Lucy Well, that's all. No more after that. I'll get you some milk. You better have something that's good for you.

Terry (*half rising*) Oh no—thank you, not milk, no.

Lucy (*going to the kitchen*) Wait there. (*Seeing* **Terry** *has half risen*) And don't jump about while you're eating, Terry.

(**Lucy** *goes to the kitchen*)

Terry You're right. She's odd.

Rosemary I said she was.

Terry No wonder he's gone off.

Rosemary Perhaps that's why she's odd.

Terry Why?

Rosemary Because he's gone off.

Terry Rubbish. And we'll have less of that, too, if you don't mind.

Rosemary What?

Terry All this business about me never going out of the house.

Rosemary It's true.

Terry It's not true and it makes me out to be some bloody idle loafer.

Rosemary All I said. . .

Terry And even if it is true, you have no business saying it in front of other people.

Rosemary Oh, honestly, Terry, you're so touchy. I can't say a thing right these days, can I?

Terry Very little. Now you come to mention it.

Rosemary Niggle, niggle, niggle. You keep on at me the whole time. I'm frightened to open my mouth these days. I don't know what's got into you lately. You're in a filthy mood from the moment you get up till you go to bed. . .

Terry What are you talking about?

Rosemary Grumbling and moaning. . .

Terry Oh, shut up.

Rosemary You're a misery to live with these days, you really are.

Terry I said, shut up.

Rosemary (*more quietly*) I wish to God you'd go off somewhere sometimes, I really do.

Terry Don't tempt me. I bloody feel like it occasionally, I can tell you.

Rosemary (*tearfully*) Oh, lovely. . .

Terry If you think I enjoy spending night after night sitting looking at you . . . (*He throws the biscuit down*) What am I eating these damn things for . . . you're mistaken. (*Thirsty from the biscuits, he grabs her orange juice glass and drains it in one*)

Rosemary That's mine, do you mind (*She rises and stamps her foot*)

Terry Come on. Let's go. (*He jumps up*)

Rosemary That was my orange juice when you've quite finished.

(**Lucy** *enters with a glass of milk*)

Lucy Now what are you doing jumping about?

(**Rosemary** *sits*)

Terry We've got to be going, I'm sorry.

Lucy Not till you've finished. Sit down.

Terry Listen, I'm sorry we. . .

Lucy (*seeing* **Rosemary**'s *distraught state*) What's the matter with Rosemary?

Rosemary (*sniffing*) Nothing. . .

Terry Nothing.

Lucy What have you been doing to her?

Terry Nothing.

Lucy Here's your milk.

Terry Thank you.

Lucy You don't deserve it.

Terry I don't want it.

Lucy Don't be tiresome.

Terry I hate the damned stuff.

Lucy I'm not going to waste my breath arguing with you, Terry. It's entirely up to you if you don't want to be big and strong.

Terry Now, look. . .

Lucy If you want to be a little weakling, that's up to you. Just don't come whining to me when all your nails and teeth fall out. Now then, Rosemary, let's see to you. (*She puts down the milk and picks up the biscuits*) Would you like a choccy biccy?

Rosemary No, thank you.

Lucy Come on, they're lovely choccy, look. Milk choccy. . .

Rosemary No, honestly.

Terry Rosie, are you coming or not?

Lucy Well, have a drink, then. Blow your nose and have a drink, that's a good girl. (*Seeing the glass*) Oh, it's all gone. You've drunk that quickly, haven't you?

Rosemary I didn't drink it. He did.

Lucy What?

Rosemary He drank it.

Lucy Terry, did you drink her orange juice?

Terry Look, there's a programme I want to watch. . .

Lucy Did you drink Rosemary's orange juice?

Terry Look, good night. . .

Rosemary Yes, he did.

Lucy Well, I think that's really mean.

Rosemary He just takes anything he wants.

Lucy Really mean.

Rosemary Never thinks of asking.

Terry I'm going.

Lucy Not before you've apologised to Rosemary.

Terry Good night.

(**Terry** *goes out*)

Lucy (*calling after him*) And don't you dare come back until you're ready to apologise. (*To* **Rosemary**) Never mind him. Let him go. He'll be back.

Rosemary That's the way to talk to him.

Lucy What?

Rosemary That's the way he ought to be talked to more often.

Lucy I'm sorry. I won't have that sort of behaviour. Not from anyone.

Rosemary He'll sulk now. For days.

Lucy Well, let him. It doesn't worry us, does it?

Rosemary No. It's just sometimes—things get on top of you—and then he comes back at night—and he starts on at me and I . . . (*She cries*) Oh dear—I'm so sorry—I didn't mean to . . .

Lucy (*cooing*) Come on now. Come on. . .

Rosemary I've never done this. I'm sorry. . .

Lucy That's all right. There, there.

Rosemary I'm sorry. (*She continues to weep*)

Lucy Look who's watching you.

Rosemary Who?

Lucy (*picking up a doll*) Mr Poddle. Mr Poddle's watching you. (*She holds up the doll*) You don't want Mr Poddle to see you crying, do you? Do you?

Rosemary (*lamely*) No. . .

Lucy Do we, Mr Poddle? (*She shakes Mr Poddle's*

head) No, he says, no. Stop crying, Rosie. (*She nods Mr Poddle's head*) Stop crying, Rosie. Yes—yes.

(**Rosemary** *gives an embarrassed giggle*)

That's better. Was that a little laugh, Mr Poddle? Was that a little laugh?

(**Lucy** *wiggles Mr Poddle about, bringing him close up to* **Rosemary**'s *face and taking him away again*) Was that a little laugh? Was that a little laugh? Was that a little laugh?

(**Rosemary** *giggles uncontrollably.* **Terry** *enters from the hall and stands amazed*)

Terry Er. . .

(**Lucy** *and* **Rosemary** *become aware of him*)

Er—I've locked myself out.

Lucy Have you come back to apologise?

Terry You got the key, Rosie?

Rosemary Yes.

Terry Let's have it then.

Lucy Not until you apologise.

Terry Look, I'm not apologising to anyone. I just want the key. To get back into my house, if you don't mind. Now, come on.

Rosemary (*producing the key from her bag*) Here.

Lucy Rosemary, don't you dare give it to him.

Terry Eh?

Rosemary What?

Lucy Not until he apologises.

Terry Rosie, give me the key.

Lucy No, Rosemary, I'll take it. Give it to me.

Terry Rosie.

Lucy Rosemary.

Rosemary (*torn*) Er. . .

Lucy (*very fiercely*) Rosemary, will you give me that key at once.

(**Rosemary** *gives* **Lucy** *the key.* **Terry** *regards* **Lucy**)

Terry Would you mind most awfully giving me the key to my own front door?

Lucy Certainly.

Terry Thank you so much.

Lucy Just as soon as you've apologised to Rosemary.

Terry I've said, I'm not apologising to anyone.

Lucy Then you're not having the key.

Terry Now listen, I've got a day's work to do tomorrow. I'm damned if I'm going to start playing games with some frustrated nutter. . .

Rosemary Terry. . .

Lucy Take no notice of him, Rosemary, he's just showing off.

Terry Are you going to give me that key or not?

Lucy Not until you apologise.

Terry All right, I'll have to come and take it off you, won't I?

Lucy You try. You just dare try, my boy.

Terry All right. (*He moves towards* **Lucy**)

Rosemary Terry. . .

Lucy Just you try and see what happens.

Terry (*halted by her tone; uncertainly*) I'm not joking.

Lucy Neither am I.

Terry Look, I don't want to . . . Just give me the key, there's a good. . .

Lucy Not until you apologise to Rosemary.

Terry Oh, for the love of . . . All right (*To* **Rosemary**) Sorry.

Lucy Say it nicely.

Terry I'm very sorry, Rosie. Now give us the key, for God's sake.

Lucy When you've drunk your milk. Sit down and drink your milk.

Terry Oh, blimey . . . (*He sits*)

Lucy That's better.

Terry I hate milk.

Lucy Drink it up.

(**Terry** *scowls and picks up the glass.* **Rosemary**, *unseen by* **Lucy**, *sticks her tongue out at him.* **Terry** *bangs down his glass and moves as if to hit her*)

Terry!

Terry She stuck her tongue out at me.

Lucy Sit still.

Terry But she. . .

Lucy Sit!

(**Terry** *sits scowling.* **Rosemary** *smirks at him smugly.* **Lucy** *sees her*)

And don't do that, Rosemary. If the wind changes, you'll get stuck like it. And sit up straight and don't slouch.

(**Rosemary** *does so*)

Terry (*taking a sip of the milk*) This is horrible.

(*Silence. He takes another sip*)

It's warm.

(*Silence. Another sip*)

There's a football international on television, you know.

Lucy Not until you've drunk that up, there isn't. Come on, Rosemary. Help Terry to drink it. 'Georgie Porgie Pudding and Pie, Kissed the girls and. . .?'

Rosemary 'Made them cry.'

Lucy Good.

Rosemary } (*together*) 'When the boys came
Lucy } out to play, Georgie

Porgie ran away.

Terry (*finishing his glass with a giant swallow*) All gone. (*He wipes his mouth*)

Lucy Good boy.

Terry Can I have the key now, please?

Lucy Here you are.

(**Terry** *goes to take it*)

What do you say?

Terry Thank you.

Lucy All right. Off you go, both of you.

Rosemary (*kissing her on the cheek*) Night night.

Lucy Night night, dear. Night night, Terry.

Terry (*kissing* **Lucy** *likewise*) Night night.

Lucy Sleep tight.

Terry Hope the bugs don't bite.

Lucy Hold Rosemary's hand, Terry.

(**Rosemary** *and* **Terry** *hold hands*)

See her home safely.

Terry Night.

Rosemary Night.

Lucy Night night.

(**Terry** *and* **Rosemary** *go off hand in hand.* **Lucy** *blows kisses*)

(*With a sigh*) Blooming kids. Honestly.

(*The telephone rings.* **Lucy**, *as she passes it, picks it up and replaces it as before. As she does so, the Lights fade to a simple spot in a call-box.* **Harry** *is there, with the receiver in his hand*)

Harry Oh, blast not again. Hallo—hallo—oh, damn and blast. (*He jiggles the receiver*) Operator? Operator? Hallo—hallo . . . Operator, there must be a fault on the line . . . The line I have been trying unsuccessfully to dial . . . Yes—six-four-one-nine. I mean, this is quite unforgivable. This is the third time I have reported it and I am still quite unable to make contact with my wife . . . Yes, well, thank you for your sympathy. Let's try a little action, shall we? Because I'm going to take this to the top . . . Yes, top . . . What? . . . No—T for Toffee, O for Orange . . . Oh, forget it. (*He rings off*) Give me strength.

Alan Ayckbourn: *Gosforth's Fête*

In *Gosforth's Fête* (1976) Ayckbourn takes the old story of a disastrous village fête. It is a classic farce situation, and one that is built up in an original way, the pace increasing until all appears to go wildly out of control. Dialogue and action perfectly interlock, and in a stage performance it is very difficult to achieve exact timing in this kind of farce. The audience's attention must be made to focus precisely on one incident after another so that they miss nothing. Well-played farce requires great discipline, and should leave an audience gasping with both laughter and admiration.

The characters in *Gosforth's Fête* are apparently the stock figures of the spinster schoolmistress, the keen scoutmaster, the bumbling but well-meaning vicar, the behatted Tory lady, and so on. In village life everybody often does know everybody else's opinon and often the most gossiped about subject (in this case, Milly's pregnancy) goes unheard by some of the people it most concerns. Ayckbourn throws his characters into a situation which is nightmare for them and a riot of mirth for us, the audience. He puts them into a context which, despite all the outrageous happenings, is just about believable. So many funny things happen to them that we may be tempted to say: 'Very funny; but things just don't happen like this in real life.' Don't they? One theatre critic remembers laughing hysterically at the scene where scalding tea pours out of the urn while people run round with a relay race of cups in order to staunch the Niagara-like flow. Some time later in a BBC corridor he witnessed 'a newly installed automatic-vending machine going bananas and dispensing endless cups of steaming hot chocolate while a frantic producer tried to cope with the merciless fluid. People turned to each other at the time and muttered "Pure Ayckbourn"!'

Characters in the play

Mrs Pearce
Milly
Gosforth
Vicar
Stewart

A tea tent. One long trestle table, the odd bench or collapsible chair. In one corner near one of the entrances, a jerry-rigged rather large valve-type amplifier with wires leading from it to outside. Another entrance at the other end of the table.
Milly, *a fresh-faced pink woman, staggers in with a box of teacups. She is wearing an overall-coat. She dumps the cups on the table. She attempts to assess the number in the box without removing them. She is involved with this when* **Emma Pearce** *comes in through the other entrance. She is smartly turned out in a feather hat, light raincoat, white gloves with smart matching bag and shoes.*

Mrs Pearce Excuse me.
Milly I'm sorry, I'm afraid we're not serving teas for another two hours. Can I help you at all?
Mrs Pearce Well, I'm Emma Pearce.
Milly Em—oh golly. Councillor Mrs Pearce.
Mrs Pearce That's right.
Milly Oh. Golly. Um. Well. Has nobody met you?
Mrs Pearce No. I saw one or two people. They seemed rather busy.
Milly Oh, yes. . .
Mrs Pearce I parked just in the lane there. Is that alright?
Milly Fine. I should think. I'm afraid we're all a bit behindhand.
Mrs Pearce Yes. Well, Mr—er—Gosfirth . . .
Milly Gosforth, yes. . .
Mrs Pearce He did say in his letter two-fifteen.
Milly He should be about—somewhere. He was. I'm Milly Carter.

(*They shake hands*)

Mrs Pearce How do you do.

Milly It's very nice of you to come.

Mrs Pearce Quite all right.

Milly Is your husband any better?

Mrs Pearce Better?

Milly Yes. Hasn't he been ill?

Mrs Pearce No.

Milly Oh. I thought that's why he couldn't come. Sorry.

Mrs Pearce No. It's just he had some business to see to. He couldn't get away. At the last minute.

Milly Oh, I see.

Mrs Pearce So you'll have to make do with me. I'm afraid.

Milly Yes . . . Oh, no, Not at all. We all tremendously appreciate your being here. Really. Super. Really.

Mrs Pearce Thank you.

Mrs Pearce And it's for a jolly good cause.

Mrs Pearce Yes, indeed.

Milly I mean, it's just what this place needs—a new village hall. Did you pass the old one on your way here? You probably did.

Mrs Pearce Was that the building on the. . .?

Milly Yes. Just along the lane there. I mean, frankly, it's an eyesore. It was put up during the war. All corrugated iron. If you're holding a meeting and it rains, you might as well save your breath.

Mrs Pearce Oh dear. The weather looks a little threatening today.

Milly Yes. I do hope it doesn't rain. I mean, we can house quite a lot of our activities in the marquee over there—or even in the tea tent if the worst came to the worst, but there's things like Mr Stokes's Wolf Cubs' P.T. display—and couldn't fit that in here for instance.

Mrs Pearce Were those Wolf Cubs, all those little boys out there in gym vests?

Milly Yes. Were they behaving themselves?

Mrs Pearce They were throwing stones at a caravan. I told them to stop it.

Milly Oh lord, good for you. They won't take a blind bit of notice. They're all little horrors. Every one of them. But thanks for trying. No, you see it's vital we get a good attendance. Absolutely vital. Mr Gosforth has worked tirelessly. I'm o/c teas. Tea lady for the day. I usually teach at the school.

Mrs Pearce Oh, how interesting.

Milly Quite a challenge, I can tell you. Most of the children round here are as thick as two planks. We don't seem to have any budding village genius. . .

(*The sound of **Gosforth**'s voice is heard off, through a loud-hailer, shouting 'Keep off there, you boys'*)

Oh, here's Mr Gosforth.

Mrs Pearce Ah.

(***Gosforth** enters. He is beery-faced, shirtsleeved, perspiring, at present a born leader of men. In one hand, he carries a battery-operated loud-hailer, in the other, a plastic carrier-bag filled with clinking bottles. He looks as if he is in the thick of battle. As soon as he has entered, he turns and glares out through the tent entrance*)

Gosforth (*bellowing through his loud-hailer*) Will all you Wolf Cubs come down off that scaffolding at once. This is your last warning. (*Lowering the loud-hailer and turning into the tent*) Bloody little vandals, swarming all over it like . . . (*Seeing **Mrs Pearce***) Ah. . .

Milly Mr Gosforth, this is Councillor Pearce.

Gosforth Oh good lord, hallo. (*He puts the loud-hailer on the table and shakes hands*)

Mrs Pearce How do you do.

Gosforth Gordon Gosforth. So nice of you to come. Sorry I wasn't there to meet you. Been having a bit of a guy-rope crisis.

Mrs Pearce Oh dear.

Gosforth We rented both these damn tents, you see. Didn't really open them up until today. Didn't have the space. When we do, we find half the guy ropes are missing off the main marquee—this one's safe enough—had to do an emergency job. Not a window left in the district with any sash cord. (*He laughs*) Now, the curriculum goes as follows. Two thirty p.m. we plan to kick-off. I'll give you a short introduction—needn't be too long—as soon as you've finished—up strikes the band—got them coming over from Hadforth—they should be here—why aren't they?—then if you can mingle about a bit if you don't mind a spot of mingling—have a go at bowling for the pig—just seen Fred Crake's trailer so the pig's arrived safely, thank God—roll a few pennies and all that sort of thing—then, at three-thirty—if you can stay till then—I hope you can—Second Little Pendon Wolf Cubs' P.T. Display, organised by Stewart Stokes—that should go on for about half-an-hour—four o'clock tea, courtesy Milly Carter and assorted ladies—four-thirty, soon as they've swallowed their biscuits—novelty races, fathers' race, mothers' race, three-legged grandfathers' race, all that sort of rubbish—five-thirty to six—final round-off with an organised sing-song with the Hadforth Band—has the Reverend managed to get the song-sheets run off?—ten pounds to a quid he hasn't—six o'clock all pack up, dismantle tents—seven-thirty all cleared away because old Swales wants the field back for his cows first thing in the morning. Hope you can stay for a bit of the fun.

Mrs Pearce Yes.

Gosforth Sure you'll want to. Milly, where is that blasted man Fairchild?

Milly He said he'd be back. He had to go on a call.

Gosforth He had better be back. Not a solitary thing is working. (*To* **Mrs Pearce**) Penalty of having a local quack who is also the electrical expert. (*He indicates the amplifier*) Rigged up the entire sound system—got all the wires down—microphones—amplifier there, you see—loud speakers, the lot. Only trouble is, not a bloody thing's working. Now he's taken off on some emergency.

Mrs Pearce Oh dear.

Gosforth Oh dear, indeed. If he doesn't fix it when you make your speech nobody'll hear a word you're saying. . .

(*There is a rumble of thunder*)

That sounds ominous. Milly, my darling. . .

Milly Yes, Gordon?

Gosforth (*handing her the carrier-bag*) These are some prizes for the races. Half a dozen bottles of sherry. Could you hide them behind the counter where the Cubs can't get at them. (*To* **Mrs Pearce**) Advantage of running a pub. Ready-made prizes always to hand (*He catches sight of something going on outside the tent behind her*) Excuse me a minute. (*Snatching up the loud-hailer and shouting through it*) Reverend, over here. Reverend, would you mind . . . (*Lowering the loud-hailer, to* **Mrs Pearce**) Useful gadget this. Saves the voice. Would you like a look round before we start, Councillor Mrs Pearce? We may be a few minutes. I think you'll find it impressive. What there is of it so far, anyway.

Mrs Pearce Lovely.

(*The Vicar enters, laughing. He laughs a lot, especially when he is nervous*)

Vicar (*laughing*) Hallo there. Bad news, I'm afraid, Gosforth.

Gosforth What's happened?

Vicar I've been finally let down on the song-sheets,

I'm afraid.

Gosforth (*clasping his head*) Oh—(*inaudibly*)—help us. Pardon the language.

Vicar No, the man who owned the duplicator has gone out of business.

Gosforth Oh well. Delete community singing. Insert community humming.

Vicar (*laughing*) Community humming, I like that . . . (*Seeing* **Mrs Pearce**) Oh, I beg your. . .

Gosforth I'm so sorry. Councillor Mrs Pearce, this is John Braithwaite, our vicar.

Mrs Pearce How do you do.

(*They shake hands*)

Vicar How do you do. Very kind of you—to turn out. And how is your husband? Better, I hope.

Mrs Pearce He's not ill.

Vicar Oh dear, seriously?

Mrs Pearce No, he's not ill.

Vicar Oh, I beg your pardon. I thought you said he got ill. He's not ill. That's better.

Mrs Pearce Yes.

Vicar There's a big difference between not ill and got ill, isn't there? No, we don't want to get those two confused.

Gosforth John, I wonder if you'd like to show Councillor Mrs Pearce the lie of the land. Take her for a turn round the tombola.

Vicar Of course. Delighted.

Gosforth If you'll excuse me, Councillor—I think I'll have to pitch in to this public address system—see what I can do with it myself.

Mrs Pearce Yes, of course.

Gosforth Twelve loudspeakers strung all the way round the field and not a squeak out of any of them.

Vicar Would you care to follow me, Councillor?

Mrs Pearce Yes, of course. See you later.

(**Mrs Pearce** *exits*)

Gosforth Yes indeed. And Vicar, would you tell those confounded Wolf Cubs to come down off that scaffolding. It was only built for loudspeakers, you see.

Vicar I will, I will.

Gosforth They're not designed to take that sort of weight, you see.

Vicar Quite. Point taken.

(*The* **Vicar** *exits*)

Gosforth In fact, as far as I can make out, they're not designed to take any sort of weight. Now then, how's my little Milly, all right?

Milly I think we're all right. Old Mr Durban is

bringing the tea urn over in a minute.

Gosforth Splendid. Now then. . .

(*Thunder*)

Oh, grief. Hark at that. Now then, where do I start with this lot. (*He looks at the amplifier on the floor*) The amplifier seems to be working okay. (*He turns on the light*) Well, anyway, the light's on . . .

Milly Gordon . . .

Gosforth (*involved*) Just a second, lovey . . . I'd better start at the business end and work round. Loose connection somewhere. That's all it can be. (*He starts to examine the mike plugs and lead, testing them from time to time*) Hallo, hallo, one, two, three, four, five.

Milly Gordon, have you a minute, please?

Gosforth Hallo, hallo. Where the hell's that damn fiancé of yours got to?

Milly I don't know.

Gosforth Well, I wish he'd stick around. He could have helped me sort this out. He's never around when you need him. Those damn Wolf Cubs of his are running amok.

Milly Gordon, have you got a minute? Please. . .

Gosforth (*sitting on a chair, still fiddling with the mike*) Darling girl, does it look as if I've got a minute?

Milly It's frightfully urgent, Gordon.

Gosforth All right, old girl, go ahead. I'll just keep fiddling.

Milly Well . . . (*She pauses*)

Gosforth Uh-huh. . .

Milly It's really rather awful. It does seem terribly as if perhaps I might be pregnant.

Gosforth Oh yes.

Milly Yes.

(*Gosforth drops the mike, as he realises what she has said. The jolt causes the mike to become live. We hear, distantly, their voices echoing away on a series of loudspeakers. They alone, in their concern, remain unaware of this*)

Gosforth Did you say pregnant?

Milly I'm frightfully sorry.

Gosforth Me?

Milly There's no-one else it could have been, Gordon.

Gosforth Oh my God. (*He rises, with the mike*)

Milly I'm really awfully sorry. What are we going to do?

Gosforth Well. . .

Milly What am I going to say to Stewart?

Gosforth Oh. . .

Milly He'll be dreadfully upset.

Gosforth Yes, I can see he might, yes.

Milly He might refuse to marry me.

Gosforth Yes, I can see he might, yes.

Milly (*her lip trembling*) I don't know what to do.

Gosforth Now, easy, easy, Milly. (*He puts his arm round her*) Now, you're absolutely sure.

Milly Yes.

Gosforth Yes. Well. This needs thinking about.

Milly What's Stewart going to say when he finds out? What's it going to do to him? Everyone knows we're engaged. How's he going to face his Cubs?

Gosforth Well, he's a good bloke. He's a Scout, isn't he, after all. He's pretty decent. Now listen, Milly, we must just get through today first. Then we'll talk about it. You see?

Milly Yes.

Gosforth Don't worry.

Milly No.

Gosforth You're not to worry, we'll sort it out. But first things first. You get your tea organised and I'll see if I can get this wretched thing to—one, two, three—ah, success, it's working—don't know what it was I did but I—ah. . .

(*They looked at each other, appalled*)

Milly How long's it been on for?

Gosforth Very good point.

(*Stewart Stokes enters in full Scout kit. Normally a pink young man—he is now red with fury*)

Milly Stewart. . .!

Stewart You bastard, Gosforth. . .

Gosforth Hallo, old boy.

Stewart You complete and utter bastard, Gosforth.

Gosforth Now keep calm, Stokes.

Stewart I'm going to kill you, Gosforth.

Gosforth Stokes, keep calm.

Stewart With my bare hands.

Gosforth I warn you, Stokes, this thing is live.

Stewart Well, switch it off, you coward, switch it off.

Gosforth I don't know how to switch it off.

Stewart Haven't you done enough? How do you think it feels to hear the news that my fiancée is pregnant by another man? Isn't that bad enough? But when you publicly announce it over four acres of field . . . in front of all my Cubs. . .

Gosforth I say, Stewart, I'm sorry.

Stewart There are Brownies out there as well, you know.

Gosforth This is still on, Stewart, this is still on.

(**Stewart** *throws down his Scout's pole, seizes the mike and tries to wrest it from Gordon's hand*)

Stewart And turn it off! Turn it off!

Gosforth Steady, steady, steady. This thing is still on. Milly, turn it off. Turn it off!

Milly Wait, wait, stop it. (*She switches the amplifier off*) It's off now. It's off.

Gosforth Thank God.

Milly Stewart, we'll have to talk about this later.

Stewart I do not want to talk about this later. I do not want to talk about it at all.

Milly Stewart, please. It's no help to anyone getting in a state.

Gosforth She's quite right, Stewart old man, she's quite right.

Stewart (*collapsing in a chair, almost in tears*) Four acres—four acres. . .

Gosforth Steady, Stewart, old boy, steady. We'll sort it out, I promise. We'll all sit down later and sort it out. Milly, crack open one of those bottles of mine, would you? Give him a glass of sherry.

Stewart I don't drink. You know I never drink.

Gosforth Well, you're in need of one now. Milly.

Milly Yes, just a minute.

(**Milly** *opens a bottle and pours some into a cup, The* **Vicar** *sticks his head into the tent*)

Vicar Excuse me.

Gosforth Yes, Vicar?

Vicar Were you aware that your ill-tidings were being broadcast abroad?

Gosforth Yes. Thank you, John, we were aware.

Vicar I see. Oh dear. I'm dreadfully sorry. . .

Gosforth Yes. Thank you, John, thank you.

(*The* **Vicar** *goes*)

Oh well, sorry, Milly. There goes your reputation as spinster of this parish.

Stewart That's not funny, Gosforth.

Gosforth Sorry, old boy, sorry.

Milly (*bringing over the cup and bottle of sherry*) Here. . .

Gosforth Here we are. Drink up, old boy, drink up.

(**Stewart** *drinks reluctantly*)

Milly Perhaps he ought to lie down in the first-aid tent.

Stewart I don't want to lie down.

Gosforth The first-aid tent isn't up yet. Someone's swiped one of their poles.

Stewart I've got things I have to do.

Milly What?

Stewart I haven't finished the platform.

(*It starts to rain*)

Gosforth You haven't? Oh lord.

Milly What platform?

Gosforth The platform upon which Councillor Mrs Pearce is supposed to make her speech twenty minutes ago. We need that finished. Can't start at all otherwise.

Milly Well, can't someone else. . .?

Stewart It's all right. I'll do it, I'll do it.

Gosforth (*at the tent flap*) Oh no. Here comes the wretched rain.

Milly Oh no.

(*Thunder*)

Oh, just look at it. Nobody'll come and the ones that are here will go home.

Gosforth Dear oh dear. Like a monsoon. Hang on. I'll try raising their morale. Try and keep them here somehow. (*He snatches up the loud-hailer and stands in the doorway*) This is only a short shower. Please feel free to shelter in the main marquee. I repeat this is only a short shower. (*He lowers the loud-hailer*) I don't think that convinced anybody.

Milly (*suddenly*) Oh, heavens.

Gosforth What is it?

Milly I left the biscuits out the back. . .

(**Milly** *hurries out, after picking up a newspaper to protect her hair.* **Stewart** *sits drinking*)

Gosforth I wouldn't drink too much of that, Stewart old boy, if you're not used to it.

Stewart Go to hell, Gosforth, you fascist.

Gosforth Your platform's getting a bit damp out there. Want a hand to drag it in?

Stewart Go to hell, Gosforth, you swine.

Gosforth All right, I'll drag it.

(**Gosforth** *goes out, as* **Milly** *comes in with a cardboard box of biscuits*)

Milly Phew! Just saved them in time. Could you give me a hand, Stewart? Stewart . . .

Stewart Huh!

Milly Oh, well. Don't then. . .

(**Milly** *goes out.* **Gosforth** *comes in through the other doorway, dragging* **Stewart's** *platform. A small, square rostrum with a rail like a wayside pulpit*)

Gosforth Pity to let this get ruined. You put a lot of effort into this. Never seen such a shower out there. The lucky-dip tub's like a water-butt already. What was there left to do on this, Stokes? Stokes? Oh, come on, stop sitting there feeling sorry for yourself, Stokes . . .

(**Milly** *staggers in with a second box of biscuits,*

holding the wet newspaper on her head)

Milly Could one of you give old Mr Durban a hand with the tea urn? He seems to have got bogged down in the mud by the gate. He's stuck.

Gosforth All right, all right, I'll go. No use expecting our Boy Scout to do anything.

(Gosforth *goes out through the other door)*

Milly Oh, Stewart, honestly, just sitting there leaving poor old Mr Durban to cope. He's over seventy, you know—and those Wolf Cubs of yours are throwing mud at each other. I wish you'd try and control them. They should be taking shelter. Oh well, don't blame me if they all go down with pneumonia.

Stewart What made you do it, Milly?

Milly What?

Stewart With a man like—Gosforth? That fascist. . .

Milly Oh, don't drag politics into it, Stewart, for goodness' sake.

Stewart What made you do it, Milly?

Milly *(brightly)* Oh, I don't know. Can't remember now.

Stewart What do you mean, you can't remember?

Milly *(taking the newspaper from her head)* Well, I suppose I can, yes. It was while you were off at the Scout Jamboree.

Stewart Oh God. . .

Milly I went across to the pub to get some brandy—for Mother—she thought she had a cold coming. She wanted some in her hot milk.

Stewart Go on.

Milly Well—Gordon was there, behind the bar as usual. It was a very quiet evening for some reason. No-one in the saloon at all. He offered to buy me a drink.

Stewart He got you drunk. *(He takes another swig)*

Milly No, he didn't. Not very, anyway. Not as drunk as you'll get if you keep going at that the way you are.

Stewart Typical. Got you drunk and then took advantage of you.

Milly Do you want to hear what happened or not?

Stewart No. Yes—I don't know.

Milly Anyway. It sort of got late—and—Mother didn't get her brandy. Gordon closed up the bar and we sat on in there talking. He told me all about his ex-wife and I talked about you.

Stewart You talked to him about me? Us?

Milly Yes.

Stewart How dare you talk to that man about us.

Milly Oh, for heaven's sake, Stewart, if you're going to be righteously indignant, do take off that stupid hat.

Stewart This is not a stupid hat.

Milly It is on you.

Stewart This is my badge of office.

Milly And those absurd baggy shorts.

Stewart You always said you liked me in my uniform. . .

Milly Well, I don't any more.

Stewart I don't know what's got into you, Milly.

Milly I don't either. I've grown up, I think. I'm thirty-four, pregnant by a man I don't much care for and I've grown up. And not before bloody time. . .

(Milly *goes out,* **Stewart** *stands unsteadily, adjusts his uniform and pours himself another drink. The* **Vicar** *enters holding a notice-board over his head which reads: 'Grand Fête Today 2.30 p.m.' In his other hand, a microphone stand)*

Vicar My goodness, my goodness. Ah, Stewart.

Stewart Hallo, Vicar.

Vicar You—er—heard the broadcast—I take it?

Stewart Yes. I did.

Vicar I'm sorry. Not the most tactful way to hear that sort of news.

Stewart No.

Vicar It must have come as a great shock to you.

Stewart To everyone. Everyone heard it, you know.

Vicar Ah, yes. But then everyone knew it, you see. Except you, that is.

Stewart They did?

Vicar Oh, yes.

Stewart How?

Vicar Well, it's a very small village, isn't it? And the spectacle of Miss Carter being let out at the side door of the 'Fox and Hounds' at six a.m. on a Sunday morning is not all that common an occurrence.

Stewart I see.

Vicar If you hadn't been at your Jamboree, I . . . *(Holding up the mike stand)* I brought this in with me. I don't know if it's vital to anything.

Stewart Oh yes, it's the microphone stand, I think.

Vicar Ah. Well. Your Wolf Cubs appear to be rolling in the mud.

Stewart Let them. Who cares.

Vicar Well no, they're enjoying themselves. I don't know what their mothers are going to say. All those clean white P.T. vests.

(Gosforth *staggers in with the tea urn, followed by* **Milly)**

Milly Can you manage?

(*The* **Vicar** *goes to help, but burns his hand on it*)

Gosforth Yes—weighs a ton . . . (*Dumping it down on the end of the table*) Right. That's it. There we are.

Milly It's a good job you rescued him. Old Mr Durban had sunk in up to his knees.

Vicar Oh dear.

Gosforth Well now. Change of plan is called for, I think—Stewart, will you lay off that stuff. I think in view of the weather an early tea is called for. Can you manage that, Milly?

Milly Yes, I think so. I've seen Mrs Winchurch around somewhere. She can help me. My other ladies weren't due till three-thirty.

Gosforth And what the hell's happened to the Hadforth Band? They should have been here half an hour ago. Right. Revised schedule of event one. Opening speech by Councillor Mrs Pearce. . .

Milly In the rain?

Gosforth She needn't get wet. We can put that platform in the tent entrance there—she can stand just inside the doorway. Anyway, even if they can't see her they can hear her. As soon as she's through—tea. Then we just pray that by the time we've finished that, this lot will have passed over. We'll have to scrub round the gym display—I don't think the instructor's quite up to it anyway.

Stewart Go to blazes, Gosforth. (*He drinks again, from the bottle*)

Gosforth And to you, old boy. Now then, let's—where the devil is she?

Milly Who?

Gosforth Councillor Mrs Pearce? Where is she? What did you do with her, Vicar?

Vicar Oh. Yes. I think I rather lost sight of her during the—broadcast. I thought she was—that's odd. Oh dear.

Gosforth (*snatching up his loud-hailer and marching to the door*) Councillor Mrs Pearce. Would Councillor Mrs Pearce kindly report to the tea tent. (*Lowering the loud-hailer*) She can't have got far.

Vicar I'll see if I can find her.

(*The* **Vicar** *runs out with his notice-board over his head. A big clap of thunder is heard.* **Gosforth** *starts fixing the mike into its stand which he arranges in front of the platform in the doorway.* **Milly** *starts to put out a few cups and saucers*)

Milly I wonder how many there's going to be of them?

Gosforth How many cups have you got there?

Milly About three hundred and fifty.

Gosforth Well, I should start with about six. (*Examining the amplifier*) My God, the rain's getting on to this thing. It'll short out completely if we're not careful (*He moves it to the side of the table.* **Stewart** *obstructs him*) Look, Stewart, would you mind . . . Milly, will you get your boyfriend out of the road, please.

Stewart I'm not her boy-friend.

Milly He's not my boy-friend.

(*The* **Vicar** *returns*)

Vicar No sight nor sound of her. I hope she's all right.

Gosforth Where the hell has she got to? She can't have vanished into thin. . .

(**Mrs Pearce** *enters through the other door. Her feather hat is limp, her shoes and stockings coated in mud. She is exhausted and soaked.* **Milly** *stifles a scream*)

Gosforth Councillor Mrs Pearce!

Vicar Good heavens.

Mrs Pearce Oh. At last. . .

Vicar Do sit down, Mrs Pearce, please

Milly What happened to you?

Mrs Pearce (*breathless*) I went—I saw your church—I thought I had time to take a quick look. . .

Vicar Yes, yes. You're very welcome to.

Mrs Pearce It started raining—I found I'd lost my sense of direction. One of your Wolf Cubs finally directed me. . .

Vicar Good boy, good boy. . .

Mrs Pearce The wrong way. I finished up in a ploughed field.

Gosforth Typical. Pack of little vandals . . . Mrs Pearce, if you're feeling up to it, I really feel we ought to start the ceremony—for what it's worth. Then we can get on with our tea.

Mrs Pearce All right.

Gosforth Feeling fit?

Mrs Pearce Yes, yes.

Gosforth Right, then. Let's get weaving. With or without the Hadforth Band, blast them. (*Switching on the amplifier*) Just pray this thing's still working.

Stewart You swine, Gosforth.

Gosforth (*ignoring* **Stewart**) So far so good. (*He climbs on the platform. He taps the mike experimentally*) One—two—three—four—success. Good afternoon to you, ladies and gentlemen—boys and girls. (*Breaking off as he sights something*) Will you Wolf Cubs not persecute that pig, please. Now keep well clear of the pig—thank you. (*Resuming*) May I first of all thank you all for braving the elements this afternoon and coming along here to support this very worthwhile cause. That cause is, as we all know, the building of the new village hall. Something that eventually can be enjoyed by each and everyone of us in this community. I won't keep you longer than I have to—I'm well aware this is hardly the weather for standing about and listening to speeches. We will, in view of the circumstances, be altering our programme of events slightly. We plan to take tea in the tea tent, that is the tent from which I am speaking to you now, immediately after we have heard from our distinguished Guest of Honour. She herself needs very little introduction I am sure. Both she and her husband have both served as councillors for this ward for many years and during that time have, I feel—and here I'm speaking over and above any purely party political feeling—have, I feel, done tremendous work both for us and for that whole community to which we all belong. Without further ado, may I call upon Councillor Mrs Pearce formally to open the Grand Fête. Councillor Mrs Pearce.

(**Gosforth** *steps down to make room for* **Mrs Pearce**. *Meanwhile, under this previous speech*)

Vicar (*to* **Milly** *in a whisper*) Do you think it would be very wicked of me to sneak a cup of tea now?

Milly (*whispering*) Not at all. Help yourself.

Vicar (*whispering*) Thank you, I will.

(**Milly** *returns her attention to the speech. The* **Vicar** *goes over and takes a cup. Anxious not to get in anyone's way, he swivels the urn round so that the tap is directly over the amplifier. He turns on the tap and starts to fill his cup.* **Stewart**, *now lying on the ground, starts to sing softly*)

Milly (*to* **Stewart**) Ssh.

(*The* **Vicar** *having poured his tea, finds he is unable to turn off the tap of the tea urn*)

Vicar Oh dear.

Milly Ssh.

Vicar Help!

Milly What?

Vicar I can't turn off the tap.

Milly Oh, Wait. . .

(**Milly** *dashes over, hands him another empty cup to catch the flow and takes the full one from him. They continue this chain of filling cups, in between time*

trying vainly to stem the flow of tea from the urn without success. This continues until **Gosforth** *has finished his speech. As soon as he has done so,* **Mrs Pearce** *steps on to the rostrum*)

Mrs Pearce Ladies and gentlemen. I seem to have brought the wrong weather with me. I'm afraid. But this is an occurrence which I don't think for once you can blame on either me or the Conservative Party. It reminds me very much of a saying my husband is very fond of quoting. The rain in Spain may indeed fall mainly on the plain—but what's left of it seems to fall mainly in Kent. Joking apart, and I don't want to turn this into a political occasion in any way—but since we have been in control of your Council—I think everyone here will agree with me—the Conservatives have made startling progress—(*gripping the microphone*) progress not only for the rich among you but also for the not so well off—not only for the rich man in his castle—but also for the poor man at his gate—if I may, I'd like to take a brief look at our recent record on Council Housing. Over three hundred new houses in less than two years. Compared, I may remind you, with the previous Labour best of only a hundred and fifty Council houses. In other words, a hundred per cent increase. Startling indeed. . .

(*Under the above*)

Gosforth (*in an urgent whisper*) What the blazes are you doing?

Milly It's stuck.

Gosforth What's stuck?

Milly The tap's stuck.

Vicar Could we possibly turn it upside down?

Gosforth Why the hell don't you leave things alone?

(**Stewart** *has found the loud-hailer and begins to croon through it, softly at first, a selection of camp-fire songs*)

Stewart Ging gang gooly gooly gooly gooly watcha. . .

Gosforth Shut up, Stokes! Milly, get that off him.

Milly (*who is preoccupied running to and fro with cups*) How can I?

Gosforth (*wrestling with the tap*) Damn and blast this thing.

Stewart Here we sit like birds in the wilderness.

Milly Shut up, Stewart.

Stewart (*at* **Mrs Pearce**) Right-wing fascist propaganda.

Gosforth Stokes! Somone get him out of here.

Stewart Long live the Revolution!

Gosforth (*moving away from the urn*) Just a minute. Keep things going, keep things going. . .

(**Gosforth** *goes to* **Stewart**, *takes the loud-hailer off him and drags him roughly to his feet*)

Come on, you, come on.

Stewart Kindly do not molest me, you adulterer.

Gosforth Come on. Out in the fresh air. (*He drags* **Stewart** *to the other entrance*)

Stewart Baden-Powell for President.

Gosforth Come on.

Stewart Home Rule for Wolf Cubs.

(**Gosforth** *drags* **Stewart** *out.* **Milly** *and the* **Vicar** *continue to drain off the urn into a growing number of cups*)

Milly We're never going to drink all this tea.

Vicar Quickly, please, quickly.

Milly I'm being as quick as I can.

(**Gosforth** *returns, wiping his hands*)

Gosforth That's fixed him. Right. Next job. Now stand clear, Vicar, stand clear.

Vicar I don't think I should, I might. . .

Gosforth (*pushing him back*) Please stand clear.

(**Gosforth** *wrestles with the tap afresh. With the* **Vicar**'s *cup no longer there to catch it, the tea pours into the amplifier below. There is a loud buzzing and howling noise from the loudspeaker system.* **Mrs Pearce**, *who is holding the mike and still in full flow, suddenly begins both physically and vocally to oscillate violently.* **Gosforth** *manages to turn off the urn*)

Done it! (*Aware of the din*) What the hell's happening?

Milly Look . . . (*She points to* **Mrs Pearce**)

Vicar Good gracious. (*He runs to* **Mrs Pearce**) Mrs Pearce. . .

(*The* **Vicar** *and* **Gosforth** *lever* **Mrs Pearce** *away from the mike. The* **Vicar** *grabs the stand and gets a shock*)

Gosforth Steady, Vicar, steady.

(**Gosforth** *hits the* **Vicar**'s *hand from the stand, and turns in time to catch* **Mrs Pearce**, *who collapses*)

Give us a hand, Milly.

Milly (*going to do so*) Right.

Gosforth Are you all right, Councillor Mrs Pearce?

Mrs Pearce (*weakly quavering*) The Conservative Party have always striven. . .

Gosforth Vicar, can you and Milly lift her over to the first-aid people?

Vicar Very well, very well.

Gosforth I'll hold the fort here.

Mrs Pearce We have always believed in a fair deal for everyone. . .

Milly All right, Mrs Pearce.

Gosforth Where the hell's that bloody Hadforth Band? It's never here when you want it.

(**Milly** *and the* **Vicar** *assist* **Mrs Pearce** *towards the other exit*)

Vicar We'll take her to the first-aid tent.

Milly It's not up.

Gosforth Then tell them to get it up. This is an emergency.

(**Milly**, *the* **Vicar** *and* **Mrs Pearce** *go out*)

(*Surveying the scene for a second*) Oh dear God . . . (*He snatches up the loud-hailer and jumps on to the platform*) Ladies and gentlemen. Sorry about this. Just goes to show these little technical hitches can happen to the best of us. There's going to be another slight alteration in our schedule. In fifteen minutes, at three-fifteen, we'll be having the home-made cake judging competition in the main marquee, and after. . . (*There is a loud crash*) Oh my God. Now I warned you Wolf Cubs, that scaffolding was unsafe. Please stand back, everyone. Let the first-aid people through. Please stand well back. . .

(*There is the sound of a brass band approaching*)

Oh dear God, what a time to turn up. (*Through the loud-hailer again*) Hadforth Band! Hadforth Band! There are Wolf Cubs on the ground requiring minor medical attention—would you please be very careful where you march. I repeat, please be very careful where you are marching.

(*He leans on the platform rail which promptly drops away. As he falls through the tent entrance, the Lights fade to a Black-out*)

Willy Russell: *Our Day Out*

The text of *Our Day Out* (1977) looks different on the page when compared with the other plays in this book. At a glance, it is seen to be episodic, jumping from one group of characters to another and from one scene to another. This is because the play was written for television, which makes demands and gives opportunities to a dramatist which are unlike those generated by writing for the stage.

Willy Russell's play is about people he knows—the inhabitants of Liverpool, his home city. The play concerns a school-outing from the city into the countryside of North Wales, a novel experience for many of the kids. The class which is taken have particular difficulties learning to read and write well, but they are bright in other ways and they speak with a vigour which Russell has captured in the dialogue which he puts into their mouths. The characters can be divided into three groups: the kids, their teachers and the other adults with whom they come into contact along the way. So much happens to all the characters during the course of this fast-moving screenplay (the name given to dramatic script which is written for the small or large screen). The changed surroundings act as a catalyst, stimulating the kids into behaving in ways in which they might not behave in school (for better or worse).

Perhaps the most interesting change is in Briggs, the stiff and strict teacher sent along by the Headmaster to ensure that the more liberal Mrs Kay does not allow the trip to degenerate into a shambles. Briggs' destruction of the roll of film is sad: he cannot trust his ability to maintain the kids' (or staff's?) respect if he lets survive the record of the day's fun. He cannot laugh at himself, and we fear that come tomorrow he will he will try to forget that he has glimpsed a different way of seeing people—and that they have seen a different Briggs. The kids and Briggs have seen that each other are human. Russell has used the playwright's oldest trick—show people under stress or in a situation which is different from their habitual one, and things will happen which mean that they will never be quite the same again.

Characters in the play

THE TEACHERS
Mrs Kay (*in her early forties*)
Susan (*early twenties*)
Colin (*early twenties*)
Briggs (*early thirties*)
Headmaster

THE KIDS
Carol (*13*)
Reilly (*15*)
Digga (*15*)
Linda (*15*)
Karen (*15*)
Andrews (*13*)
Ronson (*13*)
Kevin (*12*)
Jimmy (*12*)
Maurice (*12*)
Other kids (*all around 12 or 13*)

OTHER ADULTS
Les, *the 'lollipop man'*
The Driver
Mrs Roberts
Waitress
John
Mac
Animal Keeper
Two other Animal Keepers

*Scene: In the street. The street is in the inner city of Liverpool. **Kids** are streaming in one direction. It is approaching 9 a.m. The **Kids** are pushing, shoving, rushing, ambling, leering and jeering. A group of older kids cross the road, ignoring the lollipop man's assistance. He points them out to a passing woman, obviously disgusted. **Carol** rushes along the street wearing a school uniform which doubles as a street* *outfit and her Sunday best. She is eating half a sand-wich and clutching a supermarket carrier bag. She arrives at the roadside and, as there isn't a vehicle in sight, goes to cross without bothering to enlist the aid of the lollipop man,* **Les**. *He stops her from stepping off the pavement.*

Les 'Ey you!
Carol (*Stopping*) What?
Les Come here. Come on!
Carol (*Approaching him*) Agh ey, Les. Come on. I wanna get t'school.
Les That makes a bloody change.
Carol We're goin' out. On a trip.
Les Now listen. Are you listenin'? Y' don't across the road without the assistance of the lollipop man. And that's me!
Carol There's nott'n comin', though.
Les Now just you listen; I know it might look as though there's nothin' comin' but how do you know that a truck or car isn't gonna come speedin' out of that side road? Eh?.
Carol (*Looking*) Oh yeh. I never thought of that.
Les No. I know y' didn't. Y' never do. None of y'. That's why the government hired me to look after y' all.
Carol Ta Les.
Les Ey. Where y' goin' today then?
Carol It's somewhere far away. I forget.
Les They all goin'?
Carol Only the kids who go the Progress Class.
Les What's that?
Carol What? Y'don't know what the Progress Class is? It's Mrs Kay's class. Y' go down there in the week if y' can't do sums or writing. If y' backward like.
Les By Christ, I'll bet she's kept busy. They're all bloody backward round here.
Carol I know. Come on Les. I wanna get there.
(*Les looks up and down the road. Not a vehicle in sight*)
Les Just hold it there.
Carol There's nott'n comin'.
(**Les** *looks down the road. In the distance a car is just appearing*)
Carol Oh come on, Les.
(**Les** *holds out his arm to prevent her from crossing. Only when the car is within striking distance does he walk out with his 'Stop' sign. The car pulls to a halt.* **Les** *waves* **Carol** *across*)
Les (*Quietly to* **Carol** *as she passes*) I got him that

time. Arrogant get that one is.
(**Carol** *continues on her way. The driver of the car glares as* **Les** *waves him on*)

Scene: **The school gates.** *A coach. Various groups of* **Kids** *are scattered nearby. One group surrounds a teacher,* **Mrs Kay**, *all of them after her attention. Cries of, 'Miss, miss, miss, me mum said I could go, miss,' and 'Miss, can I come if I haven't got enough money?' and, 'Miss, can I come, miss?'*

Mrs Kay All right, all right. Will you just let me have a minute's peace and I'll get you all sorted out. Right. Now those who've got permission to come on the trip but haven't yet paid, I want you to come over here.
(*She moves a short distance away and all the kids follow her.* **Briggs** *surveys this scene*)
Mrs Kay (*Bright*) Good morning, Mr Briggs.
Briggs (*Begrudged*) Morning.
(*He turns and enters the school*)
Briggs (*To a couple of boys*) Come on, move!

Scene: The **Headmaster's** *office. The* **Headmaster** *is talking to* **Briggs**, *who was the driver of the car.*
Headmaster Well I'd like you to go with her, John. We can get Frank Collins to take over your examination classes for the day. I'd just like you to be there and keep an eye on things. I don't want to be unprofessional and talk about a member of staff but I get the impression she sees education as one long game.
Briggs Well . . . if the antics in her department are anything to go by. . .! She always reminds me of a mother hen rather than a teacher. . .
Headmaster Well, anyway, just try and keep things in some sort of order.

Scene: **The school gates. Mrs Kay** *is talking to two young teachers,* **Colin** *and* **Susan**. *Around them are excited, lively kids—not lined up but in random groups.*
Mrs Kay (*Shouting to a* **Kid**) Maurice! Come away from that road will you?
(*The* **Kid** *does so. Two older* **Kids** *come rushing out of school and up to the* **Teachers**)
Reilly Miss . . . miss, can we come wit'y'? Can we?
Mrs Kay Oh, Brian! You know it's a trip for the Progress Class.
Reilly Agh, ay, miss, we used t' be in the Progress

Class though.

Susan But you're not now. Brian. Now you can read and write you're back in normal classes.

Mrs Kay Look Brian. You know I'd take you. But it's not up to me. Who's your form teacher?

Reilly Briggsy.

Mrs Kay Well, you'll have to go and get his permission.

Reilly (*As he and* **Digga** *rush off*) You're ace, miss.

Mrs Kay Brian!

(*He stops*)

Bring a note.

Reilly (*Worried*) Ah . . . what for, miss?

Mrs Kay (*Smiling*) Because I wasn't born yesterday, Brian Reilly, and if I don't ask you for a note you'll just hide behind the corner for ten minutes and say he said you could go.

Reilly (*Knowing she's got him sussed*) As if we'd do a thing like that, miss!

Carol (*Still tugging*) Where are we goin', miss?

Mrs Kay Carol . . . Miss Duncan's just told you. Conway. We're going to Conway.

Carol Miss is that in England, eh?

Colin It's in Wales, Carol.

Carol Will we have t' get a boat?

Mrs Kay Carol . . . we're going on a coach. Look, it's there. You can get on now.

(*She shouts out to the rest of the* **Kids**)

Go on . . . you can all get on now.

(*There is a wild rush of* **Kids** *to the coach doors. The* **Driver** *appears and blocks the way*)

Driver Right. Just stop there. Don't move.

Kid Miss said we could get on.

Driver Oh, did she now?

Kids Yeh.

Driver Well, let me tell youse lot something now. Miss isn't the driver of this coach. I am. An' if I say y' don't get on, y' don't get on.

Mrs Kay Is anything wrong, Driver?

Driver Are these children in your charge, madam?

Mrs Kay Yes.

Driver Well y' haven't checked them, have y'?

Mrs Kay Checked them? Checked them for what?

Driver Chocolate an' lemonade! We don't allow it. I've seen it on other coaches madam; fifty-two vomittin' kids . . . it's no joke. No, I'm sorry, we don't allow that.

Mrs Kay (*To* **Susan**) Here comes Mr Happiness. All right, Driver . . . I'll check for you.

(*To* **Kids**)

. . . Now listen, everyone. If anybody's got any

Jean Heywood as Mrs Kay in the first television production on BBC2, 28 December 1977. (BBC copyright photograph)

chocolate or lemonade I want you to put your hands up.

(*A sea of dumb faces and unraised hands.* **Mrs Kay** *smiles at the* **Driver**)

There you are, Driver. All right?

Driver No, it's not all right. Y' can't just take their word for it. They have to be searched. Y' can't just believe kids.

(*Pause.* **Mrs Kay** *stares at him. She could blow up but she doesn't*)

Mrs Kay Can I have a word with you, Driver, in private?

(*Reluctantly the* **Driver** *gets off the coach and goes across to her. She manoeuvres it so that he has his back to the coach and the* **Kids**)

What's your name, Driver?

Driver Me name? I don't usually have to give me name.

Mrs Kay Oh, come on . . . what's your name?

Driver Suttcliffe, Ronny Suttcliffe.

Mrs Kay Well, Ronny (*Pointing*), take a look up

these streets. (*He does and she motions the other teachers to be getting the* **Kids** *on the coach*) Ronny, would you say they were the sort of streets that housed prosperous parents?

Driver We usually only do the better schools.

Mrs Kay All right, you don't like these kids. I can tell that. But do you have to cause them so much pain?

Driver (*Shocked*) What have I done? I only told 'em to wait. . .

Mrs Kay Ronny, the kids with me today don't know what it is to *look* at a bar of chocolate. Lemonade never touches their lips. (*We almost hear the violins*) These are the children, Ronny, who stand outside shop windows in the pouring rain, looking and longing and never getting. Even at Christmas, at Christmas-time when your kids from the better schools are opening presents and singing carols, these kids are left to wander the cold cruel streets.

(*Pause as she sees the effect she is having. The* **Driver** *is grief-stricken*)

Scene: **Inside the coach.** *The kids are stuffing themselves with sweets and lemonade. The* **Driver** *comes on board and by the time he turns to face the* **Kids** *there is not a bottle of lemonade or chocolate bar in sight. The* **Driver** *puts his hand into his pocket and pulls out a pound note.*

Driver Here you are, son (*to* **Kid** in front seat), run over to the shops an' get what sweets y' can with that.

(*The* **Kid** *takes the money and gets off the coach.* **Susan**, *the young teacher, leans across to* **Mrs Kay**)

Susan What did you do?

Mrs Kay Lied like hell, of course!

(*She gets up and faces the kids*)

Now, will you listen everyone. We'll be setting off for Conway in a couple of minutes.

(*Cheers*)

Now listen! We want everyone to enjoy themselves, so let's have no silly squabbling or doing anything that might be dangerous to yourselves or to others. That's the only rule we have today: think of yourselves, but think of others as well.

(**Reilly** *and* **Digga** *rush into the bus*)

Reilly Miss, miss, we're comin' wit' y', miss. He said it's all right.

Mrs Kay Brian, where's the note?

Reilly He didn't give us one, miss. He's comin' himself. He said to wait.

(**Digga** *and* **Reilly** *go to the back of the coach.* **Mrs**

Kay *looks at* **Colin** *and* **Susan**)

Colin He's coming to keep an eye on us.

Susan Make sure we don't enjoy ourselves.

Mrs Kay Ah well. We'll just have to deal with him the best way we can.

(*She sits down next to* **Carol**. *On the back seat of the coach* **Reilly** *and* **Digga** *are facing some small kids*)

Reilly Right, punks. Move!

Little Kid Why?

Reilly Cos we claimed the back seat, that's why.

Little Kid You're not even in the Progress though.

Digga We used to be though, so move.

Reilly Yeh. Respect y' elders!

(*At the front of the coach,* **Briggs** *is climbing aboard. He stands at the front and stares and glares. The* **Kids** *sigh—he is a cloud on the blue horizon*)

Briggs (*Suddenly barks*) Reilly. Dickson. Sit down!

Reilly Sir, we was only. . .

Briggs (*Staccato*) Sit down, now, come on, move!

(**Reilly** *and* **Digga** *sit on the two small kids who move to make room for them*)

Briggs Go on, sort yourselves out!

(*He leans across to* **Mrs Kay** *and speaks quietly*)

You've got some real bright sparks here, Mrs Kay. A right bunch.

Mrs Kay Well, I think we'll be safe now that you've come to look after us.

Briggs (*Looking at the* **Kids**) There's a few of 'em I could sling off right now.

Mrs Kay Oh, you are coming with us then?

Briggs The Boss thought it might be a good idea if you had an extra member of staff.

(*Stands to address the* **Kids**)

Right, listen.

(*Pause*)

We don't want you to think that we don't want you to enjoy yourselves today, because we do! But a lot of you haven't been on a school visit before so you won't know *how* to enjoy yourselves. So I'll tell you. To enjoy a coach trip we sit in our seats. We don't wander up and down the aisle. We talk quietly to our neighbour, not shout at our mates four seats down. (*Staccato*) Are you listening, girl! We look nicely out of the windows at the scenery. And we don't do anything else.

(*Throughout the speech the* **Kids** *look disappointed*)

Don't worry, I've driven in my car behind school coaches and seen it. A mass of little hands raised in two-fingered gestures to the passing cars. Yes. But we won't do that will we? Will we?

(*Chorus of:* 'No, sir.')

Briggs No, sir. We won't.

(*The* **Kid** *returning from the shop, armed with sweets, climbs onto the bus*)

Kid I've got them . . . I've got loads. . .

Briggs Where've you been?

Kid Gettin' sweets, sir.

Briggs Sweets?

Mrs Kay (*Reaching for sweets*) Thank you, Maurice.

Briggs Sweets?

(*The* **Driver** *taps* **Briggs** *on the shoulder*)

Driver Excuse me, can I have a word with you, please?

Briggs (*Puzzled*) Yes.

(*The* **Driver** *gets off the coach and* **Briggs** *follows.* **Mrs Kay** *gives the sweets to* **Susan** *who starts to dish them out. We hear a snatch of the* **Driver**'s *speech to* **Briggs**)

Driver The thing is, about these kids, they're like little souls lost an' wanderin' the cruel heartless streets. . .

(*Inside the coach,* **Colin** *has joined* **Susan** *in giving out the sweets.* **Colin** *is at the back seat*)

Reilly How y' gettin' on with miss, eh sir?

Digga We saw y', sir goin' into that pub with her, sir.

(**Susan** *is watching in the background*)

Colin (*Covering his embarrassment*) Did you?

Reilly Are you in love with her, sir? Are y'?

Colin (*Making his escape*) All right . . . you've all got sweets have you?

Reilly Sir's in love, sir's in love!

(**Reilly** *laughs and jeers as* **Colin** *makes his way down the aisle*)

Susan Watch it, Brian!

Reilly (*Feigned innocence*) What?

Susan You know what.

Reilly Agh ey, he is in love with y' though, isn't he, miss.

Digga Miss, I'll bet he wans t' marry y'.

Reilly You'd be better off with me, miss. I'm better lookin'. An' I'm sexier!

Susan (*Giving up playing it straight. She goes up to him, leans across and whispers*) Brian . . . little boys shouldn't try to act like men. The day might come when their words are put to the test!

(*She walks away*)

Reilly (*Jeering*) Any day, miss . . . any day . . .

(*Laughs*)

Digga What did she say? What did she say?

Reilly Said she fancied me.

(*At the front of the coach,* **Briggs** *and the* **Driver** *are climbing back on board.* **Briggs** *sits opposite* **Mrs Kay**. *He leans across to her*)

Briggs (*Quietly*) We've got a right head case of a driver.

(*The engine roars into life. The* **Kids** *cheer.* **Briggs** *turns round with a warning look as the coach pulls away from the school. Thousands of little fingers raise in a V-sign out of the windows*)

Scene: **Leaving the city.** *As the coach goes along the city streets the* **Kids** *are talking and laughing and pointing. On the back seat.* **Reilly** *secretly takes out a packet of Number Six cigarettes. The* **Little Kid** *sees them.*

Digga Reilly, light up.

Reilly Where's Briggsy?

Digga He's at the front, I'll keep dixie. Come on, we're all right, light up.

Little Kid Agh 'ey. You've got ciggies. I'm gonna tell miss.

Reilly Shut up you an' open that friggin' window.

Little Kid No . . . I'm gonna tell miss.

Digga Go'n tell her. She won't do nott'n anyway.

Kid I'll tell sir.

Reilly You do an' I'll gob y'.

Digga Come on . . . open that window, you.

Kid Why?

Reilly Why d' y' think? So we get a bit of fresh air.

Kid Well there's no fresh air round here. You just wanna smoke. An' smoking' stunts y' growth.

Reilly I'll stunt your friggin' growth if y' don't get it open.

(**Andrews** *gets up and reaches for the window*)

Andrews I'll open it for y' Reilly.

(**Reilly** *ducks behind the seat and lights up*)

Andrews Gis a ciggy.

Reilly Get y' own ciggies.

Andrews Ah go on. I opened the window for y'.

Digga Y' can buy one off us.

Andrews I can't. I haven't got any money.

Reilly Course y've got money.

Andrews Me ma wouldn't give me any. She didn't have any.

Digga Go 'way . . . your ma's loaded.

Andrews No she's not.

Reilly Well she should be . . . all the fellers she picks up on Parly.

Andrews Go on . . . gis a ciggy.

Digga She's always with the blacks off the boats,

your ma. And they're loaded, them blacks are.

Reilly An you must have money 'cos they pay a fortune for a bit of White.

Andrews Well *I've* got no money . . . honest.

Digga Well, y've got no ciggies either.

Andrews I'll give y'half me sarnies for one ciggie.

Reilly What's on 'em?

Andrews Jam.

Reilly I hate jam.

(*They have become lax about keeping an eye out and do not notice* **Briggs** *getting up from his seat and approaching the back of the coach.* **Digga** *suddenly looks up and sees him*)

Digga Briggs!

(**Reilly** *passes the cigarette to* **Andrews**)

Reilly Here!

Andrews Ta.

(**Andrews** *takes it and, making sure that his head is out of sight, he takes a huge drag. When he looks up,* **Briggs** *is peering down at him*)

Briggs Put it out!

Andrews Sir, sir, I wasn't. . .

Briggs Put it out. Now get to the front of the coach.

Andrews Sir, I was just. . .

Briggs I said get to the front!

(**Andrews** *sighs, gets up and goes to the front of the coach.* **Briggs** *sits in* **Andrews**'s *seat*)

Briggs Was it your ciggie, Reilly?

Reilly Sir, I swear on me mother.

Digga Don't believe him, sir. How can he swear on his mother. She's been dead for ten years.

Briggs All right, all right. We don't want any argument. There'll be no more smoking if I stay up here, will there?

(**Carol**, *who is sitting next to* **Mrs Kay**, *is staring out of the window*)

Carol Isn't it horrible, eh, miss.

Mrs Kay Mm?

Carol Y' know . . . all the thingy like. The dirt an' that. (*Pause*) I like them nice places.

Mrs Kay Which places?

Carol Y' know them places on the telly. Where they have gardens an' trees outside an' that.

Mrs Kay You've got trees in Pilot Street, haven't you?

Carol We did have till last bommy night—the kids chopped 'em all down an' burnt them all. (*Pause*) Miss, y' know when I grow up, miss. Y' know if I started to work hard now an' learned how to read, eh? Well, d' y' think I'd be able to' live in one of them nice places?

(*Pause*)

Mrs Kay Well you could try, couldn't you, love, Eh?

Carol Yeh.

(**Mrs Kay** *smiles at her and links her arm. At the back, the kids are all stifled and bored by* **Briggs**'s *presence*)

Briggs (*Pointing out of the window at the South Docks*) Now just look at that over there.

(**Digga** *looks but sees nothing*)

Digga What?

Briggs What? Can't y' see? Look, those buildings. Don't you ever bother looking at what's around you?

Reilly It's only the docks, sir.

Briggs You don't get buildings like that anymore. Just look at the work that must have gone into that.

Reilly D' you like it down here, sir?

Briggs I'm often down here at weekends, taking notes, photographs. (*Sharply*) Are you listening, Reilly? There's a wealth of history that won't be here much longer.

Reilly Me old man works down here, sir.

Briggs What does he think about it?

Reilly He hates it.

Briggs His job or the place.

Reilly The whole lot.

Briggs Well, you tell him to stop and have a look at what's around him. Yes, he might see things a bit differently then.

(**Briggs** *looks up and sees* **Linda** *kneeling up on her seat and talking to the girl behind her*)

Karen Wales is cracker.

Briggs Linda Croxley!

Linda (*Not even looking up*) What?

(**Briggs** *gets up and goes across to her. She waits until the last possible moment before sitting 'properly' in her seat*)

Briggs What sort of outfit's that for a school visit?

(*She is dressed in the prevailing pop outfit of the day*)

Linda (*Chewing. Contemptuous. Looking out of window*) What!

Briggs Don't you 'what' me young lady.

(*She shrugs*)

You know very well that on school visits you wear school uniform.

Linda Well. Mrs Kay never said nott'n about it.

Briggs You're not talking to Mrs Kay.

Linda Yeh. I know.

(*Pause*)

Briggs (*Leaning in close. Threatening*) Now listen here young lady—I don't like your attitude one bit!

Linda What have I said? I haven't said nott'n yet, have I?

Briggs I'm talking about your attitude. (*Pause*) I'm telling you now. Carry on like this and you'll be spending your time in Conway inside this coach.

Linda I don't care. I don't wanna see no crappy castle anyway.

Briggs (*Pointing*) Count yourself lucky you're not a lad. (*Pause*) Now I'm warning you, Miss Croxley, cause any more unpleasantness on this trip and I'll see to it that it's the last you ever go on. (*Pause*) Is that understood? Is it?

Linda (*Still looking out of window*) Yes. (*Sighs*)

Briggs It better had be.

(*He makes his way down to the front of the coach and takes his seat next to* **Andrews***. Across the aisle* **Briggs** *sees that* **Mrs Kay** *has taken off her shoes and has her stockinged feet curled up under her.* **Carol** *has her arm linked through* **Mrs Kay**'s *and is snuggled up to her—they look more like mother and daughter than teacher and pupil. Behind* **Briggs***,* **Linda** *is kneeling up again,* **Reilly** *and company have started smoking and there are lots of kids eating sweets, drinking lemonade and larking about. He addresses the kid next to* **Andrews**)

Briggs Right, what's your name?

(*Pause*)

Briggs Wake up!

Maurice Sir, me!

Briggs What's your name?

Maurice McNally, sir.

Briggs Right, McNally, go and sit at the back.

Maurice Sir, what for?

Briggs Never mind what for, just do what you're told, lad.

(**Maurice** *goes to the back of the coach*)

Briggs (*To* **Andrews**) Right, move up! How long have you been smoking, Andrews?

Andrews Sir, I don't smoke.

(*Pause as* **Briggs** *looks at him*)
Sir, since I was eight, sir.

Briggs And how old are you now?

Andrews Sir, thirteen, sir.

Briggs What do your parents say about it?

Andrews Sir, sir, me mum says nott'n about it but when me dad comes home, sir, sir, he belts me.

Briggs Because you smoke?

Andrews Sir, no sir, because I won't give him one.

(*Pause*)

Briggs Your father goes to sea does he?

Andrews What? No, sir.

Briggs You said 'when he comes home', I thought you meant he was away a lot.

Andrews He is, sir, but he doesn't go to sea.

Briggs What does he do?

Andrews I dunno, sir, sir, he just comes round every now an' then an' has a barney with me mum. Then he goes off again. I think he tries to get money off her but she won't give him it though. She hates him. We all hate him.

(*Pause*)

Briggs Listen. Why don't you promise yourself that you'll give up smoking. You must realise it's bad for your health.

Andrews Sir, I do, sir. I've got a terrible cough.

Briggs Well, why don't you pack it in?

Andrews Sir, sir, I can't.

Briggs Thirteen and you can't stop smoking!

Andrews No, sir.

Briggs (*Sighing, shaking his head*) Well you'd better not let me catch you again.

Andrews No, sir, I won't.

(*Pause as they each go into their respective thoughts.* **Briggs** *turns and looks at* **Mrs Kay***. She looks at him and smiles warmly. He tries to respond but doesn't quite make it.* **Colin** *walks along the aisle generally checking that everything is all right. As he gets near* **Linda**'s *seat her friend,* **Karen** *taps her and points him out.* **Linda** *immediately turns round and smiles at* **Colin***. It's obvious that she fancies him*)

Linda Sir, y' comin' to sit by me are y'?

Karen (*On the seat behind* **Linda**) Don't sit by her, sir . . . come an' sit by me.

Colin I've got a seat at the front, thanks.

Linda 'Ey, sir.

Colin What, Linda?

Linda Come here, I wanna tell y' somethin'.

Colin Well, go on.

Linda Ah ey sir, I don't want everyone to hear. Come on, just sit down here while I tell y'.

Karen Go on, sir . . . she won't harm y'.

Linda Come on, sir.

(*Reluctantly* **Colin** *sits by her.* **Karen**'s *head is poking through the space between the seats and both girls laugh*)

Colin What is it?

(*They laugh*)
You're not goin' to tell me a joke, are you?

(*The girls laugh even more*)

Well, I'll have to go.

(**Linda** *quickly links her arm through his and holds him there*)

Linda No, sir . . . listen. Listen, she said, I wouldn't tell y' . . . I will. (*Pause*) Sir, I think you're lovely.

Colin (*Quickly getting up. Embarrassed*) Linda! (*He walks away from the girls to the back of the coach*)

Linda I told him. I said I would. Ooh . . . he's ace isn't he?

Karen You've got no chance. He's goin' with miss.

Linda I know. (*Pause*) He might chuck her though an' start goin' with me. He might marry me.

Karen (*Shrieking*) Ooer! Don't be stupid, you. You won't get a husband like sir. You'll end up marryin' someone like your old feller.

Linda You're just jealous you, girl.

Karen Aaght.

(**Colin** *talks to the lads on the back seat.* **Reilly** *hides a cigarette in his cupped hand*)

Colin All right lads . . . it shouldn't be too long before we're getting into Wales.

Little Kid That's in the country, Wales, isn't it, sir?

Colin A lot of it is countryside, yes.

Reilly Lots of woods, eh sir?

Colin Woods and mountains, lakes. . .

Reilly You gonna take miss into the woods, are y', sir?

Colin (*Pause*) Now just watch it, Brian, all right?

Reilly Sir, I just meant was y' gonna show her the trees an' the plants. . .

Colin I know quite well what you meant.

(*Turns to go*)

And if I was you I'd put that fag out before you burn your hand. If Mr Briggs sees that you'll be spending the rest of the day alongside him. Now come on, put it out.

(**Reilly** *takes a last mammoth drag and then stubs out the cigarette.* **Colin** *walks back along the aisle*)

Reilly (*Shouting after him*) I'll show her the woods for y', sir.

(**Colin** *pretends not to hear.* **Reilly** *leans across to the* **Little Kid** *in the seat in front and knocks him*)

Reilly Give us a sweet you, greedy guts.

Kid I've only got a few left.

Digga You've got loads.

Kid I haven't.

Reilly Let's have a look then.

(*The* **Kid** *falls for it and shows him the bag.* **Reilly** *snatches it*) Ta!

Scene: **In the country**. *The coach is on a country road.* **Mrs Kay** *is talking to the* **Driver**

Mrs Kay Ronny, I was just wondering, is there somewhere round here we could stop and let the kids stretch their legs a bit?

Driver Well I'll tell y' what, Mrs Kay, there's a few cafés a bit further on. D' y' want me to pull into one of them?

Mrs Kay Smashing.

Scene: **A roadside café**. *Outside the café there are signs saying: 'Open' and 'Coaches Welcome'. Inside the cafe, a* **Waitress** *is working on the tables. There is also a woman,* **Mrs Roberts**, *working behind the counter.*

Waitress (*Looking up and seeing coach in distance*) Better be getting some cups ready, Mrs Roberts. There's a coach comin'.

Mrs Roberts (*Moving over to window*) Where is it?

Waitress Probably pensioners so early in the season.

Mrs Roberts (*Worried*) No. I don't . . . I don't think so.

(*She moves behind the counter and produces a pair of binoculars*)

Let me see.

(*She lifts the binoculars and looks at the coach. She can see the kids and the destination indicator which reads: 'Liverpool to Conway'. She lowers the binoculars and frowns a worried frown*)

Right! Come on, action!

Scene: **Inside the coach**. **Mr Briggs** *is addressing the* **Kids**.

Briggs Now the folk who run these places provide a good and valuable service to travellers like us . . . so remember what I've said.

Scene: **Back at the café**. *The café is alive with activity: the shutters are coming down the 'Coaches Welcome' sign is replaced by 'Absolutely no Coaches' and the 'Open' sign by one saying 'Closed'. The doors are locked and bolted;* **Mrs Roberts** *and the* **Waitress** *lean against the door.*

Scene: **In the coach**. *The coach has pulled up. The* **Driver** *and* **Mrs Kay** *are looking at the café.*

Mrs Kay Perhaps it's because it's so early in the

season. Maybe if they knew there was the chance of some business they'd open for us. I'll go and give them a knock.

Scene: **In the café**. *Inside the two women are silent, terrified. They hear footsteps coming up the drive. The door is knocked upon.* **Mrs Kay** *is on the other side of the door watched by the* **Kids** *from the coach windows. She knocks again.*

Mrs Roberts (*From within*) We are closed!

(**Mrs Kay** You couldn't possibly. . .

Mrs Roberts (*Firm*) We are closed.

Mrs Kay *moves away. As the two women hear the receding footsteps, they sigh*)

Mrs Roberts I only ever did it once, take a Liverpool coach load. I tell you not one word of a lie Miss Powell, they'd rob your eyes if you wasn't lookin'.

(*The coach pulls away. The* **Kids** *give V-signs to the café and cross their legs to stop themselves from wetting*)

Scene: **A café and shop**. *On the window a sign reads: 'Under New Management'. Inside, two men,* **John** *and* **Mac**, *are behind the counter generally preparing their place for the season.*

John Look, how many times, listen, it's only the start of the season innit? Eh? Course it is. We can't make a bloody fortune before the season's begun, can we?

Mac See, it's no that what's worryin' me. What I think, see, is we bought the wrong place. If you was askin' me, I'd say the coaches'll stop at the first café they come to. An' that's up the road.

John Some of them will, yeh. But there'll be enough for us as well. Give it a month, that's all; y' won't be able t' see this road for coaches. Thousands of schoolkids with money t' burn. We'll clean up, mate.

(*They hear the sound of brakes and of tyres pulling up.* **John** *looks out of the window*)

Now what did I say, eh?

Mac (*Looking out of window. Brightening*) Look at that. Christ, there's hundreds of them.

John Right. Let's go. Come on.

(*Moves to the counter and points out the items quickly*)

John Jelly Babies: fifteen p. a quarter.

Mac I thought they was only twelve.

John Ice cream nine p.

Mac They was only seven p. yesterday.

John Listen, mate, can I help inflation?

Mac (*Getting the picture*) Oh right. I get the picture.

John Passin' trade mate. Always soak the passin' trade. Y' never see them again so it don't matter. Bubble Gum two p.—no, make that three. Ice lollies ten p. Come on . . . get those doors open. We'll milk this little lot.

Scene: **In the car park**. *The* **Kids** *are tumbling off the coach.* **Mrs Kay** *takes out a flask and sits on a bench in the café garden.* **Briggs** *is frantic.*

Briggs Stop! Salter, walk . . . walk! You, boy . . . come here. Now stop. All of you . . . stop!

Mrs Kay (*Pouring out coffee*) Mr Briggs, they'll. . .

Briggs (*To a boy,* **Ronson**, *who is rushing for the door of the shop*) Ronson! Come here!

(**Ronson** *stops and walks back to* **Briggs**, *shrugging*)

Mrs Kay Mr Briggs . . . as long as they don't go near the road I don't think there's any. . .

Briggs All right, Mrs Kay.

(**Ronson** *stands in front of him*)

Now just where do you think you are?

(**Ronson** *is puzzled*)

Well?

(**Ronson** *looks round for help in answering. There is none*)

Ronson (*Sincerely*) Sir, Wales?

Scene: **Inside the shop**. *The counter cannot be seen for pushing, impatient* **Kids**. *The two men are working frantically as orders are fired at them from all quarters. As the orders are shouted, the* **Kids** *are robbing stuff left, right and centre—it's the usual trick but the two men are falling for it—the* **Kids** *point to jars high up, and as the men turn their backs, so racks of chocolate bars disappear into eager pockets.*

Scene: **Outside the shop**.

Briggs And don't let me catch you at it again. Now go on. Walk.

(*He watches as* **Ronson** *walks into the shop. Satisfied, he turns to* **Mrs Kay**)

Now, Mrs Kay, what was it you wanted?

Mrs Kay Well, I just thought you might like to have a sit down away from them for a few minutes.

Briggs To be quite honest, Mrs Kay, I think we

should all be inside, looking after them. Do you think it was wise just letting them all pour in there at once?

Mrs Kay Ooh . . . leave them. They've been cooped up for over an hour. They'll want to stretch their legs and let off a bit of steam.

Briggs I don't mind them stretching their legs. It's not the children I'm concerned about.

Mrs Kay Well, just who are you concerned about?

Briggs There's not only our school to think about, you know. There's others who come after us and they're dependent upon the goodwill of the people who run these places.

Mrs Kay (*Pouring out another cup of coffee*) Considering the profit they make out of the kids I don't think they've got much to complain about.

Briggs (*Taking cup*) Thanks. (*Pause*) You know, I'll have to say this to you, Mrs Kay, there are times when I really think you're on their side.

(*Pause*)

Mrs Kay And I'll have to say this to you, Mr Briggs, I didn't ask you to come on this trip.

Briggs No, but the Headmaster did.

Scene: **Outside the coach**. *The last few stragglers climb on board.*

Mrs Kay (*To the* **Kids**) Are you the last? Anyone left in the toilet?

Susan (*As she finishes counting heads*) That's the lot. We've got them all.

Mrs Kay All right Ron.

Driver Right love. (*Starts engine*)

Scene: **In the shop**. *The* **Kids** *have gone and the shelves are almost bare. The two men sit back, exhausted but satisfied.*

Mac If I hadn't seen it with m' own eyes.

John I told y'.

Mac We'll have to re-order.

John An' that's just one coachload.

Mac We must've took a bloody fortune.

John There was sixty quid's worth of stock on those shelves an' most of it's gone.

Mac Come . . . let's count up.

(*He gets up, goes to the till and opens it. It contains a lot of change but hardly any notes. He is puzzled*) Was you lookin' after the notes?

John Which notes? I thought you was takin' care of them.

Mac Well, we must of taken a load of notes. (*He looks at the bare shelves*)

Scene: **Inside the coach**. *The* **Kids** *are weighed down with sweets.*

Scene: **The shop**.

Mac The thievin' little bastards!

(*He rushes for the door.* **John** *follows. As he flings back the door he sees the coach just pulling away down the road. They run after the disappearing coach. The back window is a mass of two-fingered gestures. The two men are finally left standing in the road*)

Scene: **In the coach**. **Mrs Kay** *leaves her seat and goes over to* **Susan**'s *seat.* **Susan** *is playing 'I Spy' with a couple of girls who are sitting with her.*

(**Briggs** *moves across to talk to* **Colin**. *He is conspiratorial*)

Briggs You know what her problem is, don't you?

Colin (*Trying to keep out of it. Looking out of window*) Mm?

Briggs Well, she thinks I can't see through all this woolly-headed liberalism, you know what I mean? I mean, all right, she has her methods, I have mine but I can't see why she has to set herself up as the great champion of the non-academics. Can you? It might look like love and kindness but if you ask me I don't think it does the kids a scrap of good.

Colin Erm. . .

Briggs I mean, I think you have to risk being disliked if you're going to do any good for these type of kids. They've got enough freedom at home, haven't they, with their two quid pocket money and television till all hours, haven't they? (*Pause*) I don't know what you think but I think her philosophy is totally confused. What do you think?

(**Briggs** *waits for an answer*)

Colin Actually, I don't think it's got anything to do with a philosophy.

Briggs What? You mean you haven't noticed all this, sort of, anti-establishment, let the kids roam wild, don't check them attitude?

Colin Of course I've noticed it. But she's like that all the time. This trip isn't organised according to any startling theory.

Briggs Well what is the method she works to then? I mean, you tell me, you know her better than I do.

Colin The only possible principle behind today is that the kids should have a good day out.

Briggs Well that's all I'm saying, but if they're going to have a good and stimulating day then it's got to be planned and executed better than this.

(*While* **Briggs** *is talking,* **Mrs Kay** *has moved to have a word with the* **Driver***. Suddenly the coach swings into a driveway.* **Briggs** *is startled and puzzled*) What's this . . . where are we . . .

Mrs Kay It's all right, Mr Briggs . . . I've checked it with the Driver. I thought it would be a good idea if we called into the zoo for an hour. We've got plenty of time.

Briggs But I thought this trip was organised so that the kids could see Conway Castle.

Mrs Kay We'll be going to the castle after. (*To the* **Kids**) Now listen, everybody. As a sort of extra bonus, we've decided to call in here and let you have an hour at the zoo.

(*Cheers*)

Briggs Look, we can't. . .

Mrs Kay Now the rest of the staff and myself will be around if you want to know anything about the animals—mind you, there's not much point in asking me, because I don't know one monkey from the next.

Reilly (*Shouting from back*) Apart from Andrews, miss, he's a gorilla.

(**Andrews** *gives him a V-sign*)

Mrs Kay And yourself, Brian, the Orang Utang.

(*The* **Kids** *laugh,* **Reilly** *waves his fist*)

Digga Don't worry, miss, he's a big baboon.

Mrs Kay Now let's not have any silly name-calling.

Briggs (*Whispering in* **Mrs Kay**'s *ear*) Mrs Kay. . .

Mrs Kay (*Ignoring him*) Now as I was saying, I don't know a great deal about the animals but we're very lucky to have Mr Briggs with us because he's something of an expert in natural history. So, if any of you want to know more about the animals you see, Mr Briggs will tell you all about them. Come on, leave your things on the coach.

Kid Agh, great.

(*The* **Kids** *begin to get up*)

Scene: **The zoo.** *The* **Kids** *wander around in groups—pulling faces at the animals, pointing and running, girls walking arm in arm. They point and shriek with horrified delight at the monkeys.* **Mr Briggs** *is with a group of* **Kids** *looking at a large bear in a pit.*

Briggs . . . and so you can see with those claws it could give you a very nasty mark.

Andrews An' could it kill y', sir?

Briggs Well, why do you think it's kept in a pit?

Ronson I think that's cruel. Don't you?

Briggs No. Not if it's treated well. And don't forget it was born in captivity so it won't know any other sort of life.

Ronson I'll bet it does, sir.

Girl 1 How do you know? Sir's just told y' hasn't he? If it was born in a cage an' it's lived all its life in a pit, well, it won't know nothin' else so it won't want nothin' else, will it?

Ronson Well, why does it kill people then?

Andrews What's that got to do with it?

Ronson It kills them cos they're cruel to it. They keep it in a pit so when it gets out it's bound to be mad an' wanna kill people. Don't you see?

Andrews Sir, he's thick. Tell him to shurrup, sir.

Ronson I'm not thick. If it lived there all its life it must know, mustn't it, sir?

Briggs Know what?

Andrews Sir, he's nuts.

Ronson It must know about other ways of living, sir. Y' know, free, like the way people have to spend it livin'. It only kills people cos it's trapped an' people are always stood lookin' at it. If it was free it wouldn't bother people at all.

Briggs Well, I wouldn't be so sure about that, Ronson.

Andrews Sir's right. Bears kill y' cos it's in them t' kill y'.

Girl 2 Agh come on, sir . . . let's go to the Children's Zoo.

Andrews Let's go to the big ones.

Briggs It's all right . . . we'll get round them all eventually.

Girl 1 Sir, we goin' the Children's Zoo then.

Briggs If you want to.

Girl 1 Come on.

(**Briggs** *starts to walk away. The two girls link his arms, one on either side. He stops*)

Briggs Oh! (*Taking their arms away*) Walk properly.

Girl 2 Agh ey, sir, the other teachers let y' link them.

(**Mrs Kay** *is with another group. She sees* **Briggs**)

Mrs Kay Oh hello. How are you getting on? They plying you with questions?

Briggs Yes, they've been very good.

Mrs Kay I'm just going for a cup of coffee. Do you want to join me?

Briggs Well I was just on my way to the Children's Zoo with them.

Andrews It's all right, sir. We'll go on our own.

Mrs Kay Oh come on. They'll be all right.

Briggs Well, I don't know if these people can be trusted on their own, Mrs Kay.

Mrs Kay It's all right, Susan and Colin are walking round and the place is walled in. They'll be all right.

Andrews Go on, sir. You go an' get a cuppa. Y' can trust us.

Briggs Ah! Can I though? If I go off for a cup of coffee with Mrs Kay can you people be trusted to act responsibly?

(*Chorus of* 'Yes, sir')

Briggs All right Mrs Kay. We'll trust them to act responsibly.

Mrs Kay Come on.

(*They walk off to the zoo café*)

Scene: **The bird house**. *Two boys are slowly repeating,* 'Everton, Everton' *to two blue and yellow macaws.*

Boy Go on, just tweek it out, you dislocated sparrow . . . speak!

Scene: **The children's zoo**. *The* **Kids** *watch a collection of small animals—rabbits, gerbils, guinea pigs, bantam hens—all contained in an open pit.* **Ronson** *looks fondly at a rabbit.*

Ronson They're great, aren't they?

Carol They're lovely.

Ronson (*Bending over and stroking a rabbit*) Come on . . . come on. . .

Carol Ey' you. Y' not supposed t' touch them.

(**Ronson** *answers by picking up the rabbit and gently stroking it.* **Carol** *reaches over to join him stroking the rabbit but he pulls it close to him protectively*)

Carol Well. I'll get one of me own.

(*She bends down and picks up a guinea pig which she strokes affectionately*)

These are better anyway!

Scene: **The zoo café**. **Mr Briggs** *and* **Mrs Kay** *are waiting for coffee at the service rail.*

Briggs How many sugars, Mrs Kay?

Mrs Kay Call me Helen. I hate being called Mrs Kay all the time. Makes me feel old. I tried to get the kids to call me Helen once. I had the class full chanting it. Two minutes later they were calling me Mrs Kay again. No, no sugar, thank you.

Scene: **The children's zoo**. *More* **Kids** *have followed* **Ronson**'s *example. Quite a few of them are now clutching furry friends.*

Carol I'm gonna call mine Freddy. Hiya, Freddy. Hello, Freddy. Freddy.

Scene: **The zoo café**. **Mrs Kay** *and* **Briggs** *are sitting at a table; she lights a cigarette.*

Briggs They're really interested, you know, really interested in the animals.

Mrs Kay I thought they'd enjoy it here.

Briggs Perhaps when we're back in school we could arrange something; maybe I could come along and give them a small talk with some slides that I've got.

Mrs Kay (*Enthusiastic*) Oh, would you?

Briggs You should have asked me to do something a long time ago.

Mrs Kay Well, don't forget you've never offered before.

Briggs To tell you the truth I didn't think the kids who came to you would be too interested in animals.

Scene: **The children's zoo**. *The animal pit is empty. The children have gone.*

Scene: **The coach**. **Briggs** *and* **Mrs Kay** *approach.*

Briggs Don't worry, we'll get that arranged as soon as we get back to school.

(**Susan** *and* **Colin** *stand by the coach with the* **Driver**)

Colin (*To* **Driver**) You should have come round with us, it's a grand zoo.

Driver A couple of hours' kip—seen it all before.

Colin You'd have had a good time.

Mrs Kay All on board?

Susan Yes. We wandered back and most of them were already here.

Mrs Kay Oh! That makes a change.

Briggs All checked and present. Right. Off we go.

(*The* **Driver** *and the teachers climb on board. In the distance the* **Animal Keeper**, *polo-necked and wellied, runs towards the coach. Inside the coach the* **Kids** *sit like angels. The coach pulls away but the* **Animal Keeper** *waves it down. It stops. The* **Keeper** *strides on board*)

Mrs Kay Have we forgotten something?

Keeper Are you supposed to be in charge of this lot?

Mrs Kay Why? What's that matter?

Keeper Children. They're not bloody children. They're animals. That's not a zoo out there. This is the bloody zoo, in here!

Briggs Would you mind controlling your language and telling me what's going on.

Keeper (*Ignoring him and pushing past him to the* **Kids**) Right. Come on. Where are they?

(*The* **Kids** *look back innocently*)

Call yourselves teachers. You can't even control them.

Briggs Now look. This has just gone far enough. Would you tell me exactly what you want please?

(*A clucking hen is heard. The* **Keeper** *turns and looks. A* **Kid** *is fidgeting with his coat. The* **Keeper** *strides up to him and pulls back his coat, revealing a bantam hen. Two more* **Keepers** *come on board. The first* **Keeper** *grabs the hen and addresses the* **Kids**)

Keeper Right! And now I want the rest!

(*There is a moment's hesitation before the flood-gates are opened. Animals appear from every conceivable hiding place. The coach becomes a menagerie.* **Mrs Kay** *raises her eyebrows to heaven. The* **Keepers** *collect the animals.* **Briggs** *stares icily*)

Scene: **The coach, moments later. Briggs** *is outside talking to the* **Keepers**, *who have collected all the animals in small cages. They walk away and* **Briggs** *climbs onto the coach. His face is like thunder. The* **Kids** *try to look anywhere but at him—trying to avoid the unavoidable.* **Briggs** *pauses for a long, staring, angry and contemptuous moment.*

Briggs I trusted you lot. (*Pause*) I trusted you. And this, is the way you repay me. (*Pause*) I trusted all of you, but it's obvious that trust is something you know nothing about.

Ronson Sir, we only borrowed them.

Briggs (*Shouting*) Shut up, lad! (*Pause*) Is it any wonder that people won't do anything for you? The minute we start to treat you as real people, what happens? That man was right, you act like animals, animals! (*Pause*) Well I've learned a lesson today. Oh, yes, I have, I've learned that trust is something you people don't understand. Now, I'm warning you, all of you, don't expect any more trust from me!

(*The* **Kids** *are resigned. They have heard it all before.*

Briggs *turns to* **Mrs Kay**)

Mrs Kay. When we get to the castle we'll split up into four groups. Each member of staff will be responsible for one group.

(**Mrs Kay** *looks at him*)

Scene: **Conway Castle. Briggs,** *with a group of ordered children standing behind him, points to a spot high up on the castle. The* **Kids** *all look up, bored.*

Briggs Now you see these larger square holes, just below the battlements there—well, they were used for . . . long planks of wood which supported a sort of platform, and that's where the archers used to stand and fire down on the attackers of the castle. Now what's interesting is, if you look at the side of that tower it's not quite perpendicular. What's perpendicular mean?

Milton Sir, sir.

Briggs All right, Milton.

Milton Straight up, sir. (*Sniggers from the other boys*)

(*In another part of the castle,* **Kids** *are rushing about playing medieval cowboys and Indians.* **Mrs Kay** *sits on a bench overlooking the estuary.* **Carol** *and* **Andrews** *are with her. In a secluded passage of the castle,* **Reilly** *and* **Digga** *are smoking; they are concealed in an alcove.* **Colin**'s *voice can be heard. He approaches,* **Karen** *and* **Linda** *close behind him*)

Colin So, although these walls are nearly fifteen feet thick in places, you still have the wind blasting in through the arrow slits and with no proper heat, you can imagine just how cold it must have been.

Linda Sir, I wonder what they did to keep warm in the olden days?

Colin (*Stopping and turning*) Well, obviously they. . . Where's everybody else gone? Where are the others?

Karen Sir, they kept dropping out as you were talkin'.

Colin Oh God.

Linda It's all right, sir. Y' can keep showin' us

round. We're dead interested.

Colin (*Sighing*) All right Linda . . . what was I saying?

Linda Sir, y' was tellin' us how they kept warm in the olden days.

Colin (*Continuing down the passage*) They wore much thicker clothing . . . All right, Linda?

Linda Sir, it's dead spooky. It's haunted isn't it?

Colin Don't be silly.

Linda Sir, I'm frightened (*Linking his arm for protection*)

Colin Now, don't do that, Linda!

Linda (*Holding on*) But I'm frightened sir.

Karen (*Grabbing his other arm*) Sir, so am I.

Colin (*Firmly, freeing himself*) Now, girls, stop being silly. Stop it. There's nothing to be frightened of! Now, come on.

(*He leads them along the passage. As they pass the alcove where Reilly and Digga are concealed, Reilly leans out and just gently touches Linda's shoulder. She screams and flings herself at Colin. Karen reacts and does the same. Even Colin is slightly startled*)

Linda Sir, it touched me.

Colin What did?

Linda Oh, it did.

(*Colin looks worried. They hear laughter. Just at the point when the three of them are about to run, Reilly and Digga fall laughing out of the alcove. In the distance Briggs shouts, 'Reilly!' Reilly and Digga hear him and leg away past Colin and the terrified girls. Outside, Mrs Kay, Carol and Andrews still sit looking out over the estuary*)

Mrs Kay Why don't you go and have a look around the castle grounds. You haven't seen it yet.

Carol Miss, I don't like it. It's horrible. I just like sittin' here with you, lookin' at the lake.

Mrs Kay That's not a lake, love. It's the sea.

Carol That's what I meant, miss.

Andrews Miss, wouldn't it be great if we had something like this round our way? Then the kids wouldn't get into trouble if they had somewhere like this to play, would they?

Carol Miss. Couldn't have nothin' like this round our way could they?

Mrs Kay Why not?

Carol Cos we'd only wreck it, wouldn't we?

Andrews No, we wouldn't.

Carol We would, y' know. That's why we never have nothin' nice round our way—cos we'd just smash it up. The Corpy knows that so why should they waste their money, eh? They'd give us things

if we looked after them, but we don't look after them, do we?

Andrews Miss, miss, y' know what I think about it, eh, miss.

Mrs Kay Go on John. What do you think?

Andrews Miss, if all this belonged to us, miss, and it was ours, not the Corpy's but, ours, well, we wouldn't let no-one wreck it would we? We'd defend it.

(**Briggs** *approaches, obviously angry*)

Briggs You two . . . off! Go on. Move.

Carol Sir, where?

Briggs Anywhere, girl. Just move. I want to speak to Mrs Kay. Well, come on then.

(*The two kids, Carol and Andrews wander off. Briggs waits until they are out of hearing range*)

Mrs Kay I was talking to those children.

Briggs Yes, and I'm talking to you, Mrs Kay. It's got to stop, this has.

Mrs Kay What has?

Briggs What has? Can't y' see what's goin' on? It's a shambles, the whole ill-organised affair. Look at what they did at the zoo. Just look at them here.

(*All around the castle they can see, from where they sit, Kids running, pulling, laughing and shouting*) They're just left to race and chase and play havoc. God knows what the castle authorities must think. Look, when you bring children like ours into this sort of environment you can't afford to just let them go free. They're just like town dogs let off the lead in the country. My God, for some of them it's the first time they've been further than Birkenhead.

Mrs Kay (*Quietly*) I know. And I was just thinking; it's a shame really, isn't it, eh? You know, we bring them to a crumbling pile of bricks and mortar and they think they're in the fields of heaven.

(*Pause. He glares at her*)

Briggs (*Accusing*) You *are* on their side aren't you?

Mrs Kay (*Looking at him*) Absolutely, Mr Briggs. Absolutely!

Briggs Look! All I want to know from you is what you're going to do about this chaos.

Mrs Kay Well, I'd suggest that if you want the chaos to stop, then you should stop seeing it as chaos. All right, the Headmaster asked you to come along—but can't you relax? There's no point in pretending that a day out to Wales is going to furnish them with the education they should have had long ago. It's too late for them. Most of them were rejects on the day they were born, Mr Briggs. We're not going to solve anything today. Can't we just try and give them a good day out? At least we could try and do that.

Briggs (*The castle looming behind him*) Well, that's a fine attitude isn't it? That's a fine attitude for a member of the teaching profession to have.

Mrs Kay (*Beginning to lose her temper ever so slightly*) Well, what's your alternative? Eh? Do you really think there's any point pretending? Even if you cared do you think you could educate these kids, my remedial kids? Because you're a fool if you do. You won't educate them because nobody wants them educated. . .

Briggs Listen Mrs Kay. . .

Mrs Kay No! You listen, Mr Briggs . . . If these kids, and all the others like them, had real learning the factories of England would empty overnight. And don't you try and tell me that there's kids who, given the choice, would still empty bins and stand on production lines, but don't give me that because that's the biggest myth of all. Give them education—choice—and they'd want what we've got, what the best-off have got. And that's why you won't educate them, Mr Briggs. You're in a job that's designed to fail, because no matter what the rest of us want, the factories of England must have their fodder.

Briggs And I suppose that's the sort of stuff you've been pumping into their minds, is it?

Mrs Kay (*Laughing*) And you really think they'd understand?

Briggs Listen, I'm not going to spend any more time arguing with you. You may have organised this visit, but I'm the one who's been sent by the Headmaster to supervise. Now, either you take control of the children in your charge or I'll be forced to abandon this visit and order everyone home.

(*Pause. She looks at him*)

Mrs Kay Well . . . that's your decision. But I'm not going to let you prevent the kids from having fun. If you want to abandon this visit then you'd better start walking because we're not going home. We're going to the beach.

Briggs The beach!!

Mrs Kay We can't come all the way to the seaside and not go down to the beach!

(*She turns and walks away*)

Scene: **The beach. Briggs** *sits on a rock apart from the main group.* **Mrs Kay** *is paddling, dress held over her knees looking old-fashioned, with a group of kids. Girls are screaming in delight and boys are laughing and running. Two boys,* **Kevin** *and* **Jimmy**, *are near* **Mrs Kay**.

Jimmy 'Ey, miss, we could have brought our costumes an' gone swimmin'.

Kevin We could go swimmin' anyway, couldn't we, miss?

Carol (*Trailing behind* **Mrs Kay**) Miss, when we do have to go home?

Jimmy What? In your undies?

Kevin Yeh. Why not?

Mrs Kay No. Not today.

Kevin Agh . . . why not, miss.

Mrs Kay Because. . .

Jimmy If y' went swimming in just y' undies, the police would pick y' up, wouldn't they, miss?

Mrs Kay Look, the reason I don't want you to go swimming is because there aren't enough staff here to guarantee that it would be safe. I want to go home with a full coachload thank you.

Carol Miss, when d' we have t' go. . .

Kevin Agh, miss, I'd be all right, miss . . . I wouldn't get drowned, miss.

Mrs Kay (*Warning*) Kevin!

Kevin Oh, miss.

Mrs Kay Kevin, I've already explained why I don't want you to go swimming. . .

Kevin Oh . . . Miss. . .

Mrs Kay Carry on like that and I'll have to sort you out.

Kevin Agh. . .

(*She stops him with a warning look. He tuts. Satisfied that he won't take it any further, she turns to* **Carol**)

Mrs Kay Right. . .

Kevin Just for five minutes, miss.

Mrs Kay (*Turning and walking towards him*) Kevin Bryant . . . come here.

Kevin (*Backing away. Laughing*) Ah, miss, I didn't mean it . . . honest miss. I never meant it.

(**Mrs Kay** *glaring in mock seriousness, comes after him. He is laughing. He breaks and runs. She chases him, skirts trailing in the water, with the other kids shouting and jeering and urging her to catch him.* **Kevin** *is hardly able to run because of laughing so much.* **Mrs Kay** *charges on through the water, looking incongruous.* **Kevin** *suddenly stops, turns, bends down in the water and prepares to send up a spray*)

Kevin Don't, miss . . . don't or I'll spray y'.

Mrs Kay Kevin Bryant . . . you'll do what? . . . You wait till I get hold of you.

(*They face each other. The* **Kids** *at the water's edge chant and shout:* 'Get him, Miss', 'Duck him, Miss', 'Throw him in', 'Y've had it now, Bryant'. **Kevin** *makes the mistake of turning to the groups of* **Kids** *to answer them. In a flash she is on him and turns him upside down. She ducks him and he comes up spluttering and laughing. The other* **Kids** *cheer and laugh*)

Kevin Oh no, miss.

Mrs Kay Now who wanted to go swimming, Kevin?

Kevin Oh miss, miss. Me 'air's all wet.

(*She quickly lifts him so that she is carrying him, cradle fashion, out of the water.* **Briggs** *looks on. He turns away.* **Mrs Kay** *and* **Kevin** *walk away from the water. He shakes water from his hair*)

Kevin Miss . . . I might get a cold though. I hate that.

Mrs Kay Oh, you're like an old woman. Come on then.

(*She reaches in her bag and produces a towel. She wraps the towel round his head and rubs vigorously. Beneath the towel* **Kevin** *is beaming and happy*)

Kevin Ta miss.

Carol (*At side of* **Mrs Kay**) Miss, when do we have t' go home?

Mrs Kay What's the matter, love? Aren't you enjoying it?

Carol Yeh, but I don't wanna go home. I wanna stay here.

Mrs Kay Oh, Carol, love . . . we're here for at least another hour. Why don't you start enjoying yourself instead of worrying about going home.

Carol Cos I don't wanna go home, miss.

Mrs Kay Carol, love . . . We have to go home. It can't be like this all the time.

Carol Why not?

Mrs Kay (*Looks at her. Sighs*) I don't know, love.

Scene: **The rocks. Colin** *and* **Susan, Linda** *and* **Karen** *and some other kids are searching among the rocks.* **Reilly** *and* **Digga** *are nearby with a smaller group of followers. They are having a smoke behind a large rock.*

Andrews Gis a drag.

Digga Go an' buy some.

Andrews Don't be sly, come on.

(**Reilly** *blows smoke in their faces. As they rush for it, he drops it and stubs it out in the sand with his foot. The* **Kids** *fight for it.* **Reilly** *turns away and looks out from the rock. He shouts across to* **Colin** *and* **Susan**'s *group*)

Reilly All right, miss.

(**Colin** *and* **Susan** *look up*)

Colin (*Quietly*) Ah, here we go.

Reilly (*Shouting over*) You comin' for a walk with me then, miss?

Colin (*Standing and pointing. Shouting*) Look . . . I'm warning you, Reilly.

Susan Don't shout.

Colin I'm just getting sick of him, that's all.

Susan Well, why don't you go and have a word with him?

Colin I don't know. I just can't seem to get through to friend Brian. For some reason he seems to have it in for me.

Susan I wonder if I could get through to him.

Reilly Come on . . . what y' scared of?

Susan You go back with the others.

Colin What are you going' to. . .

Susan Go on.

(**Colin** *moves off.* **Susan** *walks slowly across to* **Reilly**)

Linda Has miss gone t' sort him out, sir?

Karen He needs sortin' out, doesn't he, sir?

Linda He's all right really, y' know, sir Y' know, when he's on his own he's great.

Karen Ooer . . . how d' you know?

Linda Shut up you.

Colin All right. All right.

(**Reilly** *smiles.* **Susan** *continues to walk slowly, provocatively, determinedly, towards him. As* **Susan** *stares straight at him.* **Reilly** *smiles bravely.* **Reilly**'s *smile gradually disappears as she gets closer. She steps straight up to him—almost against him.* **Reilly** *looks anywhere but at her*)

Susan (*Deliberately husky*) Well, Brian . . . I'm here.

Reilly 'Ey, miss.

Susan I'm all yours . . . handsome!

Reilly Don't mess, miss.

Susan (*Putting her arms round him*) I'm not messing, Big Boy. I'm serious.

(**Briggs** *in the distance walking along the beach, stops and looks. He sees them, then turns and goes back. Meanwhile,* **Reilly** *squirms*)

Susan What's wrong?

Reilly I was only having' a laugh, miss.

(*Lots of little faces peer at them from around and on*

top of the surrounding rocks)

Susan You mean . . . don't tell me you weren't being serious, Brian.

Reilly I was only jokin' with y', miss.

Susan (*Keeping him pinned to the rock, quietly in his ear*) Well, you'd better listen to me Brian. (*Pause*) You're a handsome lad, but I'd suggest that in future you stay in your own league instead of trying to take on ladies who could break you into little pieces. All right, we'll leave it at that shall we?

Reilly Yes, miss.

(*She pats him gently on the face. She pulls back and as she begins to walk away the laughter breaks out.* **Reilly** *lunges out and the* **Kids** *scatter,* **Susan** *turns and sees this*)

Susan Brian.

(*He looks up and she motions him over. She is now the teacher again*)

You know what we were saying about leagues?

Reilly Yeh.

Susan Well have you ever thought whose league Linda's in?

Reilly (*Smiling*) Linda Croxley?

(**Susan** *nods.* **Reilly** *smiles*)

Agh 'ey miss, she doesn't fancy me. She's nuts about sir. No-one else can get a chance.

Susan I wouldn't be too sure about that.

(*Turns to go*)

See you.

Reilly See y', miss.

(*He turns and walks back to his mates. As he appears they all start laughing and jeering. He stands smiling and proud*)

Reilly Well! At least I'm not like you ugly gets. (*A pause during which he grows about two feet*) I . . . am handsome!

Scene: **The beach.** *A game of football is in progress.* **Mrs Kay** *is in goal. She makes a clumsy save and the* **Kids** *cheer.* **Briggs** *watches from a distance.* **Mrs Kay** *leaves the game and goes to meet* **Colin** *and* **Susan** *who are approaching.*

Mrs Kay Wooh . . . I'm pooped.

Andrews (*Shouting from game*) Agh, miss, we've not got a goaly now.

Mrs Kay (*Shouting back*) It's all right. Carol can go in goal for you now.

(*She looks amongst the group,* **Colin** *and* **Susan** *look on*)

Elizabeth Estensen as Susan in the first television production on BBC2, 28 December 1977. (BBC copyright photograph)

Where is she?

Susan Who?

Mrs Kay Carol. She went to look for you.

Colin We haven't seen her.

Mrs Kay Well, where is she?

(**Mrs Kay** *scans the beach.* **Carol** *cannot be seen.* **Mrs Kay** *looks at* **Susan**)

You haven't seen her at all?

(**Susan** *shakes her head*)

Mrs Kay (*Looks over beach again*) Oh she couldn't. Could she?

Susan Lost?

Mrs Kay Don't say it. perhaps he's seen her.

(*She shouts across*)

Mr Briggs . . . Mr Briggs.

(**Briggs** *looks up, rises and then comes over to her*)

Susan I hope he has seen her.

Mrs Kay Yeh. The only trouble is she didn't go that way.

Briggs (*Approaching*) Is that it? Are we going home now?

Mrs Kay Have you seen Carol Chandler in the last

127

half hour?

Briggs Look! I thought I'd made it quite plain that I was having nothing more to do with your outing.

Mrs Kay Have you seen Carol Chandler?

Briggs No. I haven't.

Mrs Kay I think she might have wandered off somewhere.

Briggs You mean you've lost her.

Mrs Kay No. I mean she might have wandered off.

Briggs Well, what's that if it's not losing her? All I can say is it's a wonder you haven't lost half a dozen of them.

Colin Listen, Briggs, it's about time someone told you what a berk you are.

Briggs And you listen, sonny. Don't you try telling me a word because you haven't even earned the right. Don't worry, when we get back to school, your number's up. As well as hers. (*He motions to* **Mrs Kay**) And you (*To* **Susan**) I saw what was going on between you and Reilly. When we get back, I'll have the lot of you!

Mrs Kay Would you mind postponing your threats until we've found Carol. At the moment I'd say the most important thing is to find the girl.

Briggs Don't you mean *try* and find her?

Mrs Kay Susan . . . you keep these lads playing football. We'll split up and look for her.

(**Mrs Kay**, **Colin** and **Briggs** *walk off in separate directions*)

Scene: **The cliff**. *Below the cliff-top, the sea is breaking on rocks in a cave mouth. In the distance,* **Mrs Kay** *is shouting 'Carol, Carol', and* **Colin** *is searching the far end of the beach.* **Carol** *is standing on top of the cliff watching the waves below. She looks out over the sea. Alone on the cliff-top, she is at peace with the warm sun and small breeze upon her—a fleeting moment of tranquility.*

Briggs Carol Chandler!

(**Briggs** *approaches. On seeing her he stops and stands a few yards off*)

Just come here.

(*She turns and stares at him*)

Who gave you permission to come up here?

Carol No-one.

(*Turning, she dismisses him*)

Briggs I'm talking to you, Carol Chandler.

(*She continues to ignore his presence*)

Now just listen here, young lady. . .

(*As he goes to move towards her, she turns on him*)

Carol Don't you come near me!

Briggs (*Taken aback. Stopping*) Pardon!

Carol I don't want you to come near me.

Briggs Well, in that case just get yourself moving and let's get down to the beach.

(*Pause*)

Carol You go. I'm not comin'.

Briggs You what?

Carol Tell Mrs Kay that she can go home without me. I'm stoppin' here . . . in Wales.

(*Pause*)

Briggs Now just you listen to me—I've had just about enough today, just about enough, and I'm not putting up with a pile of silliness from the likes of you. Now come on. . .

(*He starts to move towards her. She takes a step towards the edge of the cliff*)

Carol Try an' get me an' I'll jump over.

(**Briggs** *stops, astounded. There is an angry pause. She continues to ignore him*)

Briggs Now come on! I'll not tell you again.

(*He moves forward. Again, she moves nearer to the edge. He stops and they look at each other*)

I'll give you five seconds. Just five seconds. One . . . two . . . three . . . four . . . I'm warning you, five!

(*She stares at him blankly.* **Briggs** *stares back in impotent rage*)

Carol I've told y' . . . I'm not comin' down with y'.

(*Pause*)

I'll jump y' know . . . I will.

Briggs Just what are you trying to do to me?

Carol I've told you. Leave me alone and I won't jump.

(*Pause*)

I wanna stay here. Where it's nice.

Briggs Stay here? How could you stay here? What would you do? Where would you live?

Carol I'd be all right.

Briggs Now I've told you . . . stop being so silly.

Carol (*Turning on him*) What do you worry for, eh? Eh? You don't care, do y'? Do y'?

Briggs What? About you? Listen . . . if I didn't care, why am I here, now, trying to stop you doing something stupid.

Carol Because if I jumped over, you'll get into trouble when you get back to school. That's why, Briggsy! So stop goin' on. You hate me.

Briggs Don't be ridiculous—just because I'm a school teacher it doesn't mean to say that. . .

Carol Don't lie, you! I know you hate me. I've seen

you goin' home in your car, passin' us on the street. And the way y' look at us. You hate all the kids.

(*She turns again to the sea, dismissing him*)

Briggs What . . . makes you think that? Eh?

Carol Why can't I just stay out here, eh? Why can't I live in one of them nice white houses an' do the garden an' that?

Briggs Look . . . Carol . . . you're talking as though you've given up on life already. You sound as though life for you is just ending, instead of beginning. Now why can't, I mean, if it's what you want, what's to stop you working hard at school from now on, getting a good job and then moving out here when you're old enough? Eh?

Carol (*Turns slowly to look at him. Contempt*) Don't be stupid.

(*She turns and looks down at the sea below*)

It's been a great day today. I loved it. I don't wanna leave here an' go home.

(*She moves to the edge of the cliff.* **Briggs** *is alarmed but unable to move*)

If I stayed though, it wouldn't be no good. You'd send the coppers to get me.

Briggs We'd have to. How would you survive out here?

Carol I know.

(*Pause*)

I'm not goin' back though.

Briggs Please. . .

Carol Sir, sir, y' know if you'd been my old feller, I woulda been all right, wouldn't I?

(**Briggs** *slowly holds out his hand. She moves to the very edge of the cliff.* **Briggs** *is aware of how close she is*)

Briggs Carol. Carol, please come away from there. (*Stretching out his hand to her*). Please.

(**Carol** *looks at him and a smile breaks across her face*)

Carol Sir . . . sir you don't half look funny, y' know.

Briggs (*Smiling back at her*) Why?

Carol Sir, you should smile more often, y' look great when y' smile.

Briggs Come on, Carol. (*He gingerly approaches her*)

Carol What'll happen to me for doin' this, sir?

Briggs Nothing, I promise you.

Carol Sir, y' promisin' now, but what about when we get back t' school?

Briggs (*Almost next to her now*) It won't be even mentioned.

(*She turns and looks down at the drop then back at* **Briggs**'s *outstretched arm.* **Carol** *lifts her hand to his. She slips.* **Briggs** *grabs out quickly and manages to pull her to him.* **Briggs** *wraps his arms around her*)

Scene: **The beach. Susan** *still waits anxiously on the beach whilst the* **Kids** *play football. Other* **Kids** *watch the game, including* **Linda** *and* **Karen. Reilly** *challenges* **Digga** *for the ball and gets it from him.*

Karen (*Shouting*) Go on, Digga . . . get him, get him.

Linda Come on, Brian.

(**Reilly** *gets the ball past* **Digga** *then around two more defenders, and scores.* **Linda** *cheers:* **Reilly** *sees her and winks.* **Mrs Kay** *and* **Colin** *approach.* **Susan** *looks up in inquiry;* **Mrs Kay** *shakes her head.* **Susan** *sighs*)

Mrs Kay (*As she approaches*) I think we'd better let the police know.

Susan Shall I keep them playing. . .

(*Behind* **Mrs Kay, Susan** *can see* **Briggs** *and* **Carol** *in the distance*)

Oh, look . . . he's found her.

Mrs Kay Oh, thank God. (*She turns and starts hurrying towards them*)

Colin I'll bet he makes a bloody meal of this.

Susan I don't care as long as she's safe.

Colin Yeh, well, we'd better round them up. It'll be straight off now.

(**Mrs Kay** *approaches* **Carol** *and* **Briggs**)

Mrs Kay Is she all right? Carol, the worry you've caused us!

Briggs It's all right, Mrs Kay. I've dealt with all that.

Mrs Kay Where were you?

Carol On the cliff, miss.

Mrs Kay On the. . .

Briggs Mrs Kay, I've found her. Now will you just let me deal with this.

Mrs Kay (*Shaking her head as they walk up the beach towards the others*) Carol Chandler.

Briggs Right.

(*The main group are preparing to leave as* **Mrs Kay, Carol** *and* **Briggs** *reach them*)

Briggs Right . . . come on. Everyone on the coach.

(*General 'tuts' and moans of: 'Why can't we stay', etc.*)

Come on . . . all of you, on.

Scene: **The coach.** *The staff stand by the coach doors* as the **Kids** *file by onto the coach.*

Driver Right. (*To* **Briggs**) Back to the school then?

Briggs School . . . back to school?

(**Mrs Kay** *looks up*)

It's only early, isn't it? (*To* **Mrs Kay**) Anyway, you can't come all the way to the seaside and not pay a visit to the fair.

(**Carol** *overhears them as she climbs onto the coach. She rushes inside*)

Carol (*Loud whisper*) We're goin' the fair, we're goin' the fair . . . Sir's takin' us t' the fair.

(*The word is spread like fire inside the coach. Outside,* **Mrs Kay** *is intrigued—half-smiling*)

Briggs Play your cards right, I might take even you for a ride on the waltzer.

Scene: **A fairground.** *Rock and roll music. On the waltzer the* **Kids,** *including* **Briggs** *and* **Carol** *together in a car, are spinning round.* **Mrs Kay** *takes a photograph of* **Briggs** *and* **Carol** *climbing out of the waltzer car.* **Mrs Kay, Colin** *and* **Susan, Reilly** *and* **Linda, Digga** *and* **Karen, Andrews, Ronson, Carol** *and some of the other kids are all photographed in a group.* **Briggs** *is snapped eating candy-floss, then again on the highest point of the bigwheel with mock fear on his face and* **Carol** *next to him, her eyes closed in happy terror. Then he is photographed playing darts, then with a cowboy hat on handing a goldfish in a plastic bag to* **Carol.**

Scene: **Back at the coach.** *As the* **Kids** *pile onto the coach,* **Briggs,** *still wearing his cowboy hat, stands by the coach door.*

The Kids at the fair in the first television production on BBC2, 28 December 1977. (BBC copyright photograph)

Kids (*As they get onto coach*)

Sir, thanks, sir.

Sir, that was Ace.

We had a great laugh, didn't we, sir?

Sir, we gonna come here again?

Ronson Can we come tomorrow, sir?

Briggs Oh, get on the bus, Ronson.

(*Everyone is singing as the coach moves along. One of the kids is collecting for the* **Driver;** **Reilly** *has his arm around* **Linda;** **Digga** *is with* **Karen;** **Carol,** *with her goldfish, sits next to* **Mrs Kay;** **Ronson** *has a white mouse; the back seat is now occupied by* **Andrews** *and others kid.* **Briggs** *is also on the back seat—cowboy hat on, tie pulled down and singing with them.* **Mrs Kay** *takes a photograph of them*)

Mrs Kay Say 'Cheese'.

Scene: **Back in the city.** *The city can be seen out of the coach windows. Inside the coach the kids are tired and worn out now. Some are sleeping, some are singing softly to themselves, some stare blankly out of the window.*

Linda Y' glad y' came?

Reilly Yeh.

Linda It was great wasn't it, eh?

Reilly It'll be the last one I go on.

Linda Why?

Reilly Well I'm leaving in the summer aren't I?

Linda What y' gonna do?

Reilly (*Looking out of window*) Dunno. (*Looks out of the window at the city*) It's horrible when y' come back to it, isn't it?

Linda What is?

Reilly That. (*Nods at window*)

Linda Oh, yeh. (*Resigned*)

(**Briggs,** *with* **Andrews** *asleep next to him, sees the familiar surroundings and the kids hanging about in the streets. He sits up, puts his tie back to normal, goes to straighten his hair and feels the cowboy hat. He takes it off and puts it on* **Andrews.** *He then takes out a comb and combs his hair; puts on his jacket and walks down the aisle to* **Mrs Kay**)

Briggs Well, nearly home.

Mrs Kay (*She is taking the completed film from her camera*) I've got some gems of you here. We'll have one of these up in the staff room when they're developed.

Briggs Eh? One of me?

Mrs Kay Don't worry . . . I'm not going to let you forget the day you enjoyed yourself.

Briggs (*Half laughs. Watches her put the film into its box*) Look . . . why don't you give it to me to develop?

Mrs Kay Would you?

Briggs Well, it would save you having to pay for it. I could do it in the lab.

Mrs Kay (*Handing it over*) I don't know, using school facilities for personal use.

(*He smiles at her and takes the film. He puts it in his pocket*)

Scene: **Outside school.** *It is evening as the coach turns into the street outside the school and pulls up.* **Briggs** *gets out, then the* **Kids** *pour out shouting 'Tarars' and running up the street.* **Reilly** *and* **Linda** *get off the coach together.*

Briggs Right! Come on, everyone out!

Reilly 'Night sir. Enjoyed yourself today, didn't y', sir?

Briggs Pardon?

Reilly I didn't know you was like that, sir. Y' know, all right for a laugh an' that. See y' tommorer, sir.

Briggs Eh—Linda.

(*She stops,* **Briggs** *turns*)

We'll, erm, we'll let the uniform go this time.

(*Pause*)

But Linda, don't let me catch you dressing like that in the future, though.

(*She shrugs and walks off with* **Reilly**. *The other kids make their way home.* **Mrs Kay** *gets off the coach*)

Mrs Kay Nothing left behind. 'Night Ronny.

Susan Good night.

(*The coach pulls away. The* **Driver** *toots good-bye and they wave*)

Ooh! . . . That's that. I don't know about anyone else but I'm off for a drink.

Colin Oh, I'll second that.

Susan Good idea.

Mrs Kay (*To* **Briggs**) You coming with us?

Briggs (*The school looming behind him*) Well, actually I've. . .

Susan Oh, come on. . .

Briggs No . . . I'd better not. Thanks anyway. I've, um, lots of marking to do at home. Thanks all the same though.

Mrs Kay Oh well, if we can't twist your arm.

(*Pause*)

Thanks for today.

(*She turns and goes to her car accompanied by* **Susan** *and* **Colin**. *She pulls away and toots good-bye.* **Briggs** *moves to his own car, puts his hand in his pocket and produces car keys and the roll of film. He looks at the film and then up at the school. He pulls open the film and exposes it to the light, crumples it up and puts it into his pocket. He then gets into his car, pulls away and at the junction turns right.* **Carol**, *walking along the street with the goldfish in her grasp, looks up at the disappearing car*)